Skilled workers in the class structure

ROGER PENN

Department of Sociology, Lancaster University

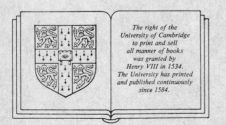

The right of the
University of Cambridge
to print and sell
all manner of books
was granted by
Henry VIII in 1534.
The University has printed
and published continuously
since 1584.

CAMBRIDGE UNIVERSITY PRESS

Cambridge
London   New York   New Rochelle
Melbourne   Sydney

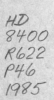

Published by the Press Syndicate of the University of Cambridge
The Pitt Building, Trumpington Street, Cambridge CB2 1RP
32 East 57th Street, New York, NY 10022, USA
296 Beaconsfield Parade, Middle Park, Melbourne 3206, Australia

First published 1984

Printed in Great Britain at the University Press, Cambridge

Library of Congress catalogue card number: 84–5796

British Library Cataloguing in Publication Data

Penn, Roger
Skilled workers in the class structure.
1   Skilled labor – Great Britain –
History – 19th century 2. Skilled labor
– Great Britain – History – 20th century
I. Title
305.5′62   HD8390

ISBN 0 521 25455 8

TM

Contents

Tables, Diagrams and Models

Acknowledgements

Many people have helped me in the pursuit of this research. I owe a massive debt of gratitude to my two Ph.D. supervisors, Dr Michael Mann and Dr Gavin Mackenzie, both of whom provided encouragement and advice during the collection and analysis of the data in this research. Dr Mackenzie has had an enormous influence on my sociological career ever since those far off days in January 1970 when he supervised my reading of Durkheim, Marx and Weber. He assisted the early periods of this research up to and including much of the data collection. Dr Mann took over supervision upon Dr Mackenzie's departure to Harvard University for a year's sabbatical. He provided a great deal of encouragement and advice during the writing of this research. I count myself extremely fortunate to have enjoyed working with two such excellent supervisors.

I should also like to thank the many social scientists in Cambridge who have assisted and encouraged this research. In particular, I should like to thank Bob Blackburn, John Barnes, Geoffrey Hawthorn, Sandy Stewart, Ken Prandy, Geoff Ingham, Cathy Marsh and last, but never least, John Holmwood. My thanks also extend to the many people in Rochdale who helped me, either by providing access to data or answering my many questions. I trust that the clergymen, trade unionists and librarians will feel that it was all worthwhile. I wish to thank Mr and Mrs H. Hemingway and Mrs E. Johnson for their help, hospitality and encouragement – my greatest sadness is that none has lived to see the final draft. I hope that they would have regarded it as a good piece of research.

Particular thanks go to Lesley Bower, who provided invaluable assistance at the beginning of the research and to Sylvia Langford and Heather Salt for their typing of the successive versions of this manuscript. I would like to thank Frank Bechhofer for his helpful critical comments on my Ph.D. dissertation, Mike Hutchinson of Lancaster University Library for much help and Alan Ainsworth for his comments on many aspects of this research. Sue Allen-Mills and Francis Brooke of Cambridge University

Press have been both helpful and sympathetic to an inexperienced author. My sister, Alison and brother-in-law, David and my father have all helped in many ways over the years and my son, Michael and daughter, Sarah have been remarkably patient and quiet while the final version of the manuscript was written. My greatest debt, inevitably, extends to my wife Brenda, whose assistance and encouragement has been tireless and constant. It is to her that I dedicate this book.

ROGER PENN

PART I

Debates and definitions

1

Orientations to the analysis of class in Britain

This book is about the nature of the British working class and, in particular, the relations between skilled and non-skilled manual workers. It will be argued that an internal division of the manual working class around the axis of skill has been a central feature of market and work relations in Britain between the mid-nineteenth century and the mid-1960's. The research will also examine whether the structuration of the British manual working class around the axis of skill in the market and at work has been translated into equivalent 'social' boundaries in the non-economic sphere. The choice of subject matter and of approach derives from an interest in the nature of the British class structure and a conviction that many misconceptions exist in the sociological and social-historical literature concerning the development of that class structure. Two major sources of these misconceptions will be subject to critical scrutiny in the next two chapters, which examine the debates about the traditional working class and the labour aristocracy.

My interest in the development of the British class structure is one shared by many social scientists. Indeed, the arguments and evidence in this work should be seen in the context of the debate about the nature of the working class that has been and continues to be one of the dominant areas of sociological inquiry in Britain. Doubtless the political culture of contemporary Britain helps to foster such interests. Certainly the Fabian socialist tradition and, recently, neo-Marxism have helped sustain an academic interest in class, but such an interest also remains a central feature of British political discourse. There is, furthermore, amongst sociologists, a persistent tendency to talk about *the changing nature of the contemporary class structure*. Lockwood, in his seminal article in 1960, went in search of the new working class and the *Affluent Worker* team located it. Roberts *et al.* (1977) have discovered a fragmentation of the British working class, whereas Braverman (1974) suggests a strong tendency for an increasing 'homogenization' of the American working class and goes on to argue that

3

this process is being repeated in all advanced capitalist societies. It was my belief when I embarked upon this research that much of the imagery of changes in the British class structure was mythical, the empirical evidence for many assertions scanty and contradictory, and that there was a cavalier approach to the appropriation of evidence into arguments. In particular, when it came to a discussion of the nature of the British class structure before 1939, there was an over-reliance on a very small number of authors.[1] It appeared as if every sociologist of class had read E.P. Thompson (1963) and Eric Hobsbawm (1964) but not their critics. One of the main thrusts of this research is to present an empirical examination of the British working class over a lengthy period and in particular to see whether there has been a significant bifurcation of the manual working class around the axis of skill and, if there has, to assess whether it had changed fundamentally between the 1850's and 1960's. The evidence is historical because the questions posed concern changes over time. However, the underlying rationale remains sociological, in as much as it is hoped that the results and their interpretation will assist a re-orientation of British sociological analyses of class.

Two main strands can be discerned within academic discourse on class in Britain. The first emphasizes the study of class consciousness, whilst the other lays emphasis on the study of *class structure*. This research lies in the latter tradition because, as will be argued in this chapter, the literature on class consciousness contains serious limitations. Furthermore, the study of class consciousness in Britain itself involves two distinct theoretical elements. Both of them – Marxism and structural-functionalism – will be examined, their affinities as explanatory systems revealed, and their modes of analysis criticized. The arena of overlap can be seen partly as a product of the general answers provided by each theoretical system to an ancient question in social theory: the problem of order.

For Marxist theory the problem of order involves an answer to the question of why capitalism has not been overthrown. The topic of capitalist stability is a perennial difficulty for Marxist intellectual systems as a result of the teleological assumptions within Marx's works.[2] Such teleology is a persistent feature of Marxist theorizing and takes the form of asserting that modern societal development follows a progressive movement towards socialism. The schema is an old one but nonetheless popular and involves the progressive evolution of the triad: feudalism–capitalism–socialism. The agency of revolutionary transformation from feudalism to capitalism is the bourgeoisie, and in the case of capitalism to socialism, it is the class that the industrial bourgeoisie creates through factory production, the industrial proletariat. This latter development embodies the fundamental contradiction within the capitalist system, that between capital and labour.

The teleological assumptions that lie behind Marxist theorizing can be seen in the currency of terms like *state monopoly capitalism: the final stage* and *late capitalism,* both of which suggest the imminent demise of the capitalist system. Even the French structural Marxists, who have been most vociferous in their denunciation of teleological versions of Marxism, fall prey to its attractions when engaged in their 'concrete' investigations of the 'current situation'.[3]

Teleological accounts are central to Marxism because they provide, amongst other things, the theoretical underpinnings that guarantee the final success of socialism. Clearly, this provides useful ideological support for Marxist political parties and intellectuals since it vindicates the ultimate correctness of their diagnoses. However, the central difficulties of this Marxist teleology are well known. State socialist societies have not resulted from the mass action of the urban factory proletariat but from the action of the peasantry in alliance with certain sections of the urban working class. For from the development of mature capitalism producing socialist revolution, it would appear that it is the periods of immediate dislocation associated with early capitalist industrialization, or those immediately succeeding defeat in war, that produce revolutionary socialist situations. The working classes of advanced capitalist societies are not revolutionary, nor even strongly socialist for the most part.

Nevertheless, the main point about these central dilemmas for Marxist theorizing is that answers to the problem of order have been located predominantly at the level of class consciousness. This has taken the form of the consolidation of the remarks made by Marx in such places as *The Poverty of Philosophy,*[4] *The German Ideology*[5] (with Engels) and *The Eighteenth Brumaire of Louis Bonaparte*[6] into a major conceptual scheme for class analyses. The main component of the model lies in the distinction between class-in-itself ('Klasse an sich') and class-for-itself ('Klasse für sich'). According to this model capitalism refers to a social system which contains, as its defining characteristic, a class of sellers of labour power. Capitalism must produce such a class – the proletariat – because it is an objective category of capitalism itself. However, this objective class-in-itself only becomes a class-for-itself endowed with revolutionary class consciousness through the medium of class struggle. These struggles, economic, political and ideological, produce class consciousness, but this can be delayed or misdirected by false consciousness.[7] Hence, the answer provided by this model to the problem of the apparent stability of advanced capitalism is that the proletariat has failed to recognize its real interests. Such false consciousness is portrayed as the result of bourgeois manipulation and hegemony, but both of these are seen as temporary phenomena. Such mechanisms as the tendency for the rate of profit to fall[8] must inevitably destroy 'bourgeois' illusions[9] since capitalism will, in the long term, fall prey to a terminal crisis and the long-awaited revolution will occur. It is evident that the generation of such a theory is not unrelated to the dominance of Leninist thinking amongst Western Marxist political parties with their emphasis on the 'Party' as a vanguard guiding the proletariat in its struggles towards a growing appreciation of the desirability of overthrowing the capitalist system. A basic assumption is that revolutions require the existence of an already constituted self-conscious revolutionary force armed with the relevant theoretical tools necessary to effect a practical revolutionary transformation. As a model of revolution, this is highly debatable,[10] but the important point to grasp is that the institutionalization of the class-in-itself/class-for-itself model has produced a strong tendency to focus class analysis in terms of the determinants of (false) class consciousness. Other aspects of class structure – in particular the 'objective' category class-in-itself – are seen as unproblematic. As a corollary, the answers to the problem of capitalist stability are focused at the level of class consciousness and specifically in terms of those elements that prevent the proletariat from perceiving its 'real' interests.

The tendency to focus class analysis on the problem of obstacles to class consciousness has affected a wide array of sociological and social historical analyses. The shared assumption of these models of social change is that revolutions are a function of radical class consciousness. Indeed, radicalization and the development of revolutionary class consciousness are often synonymous within this discourse. Nevertheless, despite the plethora of competing analyses such accounts share a similar formal explanatory structure as can be seen when they are catalogued into six sets of arguments:

Normative integration

There are two main versions of this argument.

Normative dislocation. Revolutionary class consciousness or radicalism is most likely in the period of 'anomie' between the disappearance of the 'Gemeinschaft' relations of agrarian society and the institutionalization and internalization of the norms of 'Gesellschaft' society. In other words, the working class only possesses revolutionary class consciousness in the immediate period of the transition from pre-industrial to industrial capitalism. Examples of this thesis can be found in Trotsky (1934), Bendix (1974), Kerr (1973) and Giddens (1973).

Normative lag. Revolutionary class consciousness or radicalism is most likely in the period when the working class is excluded from citizenship rights. Put another way, the working class engenders revolutionary class consciousness when the 'feudal', legal remnants of estate society persist in excluding it from nominal social equality. This argument is strongly associated with writings of T.H. Marshall (1963).

The presence of a bourgeois revolutionary tradition

Revolutionary class consciousness or radicalism is only likely if there has been a successful bourgeois revolution. The emphasis is on the revolutionary legacy of such features as a 'totalizing ideology' and a tradition of revolutionary combat. These views have been expressed lucidly by Perry Anderson (1965) and mark the rationale behind the role of the *New Left Review* in Britain in providing a surrogate revolutionary tradition. However, there is another version of this theme to be found in Parkin (1971) and in Goldthorpe and Lockwood *et al* (1969) all of whom argue that the decline of working class militancy in Britain is a function of the emasculation of the existent radical tradition by the leadership of the Labour Party. Both versions, the academic and the New Left, emphasize the need for revolutionary or radical class consciousness to be imported into the working class in an orthodox Leninist fashion. In the case of Parkin and Goldthorpe and Lockwood *et al.*, the impulse came originally from the Labour Party, whereas for Anderson it derives from the bourgeois revolutionary legacy.

Affluence

There are two main versions of this argument.

Revolutionary class consciousness or radicalism is only likely under conditions of mass misery such as pervasive poverty or widespread unemployment. Conversely, rising real standards of living weaken the revolutionary or radical impulse. This is a view held by much modernization literature, particularly the 'convergence' school. In Britain, it was extremely popular in the period of post-war affluence and was elaborated by writers like Zweig (1961), Crosland (1960) and, in the United States, from a rather different point of view, by Marcuse (1964).

Revolutionary class consciousness or radicalism is associated with conditions of falling real incomes after a preceding period of rising affluence. Historians like Labrousse (1933) and social psychologists like Gurr (1971) argue that revolutionary consciousness emerges in the immediate period of falling incomes after a sustained expansion of wealth and expectations.

Opportunity

Revolutionary class consciousness or radicalism is a feature of 'closed' social systems, where social mobility is 'blocked'. From the opposite angle, social mobility can be seen as a safety valve permitting the most able and, it is held, the most militant, potentially, to ascend the social hierarchy. This thesis received its classic elaboration in the works of Pareto (1968) and of Sorokin (1927), but contemporary versions can also be found in Parkin (1971).

Technology

There are also two opposite kinds of argument here.

Revolutionary class consciousness or radicalism is prevalent within mass production systems. With the increasing tendency towards new forms of automative technology, alienation and, concomitantly, militant class attitudes, will wither away. These ideas stem from the works of writers like Galbraith (1967) and Blauner (1964).

Revolutionary class consciousness or radicalism is associated with automative technology. The increasing contradiction between scientific–technical rationality and capitalist irrationality leads workers in technologically-sophisticated modern industries, like petro-chemicals, to a revolutionary assessment of their role. This argument is strongly associated with French theorists of the 'new' working class, like Mallet (1963) and Touraine (1966 and 1969), and has been examined empirically recently by Gallie (1978) and Low-Beer (1978).

Skill

Here we encounter two diametrically opposed theses.

The 'labour aristocracy'. Revolutionary class consciousness or radicalism is pervasive only when the working class is homogeneous. However, this homogeneity is fragmented when a skilled labour aristocracy develops within the working class. There are various versions of this general argument to be found in writers such as Engels (1953), Lenin (1971), Hobsbawm (1964), Foster (1974 and 1976) and Gray (1976). Whilst disagreeing over the precise date when a labour aristocracy can be said to emerge and over its exact social composition, all these writers argue that the emergence of sectional divisions within the working class reduces the putative level of militant working class consciousness. Furthermore, they argue that the decline of the labour aristocracy will help promote, once again, radical working class consciousness.

The 'militant craftsman'. For labour aristocrat theorists, skilled manual workers are generally seen as conservative, quiescent and dominant within working class institutions and culture. Whilst agreeing with the salience of the social distinction between skilled and non-skilled, writers in the 'militant craftsman' tradition like Montgomery (1976), Lucas (1976), Comfort (1966), Moss (1976), Hinton (1973), Williams (1975 and 1976) and Shorter and Tilly (1974), all argue that skilled manual workers have, at certain moments, constituted a revolutionary vanguard in the major capitalist societies. They further advance the thesis that with the progressive de-skilling of the labour force as a result of capitalist rationalization the working class will become homogeneous and relatively quiescent in terms of militant consciousness.

In conclusion, the Marxist problematic of the determinants of revolutionary class consciousness has intersected with a great number of sociological analyses of radicalism, not all of which are directly Marxist but which can be interpreted as 'Marxisant'.[11] As can be seen, the general problematic of obstacles to proletarian revolutionary class consciousness or determinants of working class radicalism can produce diametrically opposed empirical arguments. However, the central point here concerns not their empirical validity but their common properties as forms of argument. In general, all the arguments suffer from relatively simplistic models of social change. Specifically, they tend to contract societal developments into a pristine, dichotomous mould which has the form of saying that:

$$x \longrightarrow y \longrightarrow z$$
$$\text{not-}x \longrightarrow \text{not-}y \longrightarrow \text{not-}z$$

The assumption is that x (structural variable) leads to y (class consciousness) which itself produces z (class action). Conversely, structural obstacle (not-x) leads to false consciousness (not-y) which produces false action or action contrary to real interests (not-z). The objections to these models are several. It would appear as if diametrically opposed empirical outcomes can be derived from the same set of structural variables. This suggests that either the chronology of the arguments is imprecise or that the relationship between structure and consciousness is not quite as simple as these models would imply. In addition, the sets of variables that can be adduced to explain the non-existence of revolutionary class consciousness are multiple and could, in principle, be almost infinite. The general problem is that the structure which is held to effect class consciousness appears to be highly complex. Furthermore, the arguments listed earlier appear to operate in a discursive vacuum: it would appear as if the authors believe that to supply a variable to explain a non-event is a sufficient explanation, but the plurality of contenders for the title of efficient cause suggests that these correlations are not full explanations at all. It is, therefore, the contention of this chapter that these models of social change are dubious and that they share certain affinities with arguments located within the structural-functionalist analysis of class consciousness. However, this cannot be established until a detailed examination of the structural-functionalist framework has been undertaken.

The problem of order within structural-functionalist theory involves the general question of societal integration. Interest is focused on answers to such questions as what it is that holds the social system together and why it does not collapse. A basic assumption of this school is that without the cementing power of social forces, society itself would be impossible. The central image of structural-functionalism is of an unstable system held together in a precarious equilibrium. The mechanism that guarantees continuity is the internalization of societal values by individual members and the mutual orientation of their conduct into stable systems of action. The external arena of constraint is embodied in value systems and consequently societal stability is seen as a function of the successful internalization of these values. It is value consensus that guarantees societal integration. The notion of consensus has been notoriously difficult to define precisely within the structural-functionalist tradition and even within the work of its major theorist – Talcott Parsons. Does consensus refer to a factual consensus, a systemic strain towards general value consonance or an approximate consensus of either a systemic or factual kind? The difficulties centre around the relationships between 'system' as an heuristic theoretical tool and 'system' as an existing set of social relationships. Nevertheless, this ambiguity at the centre of structural-functionalist theorizing has been, in many respects, one of its main strengths as a theoretical framework, because it has permitted the generation of a whole range of propositions about the nature of contemporary value systems. At one extreme, it has provided the basis for the 'convergence' theorists, who argue that the logic of industrialism requires, and has produced, a universal value system in the industrialized world.[12] At the other, it has given support to Daniel Bell (1977), who argues that societal equilibrium in advanced capitalist societies is the result of the systemic tension between the differing value systems connected with the economic, political and cultural sub-systems. However, the central point about this structural-functionalist framework with regard to British class analysis is that it has supported a mode of conceptualizing social class in terms of its constitution as evaluations by individual members of society. If the problem of order is located in terms of the internalization of values, then class stability must be a function of the general consensus over relative rewards.

The emphasis on evaluation as the key conception within structural-functionalist stratification theory is clear from the works of Parsons. In 'An Analytical Approach to the Theory of Social Stratification', Parsons wrote that 'There is, in any given social system, an actual system of ranking in terms of moral evaluation. But this implies in some sense an integrated set of standards according to which evaluations are, or are supposed to be made' (1949, p.71). It was such theoretical sentiments that underpinned the original prestige inquiry conducted by the National Opinion Research Center in 1947 (1953). This study of the relative prestige accorded to a set of ninety occupations by a cross-section of the American public both appeared to give empirical support for the existence of a common value system and prompted a series of parallel inquiries in many other countries.[13] The apparent similarity in the results of these cross-national inquiries provided the empirical cornerstone for the functionalist theory of stratification. Both the original proponents of the theory, Davis and Moore (1945), and its major popularizer, Barber (1957), argued that the empirical similarities in outcomes of relative occupational prestige across different societies provided the basis for the functional theory of stratification. Davis and Moore claimed that the universal nature of evaluations of stratification must be a result of the universal necessity for stratification according to relative functional importance, while Barber stated that 'If, as we have said, there must be a pretty large degree of congruence between the functionally important roles in a society and its system of values then we should expect societies with the same kinds of functionally important roles will evaluate these roles in the same way' (Barber, 1957, p. 5).

It is unnecessary to demonstrate the theoretical and methodological weaknesses of the functional theory of stratification or the 'structural convergence' argument about invariant prestige. What is important to emphasize is that structural-functionalism, in its response to its question of societal integration, posed the answer in terms of general popular perceptions of stratification or, to use terminology avoided by Parsons *et al.*, but appropriate in a British context, 'consciousness of class'.

It was alleged attitudinal consensus of 'consciousness of class' that was challenged increasingly in the 1950's, particularly by European social scientists. The work of Centers (1959) in the U.S.A. on the different class attitudes held by the middle and working classes was accompanied by studies in Europe from Willmott and Young (1956), Bott (1957), Popitz (1957), Willener (1957), and ultimately by Lockwood's seminal article in 1960. This tradition, with increasing sophistication, attempted to demolish the assumption of consensus held by American structural-functionalists and to erect a theory of the social determinants of class imagery, as a part of a wider theoretical project of establishing conflict theory. Consciousness of class increasingly became identified with consciousness of how many classes there were in society. It was argued that the normal working class image of society was a dichotomous conflict-model, whereas the middle classes held more to an harmonious, multi-strata model. Again, it is not essential to criticize these conceptions here, but to re-emphasize the fact that whilst challenging the empirical validity of the consensus assumptions of the American structural-functionalist school in the name of 'conflict theory' they still subscribed to a version of sociological theory which focused the investigation of class in terms of consciousness and imagery.

Indeed, there are close similarities between the literature on class imagery within the conflict tradition and on class consciousness within the Marxist and Marxisant models discussed earlier. Both approaches focus the central problem for class analysis in terms of class consciousness, broadly understood. Within the conflict tradition class imagery is a function of 'n' variables, whilst for Marxist and Marxisant sociologies the radical potential of the working class is conceptualized in terms of the degree to which there are obstacles to revolutionary class consciousness. However, if we take a broad historical perspective, it can be seen that these obstacles (for example, citizenship or technology) can be conceptualized as some of the key variables that determine class imagery. The logical interconnections of the conceptual terrain have facilitated the penetration of Marxism by conflict theory and *vice versa*. This is revealed when two of the most popular debates in contemporary theories of class are examined – the 'embourgeoisement' of the working class and the 'proletarianization' of the lower middle class. Both theories are prevalent in Marxist and non-Marxist sociological discourses, and share very similar assumptions, for, in each case, relative shifts in real incomes are seen as forcing isomorphic changes in class consciousness. It is this notion of a simple relationship between class consciousness and an antecedent class structure that must be challenged. Indeed, these arguments on 'embourgeoisement' and 'proletarianization' highlight the simplistic nature of many of the class consciousness models of social change. Their central weakness is, as was suggested earlier, that they pay insufficient attention to the nature of class structure. The evidence used is often imprecise and chronologically vague. This tends to produce a mode of analysing change in the form of dichotomous ideal types which often merely embody a crude contrast between the past and the present.

This leads us to the central objection to the tradition of analysing class consciousness, namely that it often puts the cart before the horse. In particular, there appears to be an assumption that the *working class has existed or exists in some sort of pristine fashion. The main purpose of this research is to investigate the nature and existence of the working class, not to assume it.*

The conceptual tool used for this analytical purpose is the notion of class 'structuration'. The notion of 'structuration' or the degree of 'classness' is taken from Giddens (1973) and derives from Weber (1968). Giddens places considerable emphasis on the role of relative mobility chances in the structuration or boundedness of class divisions focused in the market place and in the division of labour. For Giddens, a class structure becomes more rigid, thereby exhibiting a higher degree of classness, to the extent that mobility across and within generations is restricted. The central image is of a class system that has a set of economic divisions that may or may not be translated into social boundaries. This heuristic is one shared by Goldthorpe (1980), Halsey *et al* (1980) and the many mobility researchers starting with Sorokin (1959). From the perspective of the sociology of class, it can be argued that this tradition derives from Weber's assertions that an economic class structure may or may not be translated into class conflict and class consciousness in a Marxist sense, and that social structuration is often associated with value systems distinct from the economic class structure of capitalism and which are embodied in status groups ('Stände'). The important point of this tradition in class analysis is that *it makes many issues in class investigations the subject of empirical and therefore scientific scrutiny*. Instead of bemoaning the non-revolutionary nature of the working class in advanced capitalist societies, this tradition insists that the structure of the working class itself is an empirical problem for sociological inquiry.

This research follows this tradition, but instead of placing emphasis on the openness of the working class, it focuses on the other side of the 'classness' coin – the degree of social closure. In particular, it investigates the economic division between skilled and non-skilled manual workers and, subsequently, the degree to which such economic structuration is translated into social structuration in the form of marital endogamy. The notion of closure again derives from Weber (1968), and has been the subject of sustained investigation at a conceptual level by Parkin (1979). Without agreeing with all of Parkin's contentions (indeed they are explicitly criticized in chapter 9), it is felt that an empirical analysis of those mechanisms of closure that produce varying degrees of class structuration will assist an understanding of the development of the British class structure.

This study lies within the tradition of examining class structure rather than class consciousness and draws upon recent renewal of interest in such matters amongst British social scientists. This renewed interest in class structure has four analytically distinct strands. The first involves the analysis of the labour market which has suggested the strong role of labour market structures in the internal structuration of the manual working class.[14] This interest in market phenomena has been closely paralleled by renewed interest in the sphere of work under the auspices of labour process analyses.[15] Indeed, recent work by Edwards (1979) and Gordon *et al.* (1982) has attempted to link structuration in the market with structuration at the point of production.[16] This research involves an empirical analysis of the interconnection of market and work relations which will be presented in chapters 6, 7 and 8. Recently, there has been a renewed interest by sociologists in the British tradition of industrial relations research. Indeed, there is a valuable literature from industrial relations analysts such as Fox (1974), Flanders (1970) and Turner (1962) which details how mechanisms of closure have operated within the manual working class particularly between the skilled and non-skilled. This research will make use of this tradition and attempt to give it further conceptual and empirical elaboration.

The research will involve a systematic discussion of class boundedness. It offers an explicit alternative to the Marxist literature on class boundaries exemplified by Poulantzas (1975), Carchedi (1975), Wright (1976) and Abercrombie and Urry (1983). This research accepts the existence of conventional economic class boundaries[17] and investigates both their variation over time and the extent to which these economic boundaries are translated into parallel or isomorphic patterns of social structuration.

The study was located in Rochdale between 1856 and 1964 for reasons to be given in chapters 4 and 5. The empirical material is presented in two sections. The first examines the economic structuration of the manual working class around the axis of skill between 1856 and 1964 in chapters 6, 7 and 8. The second section deals with the extent to which this economic structuration has been translated into equivalent patterns of social boundedness by means of a systematic analysis of data on intermarriage. The second section covers chapters 9 to 12 inclusive. However, before the empirical analyses are provided, it is necessary to examine critically what sociologists and social historians generally believe has been the pattern of working class development in Britain since the mid-nineteenth century, particularly concerning the internal structuration of the manual working class around the axis of skill.

2

The traditional working class

The previous chapter took the view that the emphasis within British sociology of class on class consciousness contained serious limitations. It was argued that the Marxist model of class led to a form of investigation in terms of obstacles to revolutionary class consciousness and that the conflict tradition emphasized the determinants of 'consciousness of class'. It was further argued that these structural 'determinants' and structural 'obstacles' shared certain affinities. It also appeared that both theoretical schools produced relatively simple notions about relations between class structure and class consciousness, and between class consciousness and class action. A more complex model of class structuration was suggested which would facilitate an examination of the structural constraints within which members of society operate. In particular, it was suggested that an examination of economic and non-economic structuration would permit an investigation of the *extent* to which there is a working class in Britain, and the degree to which such structuration has varied over time. However, before the research conducted in this book is presented, it is necessary to analyse what sociologists of class actually know about the development of the British working class over the last hundred years. This chapter will examine one dominant interpretative matrix – that of the 'traditional' working class and the next chapter will examine the other major framework – the 'labour aristocracy'.

This chapter on the 'traditional' working class elaborates upon some of the general points made in the first chapter. It criticizes the main sources of the notion of the 'traditional' working class in Britain – Hoggart and Williams, Lockwood and Anderson – for their meagre evidence and for their conceptual approaches. All these, it will be argued, suffer from a shared interpretative framework which involves references to an homogeneous historical working class and to certain alleged forms of class consciousness which obscure the analysis of the structuration of the British working class.

There are three sources for the dominant sociological 'knowledge' about the 'traditional' working class. The first powerful image is associated with the work of two cultural historians: Richard Hoggart (1959) and Raymond Williams (1958). The similarity of their approaches can be seen in their major works but is revealed most clearly in a conversation between them reported in the *New Left Review* in 1960. Both men were strongly concerned with the decline of working class communities in the post-1945 era of affluence and rehousing, but underlying their reflections was the third successive electoral failure of the Labour Party in 1959. For Hoggart and Williams, the collapse of Labour support was a consequence of the decline of its structural base – close-knit working class communities. Their imagery is clear; a nostalgia for the good old times when the working class lived in its solidaristic communities. By way of contrast, the present was seen as witnessing a progressive division of the working class, especially in 'the great corporations'. Hoggart (1960, p. 29) claims that 'You can see there an increasing stratification: distinctions being made at each level from apprentices all the way up.' The traditional working class is seen, on the other hand, as essentially homogeneous during the inter-war years. Hoggart locates the similarities in the fact that, economically, life for the worker was unpredictable and, socially, the worker had limited education. The working class community was an enclave in the wider social structure, characterized by very limited opportunities of escape and cemented by a strong, distinctive working class culture.

However, there is also considerable historical evidence that suggests such a conception of an homogeneous traditional working class is misleading. The Marxist theory of working class sectionalism, embodied in the theories of a labour aristocracy in Britain (which will be examined in the next chapter) and local evidence provided by Jenkins (1972) and Jewkes and Gray (1935) about the antagonistic relations between cotton spinners and piecers in Lancashire in the inter-war years do not fit neatly into the pattern of a working class 'us' and a non-proletarian 'them'. Nor does Roberts' (1971) work on communal life in Salford, which paints a picture of strong internal class differentiation. Such evidence suggests that the theory of decreasing homogeneity in the working class should remain, as yet, an hypothesis rather than a confirmed theory.

Nonetheless, very similar notions to those of Hoggart and Williams are presented by Lockwood in his articles (1960 and 1966) on the nature of the 'new' working class which provided part of the conceptual framework for the *Affluent Worker* series. In the study of working class 'embourgeoisement' Lockwood (1960, p. 249) argues strongly against false historical perspectives:

What is seen to be 'new' about the present day working class must not be discovered by a distortion of the immediate past, by an oversimplified view of the 'traditional' working class. Above all, it is important not to treat the working class – old or new – as an undifferentiated mass, although this tendency is promoted by a concentration on such factors as the level of employment in the community as a whole and on the movement of gross aggregates of economic welfare.

Lockwood also cautioned against the method so popular with pundits of comparing 'the most prosperous and least socially distinctive sections of the working class today' with 'the most socially distinctive sections of the working class of yesterday' (1960, p. 251). It is clear from this evidence that Lockwood was well aware of the dangers in the use of false historical comparisons but in his second major article, 'Sources of Variation in Working Class Images of Society' (1966) these dangers are far less emphasized. The later article provided an explanation of differences in social imagery within the working class based upon structural variations of work situation and community organization, rooted in three ideal types of the working class – 'proletarian traditional', 'deferential traditional', and 'privatized'. The implications for developmental interpretations appear to be clear, privatization is not a traditional feature of working class life, and therefore, the ideal type of traditional worker appears to be an historical approximation.

There is evident ambiguity in the concept 'traditional' worker used by Lockwood and this became clear at the Social Science Research Council Conference held at Durham in 1972 on the 'Occupation Community of the Traditional Worker'. Davis and Cousins (1975) strongly attacked Lockwood's distinction between sociological and historical concepts, stressing the necessity of a thorough historical knowledge of the 'old' for an evaluation of the thesis of a 'new' working class. Lockwood replied to this criticism, amongst others, by reaffirming the sociological rather than the historical meaning of his typology and adopting an heuristic rationale for his work. The major weakness of this defence is that Lockwood's ideal types were originally constructed to explain the 'newness' of the post-1945 working class which necessitated an historical, developmental framework. His ideal types bear a close resemblance to concrete studies of the working class[1] and Lockwood often uses words like 'emerge' to relate 'traditional' and 'privatized' ideal types of worker which, grammatically, presuppose an historical, rather than an a-historical, 'structural' sociological analysis. The most serious problem is that Lockwood's typology cannot, by its very nature, offer a theory of class developments: yet paradoxically, it has often been used for precisely this purpose, which suggests that it functions to fill a conceptual hole in the framework of sociological analysis of class structure. Such a role has been revealed in a more recent work by Goldthorpe (Goldthorpe and Bevan, 1975, p. 67), Lockwood's main collaborator in the *Affluent Worker* series, where Lockwood's concepts take on a clear historical character:

> In so far, then, as the Luton study could be taken as a pointer to the future, what was indicated was not the progressive assimilation of the working class into a predominantly 'middle class' society, but rather the emergence of a 'new' working class or, more precisely, of a new segment within the working class, whose members' priorities and aspirations, life-styles and social imagery invited comparison with those both of the white-collar employee and of the more traditional worker whether of a 'deferential' or 'proletarian' cast. But in keeping with its emergent character, the potential of this new formation within the spheres of both industrial and political action remained uncertain...

Nevertheless, despite its function for sociologists, Lockwood's version of the traditional working class must remain at best a set of hypotheses rather than an acceptable historical account.

The third major component of sociologists' imagery of the traditional working class derives from the editorial board of the influential *New Left Review*. This version was propounded in a series of articles by P. Anderson (1965) and T. Nairn (1964a, 1964b, and 1965), and their general thesis may be summarized by a lengthy quotation from the former:

> The distinctive facets of English class structure, as it has evolved over three centuries, can thus be summed up as follows. After a bitter, cathartic revolution, which transformed the structure but not the superstructure of English society, a landed aristocracy underpinned by a powerful mercantile affinal group, became the first dominant capitalist class in Britain. This dynamic agrarian capitalism expelled the English peasantry from history. Its success was economically the 'floor' and sociologically the 'ceiling' of the rise of the industrial bourgeoisie. Undisturbed by a feudal state, terrified of the French Revolution and its own proletariat, mesmerised by the prestige and authority of the landed class, it lost its nerve and ended by losing its identity. The late Victorian era and the high noon of imperialism welded aristocracy and bourgeoisie together in a single bloc. The working class fought passionately and unaided against the advent of industrial capitalism; its extreme exhaustion after successive defeats was the measure of its efforts. Henceforward it evolved, separate but subordinate, within the apparently unshakeable structure of British capitalism, unable, despite its great numerical superiority, to transform the fundamental nature of British society. (Anderson, 1965, p. 29)

Anderson's central imagery of the working class between the mid-nineteenth century and the present derives from the putative repercussions of the fusion of landowning and industrial capital in his theory. The argument is that the working class failed to achieve a 'totalizing ideology' because a 'supine bourgeoisie produced a subordinate proletariat. It handed on no impulse of liberation, no revolutionary values, no universal language' (Anderson, 1965, p. 36). In Gramscian terminology, the working class failed to develop a hegemonic position with which to combat bourgeois dominance and ended up excluded from the wider class structure. Anderson (1965, p. 34) claimed further that: 'A combination of structural and conjunctural factors in the nineteenth century produced a proletariat distinguished by an immovable corporate class consciousness and almost no hegemonic ideology ...' and that the English working class: 'has since the mid-nineteenth century been essentially characterised by an extreme disjunction between an intense consciousness of separate identity and a permanent failure to set and impose goals for society as a whole ...' For Anderson, this 'distinct, hermetic' working class culture is the sole factor in the explanation of the political situation of the proletariat over the last century, since it prevented the assimilation of Marxism into the working class. The central problems of Anderson's analysis lie in his exclusive reliance on consciousness as an explanatory category for the structural location of the working class and in his image of an homogeneous working class: both of which ignore the alternative evidence that suggests the possibility of a divided, sectionalized working class.

Indeed, these are the central problems involved in each of the three versions of class development that have been analysed. In each of them the traditional working class is seen as an homogeneous entity and its developments are explained by a putative class consciousness. This 'convergence' within the three perspectives would not appear to be accidental. Both Anderson and Lockwood base much of their respective models on the view of the homogeneous, traditional working class community popularized by Hoggart and Williams. Lockwood does not give much indication of what his conceptions are based upon in his 1960 article, but in the 1966 article on 'Sources of Variation in Working Class Images of Society' he footnotes the similarity of dichotomous class images in Britain, France and Germany and makes explicit reference to Hoggart's *Uses of Literacy* as the British exemplar. Anderson also is reluctant to give the sources for his conceptions of the British working class. However, when he does reveal his sources they amount only to a passing reference to Raymond Williams and the view that 'In England, Hoggart's matchless phenomenology has been the major contribution' (1965, p. 18). The image of an hermetically sealed working class enclave with a defensive corporate consciousness has become a dominant theme amongst many sociologists. Even in the *Berkeley Journal of Sociology* one can find an article which reproduces the very same themes. As Young (1967, p. 18), writing about the last quarter of the nineteenth century, puts it:

> Deference was still the typical style of interaction across almost caste-like boundaries which marked the interstices of the class-system . . . There were other factors inhibiting mobility. For one thing, for all the exhortations, the upward channels remained largely blocked. The reinforcement of class-cultural apartheid, growing differences of accent and vocabulary, diet, dress, and manners, customs, sports and pastimes were triumphantly confirmed by the erection of a dual education system. These were stern barriers for the ambitious. Even sterner were the strong moralistic sanctions, and communal resentments (perhaps a survival from the peasant community) against those who 'got on'. Those who aspired to get out of the community and become one of 'them' were typically ostracised.

It will come as no surprise that the evidence for these bold characterizations comes not from any analysis of actual patterns of social mobility but from two references to Hoggart's *Uses of Literacy*!

There are some clear similarities within the three general conceptions of class development that have been analysed so far. There is a clear emphasis on cultural factors and a tendency to focus class development at the level of class consciousness. For Williams and Hoggart, such an approach is integral to their work, with its particular reference to the influence of such factors as the mass media and universal secondary education in the development of British culture since 1945. Anderson and Nairn operate with a Continental variation on this theme, with an analysis heavily dependent upon Lukács and parts of Gramsci. Underlying these particular Marxist writings on class is a mode of analysis functioning overwhelmingly at the level of the superstructure. This tendency is in the mainstream of post-1945 Marxism, especially in its intellectual, university-centred form. Lockwood's work is an attempt to bridge the gap between infrastructure and superstructure, material and ideational, at a level of explanation that focuses on the material determinants of class 'imagery'. However, the analysis destroys the dimension of time by using a-historical ideal types and produces agnosticism when it comes to questions of movements in class structure. An historical approach, conversely, should be the very strength of Anderson, Nairn, Hoggart and Williams, yet, as has been shown, there are serious doubts about the validity of their historical assumptions.

Furthermore, the confusions surrounding the *precise* chronology of the traditional working class suggest that it is more of a myth than a demonstrated historical reality. By definition, the concept of the 'traditional' working class must refer to some era in the past but the actual period covered varies considerably. For Hoggart and Williams and for Lockwood, the traditional working class was seen during the inter-war period whereas for Anderson the term covers the entire span since 1848, whilst Young centres the concept on the period between 1875 and 1914. This research will examine each of these empirical possibilities in conjunction with the hypotheses derived from the analysis of the literature on the labour aristocracy in the next chapter.

Nonetheless, if the chronology of the 'traditional' aspect of the British working class is imprecise, there are two important unities within this discursive approach. The 'traditional' working class is held to have been an homogeneous entity at *some* period in British history. In other words, economically, politically *and* socially, the working class shared a relatively similar experience at certain moments but not at others. In addition, the working class is taken by all the authors to mean the *manual working class*. This shared definition will provide the point of departure for this research. The reasons for this are twofold. Firstly, this is the meaning of the term accepted generally by sociologists and social historians. Indeed, recent neo-Marxist works[2] have incorporated this conventional understanding of the working class within their accounts. The use of the term 'working class' to cover manual workers also has the support of everyday usage in Britain. Indeed, the relative uniformity of academic discourse is predicated upon the relative consensus of everyday definitions. Nevertheless, it should be realized that such a definition is both stipulative and heuristic. This definition of the working class in terms of its 'manualness' therefore possesses both contextual and intersubjective adequacy but it is *not* synonymous with the categories 'proletariat', 'labour' or 'productive workers'. It may be noted, with a certain degree of irony, that this research embodies a critique of consciousness as the organizing principle of class discourses but nonetheless incorporates a definition of class based upon intersubjective understandings. However, this would be to miss the main critical point of the research. The central weakness of the class consciousness approach is that it confuses its concepts with reality. A commitment to an initial stipulative and heuristic definition of the working class as manual workers should not be confused with the homogeneity of that class category historically. The latter requires empirical elaboration and the central critical thrust made against the literature on class consciousness in general, and the traditional working class in particular, is that it fails to probe its class concepts in a systematic, empirical way.

The central conclusion of this chapter is that the various conceptions of the traditional working class are very similar in structure and content. All three lack a basis in sustained empirical analysis – they are essentially mythical. Indeed, they share many features with a wider societal set of myths about the 'traditional', homogeneous, working class. Programmes like 'Coronation Street' on Granada Television and the vogue for Lowry prints are but the most obvious examples of a current of thought which pervades British culture. Part of the aim of this research is to put such myths under empirical scrutiny, which is not to deny the real consequences in the social world of misconceptions but to see one of the central roles of sociology as to challenge and, hopefully, rectify such ideas. However, before the empirical research is presented, it is necessary to examine the other major interpretative matrix available to British sociologists for the analysis of the structure and evolution of the working class – that of the 'labour aristocracy'.

3

The labour aristocracy

The concept of the aristocracy of labour derived from the first great historical crisis of Marxist theory. Marx's notion of the increasing immiseration of the proletariat appeared by the 1880's to lack a correspondence with the reality of working class development in Britain; and it was as a response to this contradiction between theory and reality that Engels (1953) formulated the concept of a working class elite. This 'aristocracy' owed its privileged economic position to the peculiar monopoly enjoyed by British industry in the world market in the period between 1850 and 1880. The non-revolutionary behaviour of the British proletariat was a direct, but temporary, consequence of the 'super-profits' derived from British economic hegemony. The proletarian elite was concentrated in the prosperous trade unions which were sharply divided from the majority of the working class whose conditions had changed little since the publication of Engels' *The Condition of the Working Class in 1844* four decades earlier. However, if Engels initiated the concept of a labour aristocracy, it was Lenin (1971) who systematized the notion into a theory of capitalist development as a whole. For Lenin, the aristocracy of labour referred to those groups of workers in the imperialist countries like Britain and France, whose wages were 'artificially' high as a result of the 'super-profits' generated by these monopoly–capitalist, imperialist nations. This upper stratum within the working class provided the material base for the reformist labour leadership so detested by Lenin.

When one descends from the level of abstract theory and polemic to empirical historical studies, the question of the existence of an aristocracy of labour in nineteenth century Britain becomes more difficult to assess. What is known centres around two distinct levels: the macro- and the micro-historical. The macro-historical approach is evident in Hobsbawm's (1964) pioneering study of the 'Labour Aristocracy in Nineteenth Century Britain' which defines the labour aristocracy as: 'certain distinctive upper strata of the working class, better paid, better treated and generally

regarded as more respectable and politically moderate than the mass of the
proletariat' (Hobsbawm, 1964, p. 272). It is this combination of both a
privileged economic position and conservative political behaviour that
shows the continuity of Hobsbawm's analysis with that of Engels and
Lenin.

Hobsbawm recognizes the multiplicity of criteria that constitute the
labour aristocracy; 'level and regularity of earnings', 'prospects of social
security', 'conditions of work', 'relations with the social strata above and
below', 'prospects of future advancement and those of his children'. The
first two criteria refer to a typical market situation and the third,
'conditions of work', refers to the pattern of authority relations within the
work situation. The final two criteria refer to the relational aspect of class.

However, despite this complex model, Hobsbawm relies almost exclusively on wage rates as an index of social class. Yet it is hard to see how
the information provided on wage rates can support Hobsbawm's general
interpretation. In particular, it is not clear why Hobsbawm assumes a
necessary relationship between affluence and conservatism. As Piva (1975)
has pointed out, such an unexamined assumption closely parallels the
assumptions of the 'embourgeoisement' debate in the 1950's and 1960's
and reflects that general tendency for sociologists to 'read off' changes in
politics as a simple reflection of changes in patterns of income criticized in
the first chapter.

With reference to the problem of the labour aristocracy in nineteenth
century Britain, wage differentials *per se* cannot support Hobsbawm's
thesis. Certainly they may be seen as a necessary feature of a labour
aristocracy as a distinct stratum but a further demonstration requires that
this economic potential becomes actualized in politics and in patterns of
social interaction. Hobsbawm attempts to make the latter association by
claiming that 'Socially speaking the best paid stratum of the working class
merged with what may be loosely called the lower middle class. Indeed the
term "lower middle class" was sometimes used to include the aristocracy of
labour' (Hobsbawm, 1964, p. 273). The evidence to support this view that
the skilled labour aristocracy belonged to a composite 'lower middle class'
is very weak, being based almost exclusively on the social background of
'Pupil-Teachers' (teacher trainees). There is no evidence provided on the
relational or associational indices of social class behaviour such as marriage
or residential patterns, membership of voluntary associations or the formal
and informal networks of interaction either at work or within the larger
local community structures. Hobsbawm also holds that 'If the boundaries
of the labour aristocracy were fluid on one side of its territory, they were
precise on another. An "artisan" or "craftsman" was not under any

circumstances to be confused with a "labourer"' (Hobsbawm, 1964, p. 275). Yet the evidence for this is based, not on any systematic analysis of social interaction, but upon the nature of trade unions in the nineteenth century, which as organizations of the skilled encountered a large and permanent army of unemployed and under-employed unskilled workers capable of 'blacklegging', or even more insidiously over the long run, of diluting the apprenticeship system that acted as the major structural prop to the privileged market position of many craftsmen. Indeed, if Hobsbawm wishes to characterize the aristocracy of labour in skilled terms, then the fundamental criterion ought not to have been factors like status, wages and security but the factor which guarantees these, which is control over the access to the trade which is necessarily exercised in times of labour surplus against the mass of workers. It is social mechanisms of exclusion like apprentice regulations and not simply relative wage levels that offer the strongest basis for the theory of a labour aristocracy. These arguments feature strongly in the discussion about the social bases of 'skill' which forms the core of chapters 4 and 8.

Pelling (1968) has tested Hobsbawm's thesis that there existed in the period from 1840 to 1914 an elite of comparatively prosperous artisans confronting the 'distinctly poor'. In order to do this, Pelling prefers to use the assessments made by social investigators like Booth (1902) and Rowntree (1902) of total family incomes as a more reliable indicator of differential economic resources than individual wage rates. Booth's research about London discovered that upper working class families 'consort together in a free and friendly way' with families from lower middle class and more proletarian backgrounds. It would appear that in London in the late nineteenth century, far from there being a small working class elite, there was a broad group of comparatively affluent workers. Pelling reports that Rowntree in York also found a broad band of relatively well-off workers, and that Bowley and Burnett-Hurst (1915) found relative affluence in Northampton and Stanley and the classic labour aristocrat pattern *only* in Reading. These figures indicate that when family income is used to discover the material differentiation amongst the working class the existence of a labour aristocracy in most towns is by no means clear. However, these family income statistics refer only to the last few years of the nineteenth century and we know very little for previous years.

Pelling (1968, p. 55) also dismisses Lenin's claim that the upper stratum furnishes the bulk of the membership of co-operatives, trade unions, sporting clubs and numerous religious sects, by showing the wide appeal and membership of co-operative and friendly societies. However, the most important part of Pelling's study is his analysis of the alleged conservatism of the artisan in contrast with the militancy of the labourer. He turns this upon its head with documentary evidence, of which the most significant is a quote from Mayhew (1861, p. 233):

> The artisans are almost to a man red hot politicians. They are sufficiently educated and thoughtful to have a sense of their importance in the state . . . The unskilled labourers are a different class of people. As yet they are as unpolitical as footmen, and instead of entertaining violent democratic opinions, they appear to have no political opinions whatever; or if they do possess any, they rather tend towards the maintenance of 'things as they are' than towards the ascendancy of the working people.

The thesis of the conservatism of the union leaders is also very dubious. The whole idea of a trade union was deviant to the laissez-faire doctrines of Victorian middle class ideology. If this is the point of reference it is hard to see how unions with their concomitant striking and picketing can be classified as conservative. Only if one assumes *a priori* a necessary connection between working class institutions and socialist revolution does this make any sense. These issues will be discussed in greater detail in chapter 6.

The main problem with this macro-historical debate about the aristocracy of labour is that it lacks empirical specificity. Evidence is taken from widely divergent sources to support the respective cases and there is a strong tendency to shift from one area of analysis to another in a haphazard fashion. As Piva (1975, p. 290) states, 'the weakness of both the aristocracy of labour and the embourgeoisement theories is that their proponents have been too quick to generalize from data which they have collected', and, it must be added, to gloss over the differential nature of the evidence itself. Little is known about specific patterns of inter-class and intra-class behaviours in actual historical situations. In a real sense it would appear clear that a necessary condition for the establishment of the existence of a certain type of class structure in a national context must be a series of local specific studies. Without a coherent picture of actual patterns of class behaviour in various localities over a period of time, it would appear impossible to verify any proposition about the national class structure.

To a certain extent the micro-historical approach to class relations in the nineteenth century fills some of the gaps and uncertainties left by the macro-debate. This approach has developed considerably over the last decade, mainly as a result of an increasing interest in local historical phenomena, but partly due to the greater sophistication of sociologists and social historians in their use of quantitative data. The study of marriage records and residential patterns, for instance, can be used as sensitive indicators of such class behaviour as social distance and interaction patterns. Membership of voluntary associations, especially churches and friendly societies, can reveal a great deal about the local class structure. The evidence may often be less than complete but, when compared with previous historical periods, there is a large amount of potentially valuable data.

For example, Neale (1972) has used a five class model to analyse and explain political behaviour in his local study of Bath during the period between 1800 and 1850. His model involves the decomposition of the concepts of a single middle class and a unitary working class. It appears to make more sense to talk, in Bath at least, of the middle classes and the working classes. The latter are subdivided into working class A and working class B, whilst the former are divided into the 'middle class proper' and the 'middling class'. The handling of the working class is somewhat unsatisfactory, since his own definition of class as a political phenomenon organized around conflict makes it hard to see how 'working class B' – the 'agricultural labourers, other low-paid and non-factory urban dwellers, domestic servants, urban poor . . .' – could ever qualify as a political class, since there is a very limited potential for mobilization of this aggregation of status groups as a political class, as Marx argued cogently in relation to the nineteenth century French peasantry.

Nevertheless, it is Neale's distinction between the 'middle class proper' and the 'middling class', that is of most relevance for the question of the position of skilled workers in the class structure. The 'middling class' comprises a political alliance of 'petit-bourgeois', 'aspiring professional men, other literates and artisans' (1972, p. 30). Of course, Bath during this period was by no means an industrializing centre and its typicality must be doubted. Nevertheless, the important point is that Neale suggests strongly that the manual/non-manual division is not necessarily a universally significant feature of class structuration, even if his class criteria are exclusively political. What would be interesting to know is whether the 'middling class' constituted a class based upon the criterion of interaction at more intimate levels than politics. A study of marriage and residential patterns, interaction behaviour in voluntary associations other than the political, and social mobility at the time would greatly extend our knowledge of Bath's stratification patterns.

If Bath appears to be peripheral to the general development of nineteenth century Britain, Foster's (1974) comparative study of Oldham, Northampton and South Shields focuses on the heartland of early industrial capitalism. His theme is the development and decline of a revolutionary class consciousness in Oldham in the period from 1790 to 1860. In the first part of the period, from 1790 to 1820, the old pre-industrial capitalist type of social structure broke down in the face of the

new economic crises inherent in the development of industrial capitalism;
the recurrent cyclical slumps, the shifting focus of conflict from prices to
wages and the resulting polarization of the community between owners and
workers. These economic dislocations, combined with militant Jacobin
ideology, served to produce a complete breakdown in the traditional modes
of social control. The authority systems sustaining the old social structure
all had one thing in common; namely they denied any legitimate expression
of labour interests. It was this denial of authentic labour interests that
provided the spark that ultimately fused the working class community:

> As soon as the basic area of conflict started to shift from prices to wages,
> the very tightness of the old systems of control (above all their outlawry of
> a separate labour identity) proved their greatest liability. In the new
> conditions it was precisely the men who were themselves beyond the law,
> the previously isolated radicals, who were now (uniquely) in a position to
> express the interest of the great majority. (Foster, 1974, p. 34)

The development of a mass revolutionary class consciousness really
occurred in earnest in the 1830's and 1840's and centred on the espousal of
illegal unionism and the rejection of state power which 'compelled the
formation of a labour community'.

The typical authority relationships of the new factory environment were
exacerbated by the economic realities of the early cotton industry. Over-
capitalization and reduced profit rates necessitated wage cuts and
produced a complete polarization of the community. Foster uses marriage
records and census returns to show that this development of an antagonistic capitalist–worker relationship also witnessed a breakdown of social
distance within the working class. However, his tables do not offer
unequivocal support to this textual argument as he appears to assume.
Foster (p. 127) states that 'Shields...has the least intermarriage and
conversely...Oldham has the most intermarriage'. Yet this conclusion is
based upon his table 5 which shows that the relative frequencies in the three
towns of a labourer family intermarrying with a craft family are: for
Northampton 77%, Oldham 80%, and for Shields 70% (100 = a random
distribution). However, these percentages hardly reveal dramatic differences. When Foster (p. 126) presents data on the relative chances of a
labourer family living next door to a craft family (table 4), he shows that for
Northampton in 1851 it was 104%, Oldham in 1841 was 108%, but in 1851
it had fallen to 88%; whilst for Shields in 1851 it was 80% (again,
100% = random distribution). Foster then proceeds to argue in the
notes at the back of his book that using the significance test described
in his appendix 2,[1] the figures for Oldham in 1841 are significant at the
20% level (chi-square = 1.87) against those for Oldham in 1851 but only at

the 5% level (chi-square = 3.82) against those for Shields in 1851 and that consequently Oldham represents stronger levels of class homogeneity than Shields. Such an argument is, statistically speaking, nonsense.[2] When we examine this appendix, it becomes apparent that Foster has made the serious error of confusing the meaning of the chi-square test. Chi-square indicates whether two factors are independent or, in other words, if there is an interaction effect. Foster seeks to establish whether the *magnitudes* of interaction differ between two towns. This is impossible with a simple chi-square test, since *chi-square is a test of statistical significance and not of the strength of a relationship*. Indeed, statistical significance bears no simple connection to strength of relationship since significance is affected by the size of the sample. It would appear that if Foster wanted to achieve the conclusions desired, he should have followed a more complex procedure.[3] Firstly, he should have tested for an interaction effect. Then he should have standardized his results and tested the standardized scores for strength of relationship.[4] Consequently, given Foster's errors, *no reliance can be placed upon his specific interpretation of the material during the period between 1841 and 1851*.

If Foster's arguments about the homogenization of the working class in Oldham in the 1840s are fanciful, there are nevertheless other important arguments in Foster's text about the emergence of a labour aristocracy in the 1850's and 1860's. According to Foster, the cotton and engineering industries in Oldham witnessed the emergence of a 'new structure of authority, one in which the skilled top third acted as pacemakers and taskmasters over the rest' (Foster, pp. 228–9). The violent conflict during the 1851 Engineers' Lock-out ensured a change from the old craft elite to a new labour aristocracy because new technological systems destroyed the craft engineers' insulation from employers' control and identified the new skilled workers with management. The same process occurred in the cotton industry but with less violence, since the skilled spinners were in a precarious position confronting the mechanization involved with the automatic spinning mule. In both industries, it was the greatly increased use of payment by piece-rates that facilitated the use of skilled workers as pacemakers for the rest of the workforce, 'Instead of enforcing discipline against the management they were now to do so on its behalf' (Foster, p. 231). It was this new division of authority riven within the previously homogeneous, solid, Oldham working class that explains the development of two distinctive working class patterns: the 'bourgeois' temperance, adult-educational, religious elite of skilled workers and their cultural negation – the profane, anti-intellectual, beer-swilling 'proletarian'.[5]

Foster's study seeks to explain the emergence of a labour aristocracy in

Oldham during the 1850's and 1860's in terms of a profound cultural shift within the manual working class associated with an increased use of piece-rate payment systems and the deliberate division of the working class by the capitalist employers. As was shown, the quantitative material in Foster's text does not support any of his interpretations, since these are based upon a confused statistical analysis, and it is far more likely that Musson (1976) is correct in arguing that the Oldham class structure changed very little over the period under discussion. Moreover, it will be argued in chapters 6 and 8 that Foster's belief that it is capitalist employers who create a divided working class (an assumption which appears to be an article of faith amongst many romantic Marxist social commentators) is entirely misconceived, since it ignores the active role of organized labour in the internal stratification of the British manual working class. However, apart from the difference in value systems and membership of certain voluntary associations, we do not know whether the authority division within the work milieu was translated into non-work limitations upon social interaction or solidified in distinct barriers to marriage or neighbouring.

Gray's (1974 and 1976) study of Edinburgh in the last half of the nineteenth century suggests that such barriers to social interaction did exist in the 1850's and 1860's, but began to weaken towards the later part of the century. The material differences within the Edinburgh working class were complex and were mirrored by status differences and more significantly by differences in social interaction. *The Reformer* wrote that the skilled labour aristocracy was: 'generally the elite of the working men, and so far removed from the operatives and labourers at the lower end of the scale that they have not many sympathies in common, and not much intercourse with . them' (29 March 1873), and this is supported by the evidence of residential segregation and from the marriage certificates for the period 1865 to 1869 presented by Gray: 'in all the skilled trades, marriages to the daughters of other skilled workers account for the largest single category; more significantly perhaps the printers, book-binders, masons, joiners, engineers, and ironmoulders have more marriages to daughters of business and white collar groups than to the daughters of unskilled workers' (Gray, 1974, p. 24). Gray's data also bear out the picture drawn by Hobsbawm of skilled labour aristocrats being members of a lower middle class. From his evidence of leisure activities in voluntary associations, Gray argues that the social contacts of artisans were with a relatively fluid and transitional lower middle class. This 'middling class' espoused middle class individualism as its creed with an emphasis on 'self-help' and 'respectability' very similar to the ideology of the Oldham labour aristocrats. Yet, despite the similarities within this 'middling' or lower middle class, the individualism of the skilled workers often involved a considerable degree of collectivism. Trade unions and friendly societies might couch their rationale in the language of Victorian individualism yet the reality was often something entirely different, and it was this difference in the interpretation and meaning of 'self-help' and 'thrift', focused upon their economic status as workers, that indicates the volatility and instability of the 'middling class' to which the skilled labour aristocrats belonged from the mid-century to the onset of the 'Great Depression' in 1873.

This fundamental instability was revealed in the 1880's and 1890's as the position of the skilled workers was changing as a result of transformations in both their market and work situations. Gray only deals with this fleetingly, but the effects in terms of differential patterns of class interaction were definite:

> A comparison of patterns of marriage in the 1890's with those of the 1860's reveals in most of the skilled trades a higher rate of marriage to daughters of semi and unskilled workers and a lower rate of marriage to daughters of business and white collar groups; perhaps most revealing, the two unskilled occupations analysed (building labourers and carters) both have an increased proportion of marriages to daughters of skilled workers. (Gray, 1974, pp. 30–1).

The labour aristocrats became, instead of a 'middling' or lower middle class, more and more an integral part of the manual working class, providing the leadership and membership of the proliferating socialist cells. In the later part of the nineteenth century, the labour aristocrats became the 'organic intellectuals' of the working class and had a profound impact on the nascent working class movement and provided a great stimulus to the Labour Party when it was formed in 1900.

It is clear from this analysis that the concept of the labour aristocracy means different things to different writers and that the types of evidence produced for its existence vary considerably according to context. If the concept is to be used by sociologists of class as an heuristic device, it must be operationalized in a clear way, but this is by no means easy. Certainly, the picture painted by Foster and Gray in particular is more complex than Hobsbawm's. From their arguments discussed above, it would appear as if a 'composite theory' of the labour aristocracy can be generated from these micro-level, localized studies of the British class structure before 1914. This theory would argue that the chronology of working class sectionalism follows a certain trajectory which can be seen in terms of three stages:

1) The industrial revolution created an homogeneous manual working class.
2) The period after 1848 witnessed the progressive disintegration of this factory proletariat and the emergence of a labour aristocracy.

3) This sectionalism began to break down in the 1880's and 1890's when a new 'homogeneous' working class emerged.

This theory pervades many historical and sociological versions of class development in Britain. It has been challenged at the macro-level by writers like Pelling (1968), Musson (1976), and Moorhouse (1978). The purpose of this research is to subject the theory to empirical scrutiny in a localized, micro-context. The place chosen for this investigation, Rochdale, has many advantages for such a 'test'. By 1851 it had become an industrialized community and factory production dominated the occupational structure. Furthermore, it contained two of the most important industries involved in the debate about the labour aristocracy – cotton and engineering. Most important of all, it possesses very good sources of data from which a sustained analysis can be generated. In particular, there are good records on relative wage differentials within the working class over a long period and, in addition, more than adequate materials on the pattern of intermarriage in the town. Given that such data have provided the empirical cornerstone for much of the 'composite theory' of the labour aristocracy and that a town like Rochdale ought to be an ideal location for the existence of an aristocracy of labour, this research should provide a critical test of its adequacy.

One of the central features of the literature on the aristocracy of labour in Britain is that it focuses generally on a skilled manual 'labour aristocrat' stratum separated from a non-skilled manual 'proletarian' residual. Whilst advocacy of a labour aristocracy theory is not coterminous with a belief in the centrality of a skilled:non-skilled manual bifurcation within the working class it forms the central thrust of much interpretation. This research will operationalize the concept of the labour aristocracy in these terms with reference to the relations between skilled and non-skilled manual workers in the Rochdale cotton textile and engineering industries.

Logically there would appear to be four distinct modes of conceptualizing the position of skilled manual workers in the class structure:

1. *Proletarian*: skilled manual workers constitute an integral part of the manual working class.
2. *Bourgeois*: skilled manual workers form an integral part of the middle class –
   (A) the middle class is seen as an undifferentiated class ('embourgeoisification' proper)
   (B) skilled workers constitute an integral part of the lower middle class
3. *Differentiated*: skilled manual workers constitute a class apart ('in themselves').

4. *Classless*: skilled manual workers are individuated as an entity to the extent that their class membership is independent of their identity as skilled manual workers.

The purpose of this research is to examine which of these models best approximates to the evidence on the position of skilled manual workers in Rochdale between the mid-nineteenth century and the mid-1960's. However, in order to achieve this, a general model of the position of skilled manual workers in the class structure will be suggested. This model will incorporate both the 'composite theory' of the labour aristocracy, which focuses on the period from about 1810 to 1914, and more recent sociological work. This is not to say that the notion of the labour aristocracy has vanished from Marxist accounts of twentieth century class structures. This is far from the case; the concept possesses an elasticity of usage bewildering in its range,[6] but it is given a certain coherence by the fact that it refers to any and all sectional divisions within the category 'labour' in Marxist discourses and functions to explain the failed teleology of Marxist theory. However, if we wish to retain a focus on the relationships between skilled and non-skilled manual workers in Britain in the twentieth century, it is more useful to incorporate sociological material into the model.

The central image portrayed by contemporary sociology in relation to skilled manual workers is of structural differentiation over the last sixty years. This theory has a strong basis in the notions of the homogeneous 'traditional' working class discussed in the previous chapter. Its main theoretical exponent is the conflict theorist, Dahrendorf (1959), who argues that there has been a 'decomposition of labour'. By this, Dahrendorf means that the tendency towards de-skilling and homogenization of manual work evident in the growth of routine semi-skilled work earlier in the twentieth century has been reversed as a result of the 're-skilling' of the labour force since 1945. This process of the 'decomposition of labour' is seen as involving the combination of traditional modes of rationalized work tasks with more sophisticated skilled work associated with the design, operation and maintenance of modern systems of production. Dahrendorf's theory has received empirical backing from Mackenzie's (1973) study of skilled craftsmen in Rhode Island. Mackenzie suggests that there has been a progressive structural shift in the American class structure which has witnessed the differentiation of skilled manual workers away from the rest of the manual working class but not towards assimilation by the lower middle class. Indeed, it is this awareness of the distinct structural position of skilled manual workers within the class structures of advanced capitalist societies that prompted Mackenzie's (1974) critique of the *Affluent Worker* series. Mackenzie recognized that Goldthorpe and Lockwood *et al.*'s refutation of the embourgeoisement thesis could not be complete since it failed to investigate systematically the position of skilled manual workers, who are generally the most well-paid within the British working class. Part of the aim of this research is to take up this issue suggested by Mackenzie in an attempt to discover if there is any truth in the view that British skilled manual workers have been 'embourgeoisified' in the twentieth century.

The general model of skilled manual workers in the British class structure can now be outlined:

1. The industrial revolution created an homogeneous manual working class.
2. The period after 1848 witnessed the progressive disintegration of this factory proletariat and the emergence of a labour aristocracy of skilled workers.
3. This sectionalism began to collapse in the 1880's and 1890's and a new 'homogeneous' working class developed.
4. This 'homogeneous' working class continued until the 1940's.
5. During the post-1945 period there was a progressive redifferentiation of the manual working class and skilled manual workers re-emerged as a distinct class or stratum.

It is the purpose of this research to investigate whether this model is correct by means of an empirical investigation of material collected in Rochdale about the changing relations between skilled and non-skilled manual workers in the town between 1856 and 1964. The model will be probed initially in terms of the economic structuration of the manual working class around the axis of skill by means of evidence on trade union organization and earnings differentials. Subsequently, the model will be assessed from the perspective of the social structuration of the manual working class with the help of data gathered on intermarriage. However, before this analysis can proceed, it is necessary to clarify the concept of skill and to describe briefly the salient characteristics of Rochdale. These two tasks form the basis of the next two chapters.

4

Theoretical orientations to skill

In the first chapter of this research it was argued that it is vital to analyse the empirical structuration of the working class and not simply to assume some sort of pristine class homogeneity. A further argument was presented suggesting that popular sociological notions of a 'traditional' working class were mythical. In particular, it was held that such notions provide an unreliable historical bench-mark against which to assess the 'newness' of the post-1945 working class. If the notions of an homogeneous, 'traditional' working class do not contribute a useful departure-point for the historical analysis of working class structuration, the corpus of studies engaged in the investigation of the 'labour aristocracy' in the nineteenth century and the sociological literature on skilled manual workers in the twentieth century do provide such a focus, since, despite the welter of competing definitions, a general model concerning the development of historical relations between the skilled and non-skilled can be extracted and empirically examined. It is the purpose of this research to examine the nature, duration and variability of internal skilled relations within the British manual working class between 1856 and 1964, in an attempt to discover the appropriateness of the model constructed in chapter 3. However, before such an analysis proceeds, it is necessary to ask what light conventional sociological theories shed upon the nature and evolution of skilled work.

The issue of changes in the level of skill amongst the labour forces of advanced capitalist societies has become a major topic of interest for British sociologists. A meeting held at the London School of Economics in 1978 under the auspices of the British Sociological Association Industrial Sociology Group on 'Braverman and Deskilling' attracted an audience of over a hundred.[1] Thirty or more researchers gave papers to the ensuing S.S.R.C. conference on 'Deskilling and the Labour Process' later that year. Wood (1982) has produced a compendium volume from that conference and both More (1980) and Lee (1979 and 1981) have published additional material on the subject. One major factor in this upsurge of interest involves an increasing recognition by both Marxist and non-Marxist sociologists that skill is a central issue in the development of contemporary class structures.

The reception of Braverman's *Labor and Monopoly Capital* (1974) was part of the general burgeoning of neo-Marxist analysis in the 1970's with its particular emphasis on the political economy of the labour process (see Friedman, 1977a, 1977b and the Brighton Labour Process Group, 1977). Braverman's emphasis on the de-skilling of work in the twentieth century stimulated considerable research, notably in the areas of women's paid labour (Beechey, 1978), micro-electronics (Downing, 1980) and clerical proletarianization (Crompton, 1978). It was also apparent to non-Marxist sociologists that the skilled divide within the manual working class required investigation. Mackenzie's (1974) critique of the *Affluent Worker* series was seminal. Mackenzie argued that Goldthorpe and Lockwood *et al.*'s refutation of the 'embourgeoisement' thesis could not be regarded as conclusive since it applied only to affluent semi-skilled assembly-line workers and not to (even more) affluent skilled craftsmen. Events in the engineering industry over the last few years have demonstrated the continued significance of differences around the axis of skill within the manual working class. The British Leyland toolroom[2] and Heathrow maintenance engineers' disputes in 1977, the significant swing in support to Thatcherism by skilled manual workers (K. Coates, 1979, p. 31) in the 1979 General Election, mainly as a result of Labour Government incomes policies that 'squeezed' skilled differentials, and the evident hostility between the Amalgamated Union of Engineering Workers (A.U.E.W.) and the Transport and General Workers Union (T.G.W.U.) recently at British Leyland have all continued to suggest that skill remains a topic that merits serious sociological inquiry. Gallie (1978) and Maitland (1980 and 1983) have provided further evidence that, in addition to divisions derived from earnings differentials and status, the separate industrial organization of skilled maintenance engineers and non-skilled production workers (and particularly the dependence of the latter upon the former) produces objective conflicts of interest at work between elements within the manual workforces in chemical and tyre factories in advanced capitalist societies. Given these common concerns amongst sociologists about questions of skilled manual workers in advanced capitalist societies, it is worth asking two questions about skill itself. Firstly, what theories of skill are available to sociologists? Secondly, how adequate are these theories, particularly for a characterization of trends in manual work in Britain?

There are two dominant, and apparently contradictory, grand-theoretical interpretations of skilled work in advanced societies: post-industrialism and Marxism. Post-industrialist theorists paint a picture of an increasing demand for, and provision of, skilled workers in advanced industrial societies. This secular model will be termed the 'skilling'[3] thesis. The general argument as found in writers like Bell (1974), Touraine (1969) and, to an extent, Habermas (1976), is that advanced industrial society requires an increasingly educated work force. Arguments are put forward about the growth of 'knowledge' as a new factor of production and the concomitant growth of knowledge-producing (universities, research institutes) and knowledge-consuming (electronics) industries. Indeed, it can be argued with considerable force that post-industrial theories are all primarily theoretical sociological reflections upon empirical work conducted by American labour economists concerned to explain the rapid and dramatic growth there of the service sector of employment. This connection is less obvious in Touraine or Habermas, since their arguments derive more from assertions based upon fragmentary and limited evidence than from systematic reflection upon empirical research; but it is quite explicit in Daniel Bell, who openly acknowledges his debt to the pioneering work done by the American labour economist, Fuchs.

For Fuchs (1968), the major explanatory variable in the growth of the service economy is change associated with the development and implementation of advanced technology. His thesis suggests that the evolution of new advanced technologies – electronics in general, and computers in particular – requires an increasingly educated workforce for its development. Emphasis is increasingly put on investment in manpower or the production of 'human' capital. Proponents of human capital theory like Becker (1964) at Chicago, who provide the theoretical basis for Fuchs' work, argue that more and more capital investment takes the form of training and that the workforce becomes increasingly 'valuable' as an input for production. It is the putative effects of, on the one hand, the growth of the 'knowledge-industries' and, on the other, of increasingly sophisticated technology that produce a secular 'skilling' of the labour force under advanced industrialism.

Advanced industrial societies have witnessed an increase in the sophistication of technology, an expansion of knowledge-producing and knowledge-consuming industries and also a dramatic increase in general levels of education. However, there are certain features of the correlation between increased formal education and expanding knowledge-related industries that should lead to a certain scepticism about the validity of post-industrialist theories of 'skilling'. Firstly, increasing years spent at school do not necessarily lead to an increase in the 'skills' of the incumbents. Sources as wide apart as the *Black Book* on education and radical sociological research typified by Willis (1977) and Corrigan (1979) cast

serious doubt on the likelihood of there being a simple, positive relationship between years of formal education endured and industrial
competence. Secondly, for Britain at least, research has suggested that the
formal education system is a poor indicator of future occupational
attainment since it ignores the crucial role of part-time, post-school
education in the accumulation of industrially-relevant educational creden-
tials.[4] Without a more complex model of levels of education and training
than merely years spent in school, post-industrialist theories remain, at
best, conjecture. Thirdly, the undoubted sophistication of the products of
advanced electronic technology does not necessarily require the existence
of high levels of skill in its routine production. The extensive division of
labour and functions within the enormous multi-national corporations
that produce such commodities as computers, video-recorders and calcu-
lators, may well decrease the proportion of technically-sophisticated
personnel required for research and development and for production
within the overall workforce. That the hypothesis of decreasing need for
skill is likely is suggested by the widespread *manufacture* of such
commodities in Taiwan, Hong Kong and South Korea – countries not
renowned for their post-industrial structures. Given the high ratio of
capital to labour in such ventures, it would seem difficult to explain the
massive increase in the provision of educational services in advanced
industrial societies simply in terms of technological exigencies. Indeed, a
technologically deterministic argument might suggest that there is a good
case for reducing educational expenditure and provision, since new
technologies make it increasingly irrelevant. Finally, if one examines the
expansion of the service sector carefully, it becomes apparent that the
fastest growing and largest sectors are not technically qualified personnel
but clerical and sales-workers, teachers, social workers and medical
workers.

If the post-industrialist theory of 'skilling' lacks a certain prima-facie
plausibility, it is still worth asking what evidence there is, in Britain at least,
about changes in levels of training amongst manual workers. The situation
appears confused. Recent newspaper articles and television programmes[5]
all echo the conclusions of the Carr Committee Report (1958) which
argued that serious structural shortages of skilled manpower had emerged
in the post-war period, particularly in the engineering industry. Furthermore, both Liepman (1958) and Williams (1958) severely criticized the
attitudes of the Amalgamated Engineering Union in the 1950's towards
industrial training. However, Lee (1979) has challenged the dominant view
that the Engineering Union simply uses apprenticeship restrictions as a
means to restrict labour supply and enhance relative wages and status, and
presents evidence on the deliberate policies utilized by many engineering

employers of engaging apprentice-labour as a cheap substitute for skilled craftsmen.

The confusion surrounding levels of skill in the post-1945 engineering industry is apparent. On the one hand, employers, Government inquiries, National Economic Development Office Reports (1977 and 1980), and even trade unions complain about the lack of skilled engineering craftsmen, yet, on the other hand, it is argued that apprentices are employed in many firms as cheap forms of labour. However, if the latter point is true, the investigator is led to ask how untrained apprentices can perform the tasks of apprentice-served men. This apparent paradox can only be solved after a detailed analysis of the historical evolution of skill in industries like engineering, which remains a task to be accomplished by social scientists.

However, if the focus of inquiry about levels of skill and training amongst the manual working class is shifted from the recent post-war era to a time-span of, say, a hundred years or more, it becomes much clearer that levels of industrial training *have* witnessed a general and persistent decline. In the engineering industry, length of apprenticeship has declined from seven years to five, and, at present, stands at either three or four years. Such reductions have been paralleled in other apprenticed trades like printing,[6] building,[7] and shipbuilding.[8] It is now possible to gain the basis of a craft skill at a Government Training Centre in six months and it is the actual state of the local labour market and particularly the power of skilled trade unions that determines whether individuals with Government Training Centre skills are recognized as being on a par with apprentice-served craftsmen in any particular area.[9] That such individuals are so recognized *de facto* in certain areas must suggest strongly that a basic level of skill in these trades can be attained in six months, yet there is still a lack of research into the question of whether such G.T.C. men actually achieve full levels of skill subsequently or whether they become effectively tied to specific internal labour markets.

Consequently, in a broad historical context, it would appear that the general levels of industrial training have decreased for skilled manual workers in Britain. It might be argued that increased levels of skill produced in schools have facilitated this decrease in post-school training, so that the overall degree of skill has remained constant or, perhaps, even increased. However, anyone who has attended a 'vocational' comprehensive school will not need the evidence from educational sociologists like Willis (1977) and Corrigan (1979), to be persuaded of the improbability of such a contention. In reality, the levels of technical expertise generated at school in subjects like metalwork are so rudimentary that nobody could argue seriously that they have compensated for the decline in skill associated with diminished periods for apprenticeships. A more serious criticism of the relevance of the evidence outlined on skilled manual work would be that post-industrial theory is not focused on manual workers at all, but on the greatly expanded non-manual sections of the workforce in the twentieth century. Such a viewpoint would hold that decreasing levels of skill and training within the manual working class are compensated for by increasing levels of skill within such occupations as draughtsman, designer, systems analyst and production manager. If such a view were correct, it would contradict the central image of post-industrialist theory (and its ally, human capital theory) of an increasingly skilled *manual* working class. Consequently, given its implausibility conceptually and empirically, the 'skilling' thesis must be rejected as a possible model from which to approach the analysis of trends in the historical development of the British manual working class.

The second major theoretical orientation towards secular trends in skill – the Marxist theory of the 'de-skilling' of the working class – would appear, therefore, to be more plausible, at least on a prima-facie basis. However, it will be shown that, even if there is an apparent identity between Marxist prognoses and empirical developments in levels of skill amongst the workforce, the latter in themselves cannot corroborate the former.

Marx's theory of 'de-skilling' is rooted in his theory of capitalist development and it stands or falls as a theory upon this conceptual base. It will be shown that Marx's theory of capitalist development is incoherent and consequently Marx's derivative theory of de-skilling cannot provide an adequate foundation for the analysis of trends in levels of skill amongst the workforce of industrial capitalist societies.

Marx's theory of capitalist development has certain key features. It is inherently teleological at the level of systemic properties of societies (or 'social formations'). Such teleology is a persistent feature of Marxism and its difficulties are well known (see Giddens, 1973). Amongst its main problems is the historical evidence which demonstrates that the working classes of the advanced capitalist societies are not revolutionary nor even strongly socialist. Marxist teleology has its roots in Hegelian dialectics which are themselves rooted in a rationalistic re-interpretation of Christian eschatology. However, what appears to be less well-recognized is that Marx's teleology of class development is strongly anchored in the economic analyses of *Capital* itself. In particular, the notions of the progressive polarization of the class structure, the proletarianization of intermediary and transitional classes, the homogenization of the proletariat and the 'de-skilling' of the workforce, are all derived from this theory of capitalist development. Indeed, there is no doubt that Marx felt that his economic theories provided the theoretical justification for his general model of class development. This can be seen when Marx cites *The Communist Manifesto* in Chapter XXXII of *Capital : Volume 1*, where he argues that:

> The advance of industry, whose involuntary promoter is the bourgeoisie,
> replaces the isolation of the labourers, due to competition, by their
> revolutionary combination, due to association. The development of
> Modern Industry, therefore, cuts from under its feet, the very foundation
> on which the bourgeoisie produces and appropriates products. What the
> bourgeoisie, therefore, produces, above all, are its own grave-diggers. Its
> fall and the victory of the proletariat are equally inevitable... Of all the
> classes, that stand face to face with the bourgeoisie today, the proletariat
> alone is a really revolutionary class. The other classes perish and
> disappear in the face of Modern Industry, the proletariat is its special and
> essential product... The lower middle-classes, the small manufacturers,
> the shopkeepers, the artisan, the peasant, all these fight against the
> bourgeoisie, to save from extinction their existence as fractions of the
> middle-class... they are reactionary, for they try to roll back the wheel of
> history.
> Karl Marx und Friedrich Engels, 'Manifest der Kommunistischen Partei',
> London, 1848, pp. 9, 11. (Marx, 1970, p. 715)

Let those who argue that Marx's *Capital* does not involve a theory of
capitalist development take note of Marx's own chapter heading which
precedes the above citation – 'The Historical Tendency of Capitalist
Accumulation'. Only the most blinkered can fail to see the necessary
connection between Marx's pessimistic teleological economic theory and
his version of class developments in capitalist societies.

Marx argues in *Capital* that, under capitalism, entrepreneurs are forced
through the mechanisms of competition and the expansion of capital to
rely increasingly on 'dead-labour' [labour embodied in the form of
machinery] in the sphere of production. In this respect, Marx echoed a
common pessimism amongst early Victorian political economists about the
likely results of increased mechanization for society as a whole; a feeling
expressed with lucidity by Ricardo (1973) in his chapter 'On Machinery' in
the *Principles of Political Economy and Taxation*. The increasing application of capital-intensive mechanization produces, according to Marx,
a constant tendency towards redundancy and unemployment of labour.
The main social effect of mechanization – widespread unemployment – facilitates the continuous reproduction of a 'reserve army of labour'
under capitalism; 'a law of population peculiar to the capitalist mode of
production' (Marx, 1970, pp. 591–2). The reserve army of labour itself
provides the mechanism whereby wages paid to labour remain at
subsistence level.

This central image of a capitalist system that forces competing capitals to
replace 'living labour' (workers) with 'dead labour' (machinery) also

provides the foundation for Marx's theories of the rising organic composition of capital and the concomitant theory of the tendency for a declining rate of profit. The organic composition of capital is the value-ratio between machinery and labour power. It has been shown that Marx's theoretical project is incoherent at this point. Both Robinson (1942) and Sweezy (1942) have demonstrated that, for the tendency towards a rising organic composition to produce a falling rate of profit, the rate of exploitation must remain constant – which violates the assumption of subsistence wages, since a constant rate of exploitation coupled with a rising organic composition *must* increase real wages, since the proportion of time spent by labour producing the increased production which results from greater capitalization remains constant.[10]

This is a very serious weakness in Marx's argument, since profits are the motor of the capitalist economy. In essence, all that Marx's arguments suggest is that, in a simplified, abstract model of capitalism, profits are affected by the level of wages: a conclusion quite acceptable to neo-Ricardian and post-Keynesian economists.

There are further internal theoretical difficulties associated with Marx's assumption that increasing technical change must lead to a rise in the organic composition of capital. As Sweezy points out, there is a theoretical ambiguity in Marx's formulations:

> In physical terms it is certainly true that the amount of machinery and materials per worker has tended to grow at a very rapid rate for at least the last century and a half. But the organic composition of capital is a value expression; and because of steadily rising labour productivity, the growth in the volume of machinery and materials per worker must not be regarded as an index of the change in the organic composition of capital. Actually, the general impression of the rapidity of the growth of the organic composition of capital seems to be considerably exaggerated. (Sweezy, 1942, p. 103)

The 'de-skilling' thesis in Marx is intimately linked with the previous formulations. For Marx, the 'logic' of capitalist competition necessitates the revolutionization of the techniques of production. This takes the form of increasing mechanization and, as a corollary, the displacement of skills. In a literal sense, the workforce is proletarianized; it has nothing to sell on the labour market, except its wives and children. 'De-skilling' is one major component of the overall theory of proletarianization under capitalism; the other being progressive elimination of the petty bourgeoisie. The 'de-skilling' thesis is, in consequence, tied to notions of the progressive polarization of the capitalist class structure into a small capitalist class and an ever-expanding and indigent non-skilled proletarian class.

However, if there is a series of problems associated with the articulation of various elements (such as the organic composition and subsistence wages) within Marx's overall pessimistic teleology, there are also crucial problems connected with his interpretation of technical change under capitalism. In reality, capitalists seek to minimize *costs* and this must involve both means of production and labour, since both can have an effect on productivity. Consequently, capitalists will seek to introduce 'capital-saving' and 'labour-saving' processes in order to prevent a rise in costs; otherwise, rising costs, under a competitive model of capitalism, must inevitably reduce profitability.[11] Clearly, this affects the status of the Marxist model of de-skilling, for it must include changes associated both with new machinery and with transformations of the labour process caused by alterations in the actual organization and manning of existing machinery.

Apart from the complexity of capitalists' strategies (and their managerial agents), another central problem is connected with Marx's central imagery of a falling rate of profit associated with increasing mechanization. Howard and King have demonstrated that unless technical change is 'inherently irreversible' (1975, p. 209), it is unclear why a reversion to older forms of technology would not occur. However, this suggests that new forms of production may be more profitable and this leaves scope for the entry of a neglected force within Marxist analyses – offensive and defensive strategies by sections of the working class in order to enhance their relative share of the surplus.

Indeed, it is the failure to incorporate the role of organized strategies by sections of the working class that seriously weakened the most stimulating recent Marxist analysis of de-skilling, Braverman's *Labor and Monopoly Capital* (1974). Braverman, unlike Marx, is far more aware of the different forms of capitalist-managerial strategies in the routinization of work. His study of the 'degradation of work' in twentieth century America deals with both increased mechanization and changes in the organization of existing technologies. However, Braverman fails to provide conceptual space[12] for working class reactions to such managerial strategies, since he believes that the labour process is both analytically and substantively separate from political struggles.[13] Braverman is quite explicit on this point. He states clearly at the beginning of *Labor and Monopoly Capital* that: 'No attempt will be made to deal with the modern working class on the level of its consciousness, organization or activities.' (Braverman, 1974, pp. 26–7).

The incorporation of such factors as working class organizations and their offensive and defensive strategies within the economy is the great strength of neo-Ricardian and post-Keynesian economics. These theories are less deterministic than Marx's, since they adopt the central image of a 'balance of forces' for the determination of relative shares between capital and labour. This metaphor of relative power in the processes of distribution within industrial capitalist societies leads directly towards the incorporation of sociological and historical factors, since these become crucial for an understanding of the structuration of the capital: labour relationship. In particular, these theoretical approaches lead directly towards the analysis of the structure of labour market behaviour which constitutes the pivotal arena for income distribution. It is apparent that there is an affinity between the concerns of neo-Ricardian and post-Keynesian[14] economics and recent interest by sociologists like Blackburn and Mann (1979) and exemplified in the symposium in the *Cambridge Journal of Economics* (Elbaum *et al.* 1979) on the labour process. Clearly the investigation of labour markets and the analysis of relations between trade unions and management are of considerable interest for such economic theories. Furthermore, the neo-Ricardian and post-Keynesian emphases on the impossibility of providing abstract, *a priori* answers to *actual, empirical* outcomes of distributive struggles is highly compatible with Weberian[15] emphases on the variability of class relations and the absolute necessity for empirical investigations of their structuration.

Some may argue that there is no substantive difference between Marxist and neo-Ricardian, post-Keynesian and contemporary sociological approaches since all emphasize the notions of 'class struggle' and 'class conflict' as central for an understanding of the nature of capitalist society. Nothing could be further from the truth! The notions of 'class struggle' and 'class conflict' have quite different meanings for the two forms of analysis. Marxism regards class struggle as the motor which will generate the destruction of the capitalist system. Neo-Ricardian, post-Keynesian and 'class structural' approaches regard 'class conflict' as an essential part of the capitalist system, and remain agnostic about the durability of that system. Furthermore, the underlying frameworks and models are quite distinct. Marxism is deterministic, deductive and pessimistic, whereas these other economic and sociological schools emphasize the indeterminate and the empirical.

What kind of a model of skill can be derived from these theoretical discussions? Firstly, it should be clear that neither the post-industrialist nor Marxist models are adequate. Post-industrial arguments about the secular 'skilling' of the workforce would appear unlikely as a first approximation for the sociological analysis of the historical development of the British manual working class. Marxist 'de-skilling' theories are both internally incoherent and contain a conceptual blind-spot concerning reactions by manual working class organizations, particularly trade unions, to capitalist-managerial strategies to de-skill the labour process. Indeed, both theories are technologically deterministic, in as much as they both assume that technological change produces isomorphic changes in the division of labour. Such an assumption will be treated as an empirical hypothesis in this research rather than as a theoretical *a priori*.

The model that would seem most appropriate at this stage of the argument contains three elements. Firstly, industrial capitalist society involves a structured conflict between capital and labour. This conflict is fundamentally asymmetric because of the essential characteristic of industrial capitalism: the separation of the direct producer from the means of production as an effect of capitalist ownership rights. However, the determination of the proportion of the surplus product that will accrue to either capital or to labour cannot be predicted *a priori* and, therefore, *a fortiori*, no unilinear immanent tendency towards secular decline (or rise for that matter) in the rate of profit can be determined. The determination of the rate of profit cannot be deduced independently of the legal, political, ideological and economic conditions that envelop production.

Secondly, the asymmetric conflicts between capital and labour over wages (the distribution of the surplus) and over technology and the division of labour (the 'managerial prerogative') are conducted within variable structures. One key element of these variable structures of asymmetric conflict is the nature and structure of the labour market.

Thirdly, the model hypothesizes that under certain circumstances[16] organizations of workers (generally in Britain trade unions, but also 'informal' groups of workers) can strongly delimit the effectiveness of the managerial prerogative. Two key variables in such delimitations of the managerial prerogative by skilled manual workers would appear to be:

(a) strength of workers' organizations;
(b) degree of 'tightness' or 'slackness' within the local labour market.

Clearly, this model is making at least two empirical historical assumptions. Firstly, that workers can organize either formally or informally[17] and, secondly, that skilled manual workers organize separately from the non-skilled.[18] If both assumptions are granted, it is possible to hypothesize four empirical outcomes in the degree of delimitation of the managerial prerogative by organized skilled labour as illustrated in Model 4.1.

The model as outlined suggests that when strongly organized skilled manual workers confront management in 'tight' labour markets, management will acquiesce to their demands in order to secure skilled labour which is in short supply and in the knowledge that the power of organized skilled labour will prevent their costs out-distancing their competitors. Overt industrial conflict is likely to be brief. On the other hand, in situations where skilled manual workers are weakly organized and the labour market

Model 4.1. *A model of the various forms of delimitation of the managerial prerogative by skilled manual workers*

	Strength of skilled labour	
Type of labour market	Strongly organized	Weakly organized
Strong demand for skilled labour ('tight')	Managerial prerogative strongly restricted by skilled workers	Managerial prerogative strong but scope for 'picking off' employers if some firms are more formally organized than others
Weak demand for skilled labour ('slack')	Managerial prerogative strongly challenged by organizations of skilled workers, but these organizations are themselves subject to challenge by management	Managerial prerogative strongly implemented

is slack, a strong managerial prerogative is to be expected and conflict will take the form of individualistic actions (high absenteeism and high labour turn-over) and will be sporadic. In situations where the labour market is 'slack' and skilled manual workers are strongly organized, strong attempts to implement managerial prerogatives will be met by equally fierce resistance. On the other hand, where the labour market is 'tight' yet skilled manual workers remain weakly organized, a situation of 'picking off' firms will be experienced. 'Picking off' refers to the twin processes of organizing a particular firm, either by a recruitment drive or (but often associated with such a drive) getting union members to go and work at a particular firm. Once a firm is organized in these ways, the firm can be 'picked off' by means of strike action: a central claim of which will be trade union recognition.

This model is fairly simple and relatively unsophisticated. Obviously a whole set of exogenous variables affects the strength of organized labour and the demand for labour within the local labour market. The structure of capital and the nature of the product market are two such key variables. If capital is sufficiently mobile it can pre-empt factors like strong union organization and shortages of skilled labour, by relocating production to where unions are weak and skilled labour available. However, as often as not, the availability of skilled labour is tied to traditional centres of production and, consequently, capital must either find new ways of producing without such skills or weigh up the costs of training labour in the new locations.

The nature and state of the product market is also significant since it affects the degree to which withdrawal of co-operation by workers damages employers. For example, in circumstances of declining overall trade, the common interests of capitalists and of workers may inhibit trade union action which could cause a loss of markets and a decline in employment prospects. In other circumstances, empty order books may lead management to challenge traditional union powers over the managerial prerogative in order to provoke strikes[19] and save upon costs. A main aim of this research is to examine and analyse empirical material gathered on trade union structuration and the course of wage differentials within the manual working class in Rochdale between 1856 and 1964, in order to ascertain the extent to which the simple model outlined above is sufficient to grasp the essential relations between skilled manual workers and management; and how far additional variables need to be introduced into the analysis.

What are the conceptual assumptions behind this model? They cannot be Marxist in any strict sense because of what has been argued earlier about the characteristics of Marxism. It is the emphasis on teleological, deterministic, 'tendencies' that produce an effect on the 'phenomenal forms' of social development which constitutes the distinctiveness of the Marxist model. Such models are both theoretically incoherent and empirically implausible and it is to be hoped that the model outlined above is neither. It might be argued that the model is Marxist in a weaker sense, particularly given its use of concepts like capital and labour, endemic structural conflict and the like. However, such an orientation is unhelpful since it fails to recognize that the model presented above is compatible with both neo-Ricardian *and* post-Keynesian economics and also with all variants of Weberian conflict theory. Marxism, as a theoretical school, should not be collapsed into other forms of analysis because a method of *ad hoc* incorporation produces two damaging consequences. Firstly, it ignores the specific claims of Marxist analyses and, secondly, there is a persistent tendency for a whole array of implausible concepts, like the tendency for the rate of profit to fall, to enter in the wake of the assimilation of a few, apparently innocuous, Marxist conceptions. This is not to take a position of sociological 'purism' but to accept the distinctiveness of Marxism and not to wish to incorporate it.

The argument in the first four chapters has examined the dominant emphasis in British class analysis on class consciousness and found it lacking in certain key respects. It has been argued that one central area for fruitful analysis of internal class structuration lies in the area of divisions, distinctions, conflicts and contradictions associated with the processes surrounding local labour markets. It was argued further that an historical perspective was essential if an attempt were to be made to discuss changes in the internal structuration of the manual working class. The notion of a 'traditional' working class was held to be unhelpful for such a venture, whereas the notion of an endemic, variable structural distinction between skilled and non-skilled manual workers in Britain was seen as providing a useful point of departure. This research is an attempt to specify empirically the varying structuration of the manual working class around the axis of skill. As has been shown in this chapter, post-industrial 'skilling' and Marxist 'de-skilling' theories both contain serious weaknesses in their interpretations of secular trends in skill. However, a simple, heuristic model of relations between skilled unions and management was suggested and will be examined in relation to the evidence presented. However, if the analysis is to be empirically informed, it must set limits for the incorporation of relevant data. It was decided to focus the analysis on Rochdale in Lancashire. I chose Rochdale because it permitted an extensive analysis of an industrialized environment and because it contained two major industries that have failed to come under the spotlight of contemporary British sociology – textiles and engineering. I chose the beginning date of the study as 1856 because by that time (the date of the incorporation of Rochdale as a Municipal Borough) the town was clearly an industrialized, urban environment. The study ends in 1964 for reasons that will be clarified in the next chapter of this research. This next chapter will discuss the social structure of Rochdale and the nature of evidence used in the empirical analyses. However, it is worth pointing out again that one central thrust of the empirical investigation of relations between skilled and non-skilled manual workers is to ascertain whether relations as structured at the workplace are isomorphic with relations as structured in the community. Hence, the next chapter will deal not only with the nature of the evidence relating to workplace structuration (trade unions and wage differentials) but also with evidence pertaining to social endogamy (intermarriage).

5

Aspects of the social structure of Rochdale, 1856–1964

The location of the study

It is clear from the discussion in chapter 3 about the labour aristocracy and from the model of relations between skilled manual workers and management elaborated in chapter 4 that there was a need to find a specific location in which to test the propositions put forward in both chapters. Given the contents of both chapters, it was felt necessary that such a study should be conducted in an industrialized environment over a lengthy period of time. An industrialized location was essential in order to avoid those additional complicating factors associated with industrialization. It was also felt that there was a need to examine at least two industries in the same place in order to see whether changes in one industry paralleled developments in another. In particular, it would be useful to have data on two major industries that have provided much of the evidence for the thesis of a labour aristocracy in Britain: cotton and engineering. Rochdale represents an ideal setting for such a study since it was industrialized by the 1850's,[1] contains the two industries, cotton and engineering, and has good sources of data. The rest of this chapter will provide a brief history of industry in Rochdale, comments upon the relevance of the material examined for sociological portraits of British social structure and a discussion of the data sources themselves.

A brief history of industry in Rochdale[2]

Rochdale lies on the eastern edge of industrial Lancashire, close to the Pennines which separate Lancashire from the West Riding of Yorkshire. Manchester lies eleven miles to the south-west, Bury six miles to the west and Oldham six miles south. Although a famous centre for cotton production, Rochdale has never been a 'cotton town' like Nelson or Colne, in the sense of being almost exclusively dependent on cotton for the

49

livelihood of its inhabitants. Despite the fact that around the turn of the nineteenth century Rochdale was the largest ring spinning centre in Britain, it has always been characterized by a varied economic infrastructure.

The main industry before the Industrial Revolution was wool. During the seventeenth and eighteenth centuries local wool, instead of being exported to the Continent as in previous centuries, was warehoused by local merchants who 'put it out' to cottagers for spinning and weaving in the domestic system of pre-industrial mercantile capitalism. During the first half of the nineteenth century, steam machinery was introduced into the woollen industry and Rochdale became a major centre for factory-produced woollen products. However, despite the dominance of woollen production at the moment of Municipal Incorporation (1856: the date when the substantive material analysed in this book commences), the first fifty years of the nineteenth century saw the tremendous growth of the cotton industry and the transposition of Rochdale from the West Riding woollen zone to a world centre for cotton production.

Local historians have found it difficult to specify the exact moment when cotton production began in Rochdale, but there is no doubt that the first factories were built during the 1790's. It was during the two subsequent decades of Napoleonic Wars that cotton in Rochdale became firmly established, as Lancashire as a whole took a progressive stranglehold on the world market. The simultaneous development of factory production in the woollen and cotton industries stimulated the growth of other local industries, particularly coal mining and textile machinery production. The coal industry became increasingly unimportant after the mid-nineteenth century, with the working-out of profitable seams, and does not feature in the analysis presented in this research. Textile machinery developed after about 1810, and by the early 1850's the major enterprises that span the period covered in this research (1856–1964) had come into existence and were well established. The second half of the nineteenth century saw the progressive growth of a more generalized engineering industry which produced such machinery as machine tools, electrical switchgear, springs, cranes, hydraulic hoists and, of course, the many fish and chip frying machines evident all over Britain. A more recent important development has been the growth of asbestos goods production and Rochdale now contains one of the largest factories in the world producing asbestos yarn.

Rochdale has been over the last century or so a predominantly 'two-industry' town and hence is a more complex social and industrial phenomenon than the 'one-industry' communities like mining villages that have occupied so much sociological attention. Nevertheless, until the post-1945 era, there can be little doubt that cotton manufacture was the predominant industry after 1850, both in terms of employment and of

Table 5.1 *Numbers of workers (male and female) employed in the textile and engineering industries*

	1861	1871	1881	1891	1901	1911	1921	1931	1951	1961
Males in engineering	929	N	1,567	1,443	3,966	5,529	5,627	4,238	5,074	4,580
Females in engineering	1	O	1	18	—	103	143	27	364	480
Total employed in engineering	930		1,568	1,461	3,966	5,632	5,770	4,265	5,438	5,060
Males in cotton	5,467	D	5,229	5,902	5,540	10,224	8,638	6,324	4,399	3,101
Males in wool	3,270	A	2,153	1,928	—	—	—	—	—	—
Women in cotton	6,117	T	8.075	8,409	9,218	13,592	13,018	12,331	8,406	6,380
Women in wool	2,088	A	2,272	3,007	—	—	—	—	—	—
Total employed in cotton	11,584		13,304	14,311	14,758	23,816	21,656	18,655	12,805	9,481
Percentage: engineering/ cotton	8.03		11.79	10.21	26.87	23.65	26.64	22.85	42.47	53.37

Source: The decennial Censuses, 1861–1961[3].

determining the periods of expansion and contraction in the town. This can be seen from Table 5.1.

The causes of the decline of the Lancashire cotton industry have been recounted many times, since along with the other dwindling staple industries, they have been the subject of much analysis. Freeman *et al.* (1966, p. 121) summarize the position:

> Though in Victorian Manchester it seemed that Lancashire monopolized the world's cotton industry almost by divine dispensation, it is now clear that some contraction ... was, from the first, inevitable. Lancashire had no unique range of advantages for the cotton industry, which it acquired almost by historical accident. In its more rudimentary forms this is a simple manufacture which has naturally become the spearhead of industrialization in many parts of the tropical world, and perhaps the most widely dispersed of the world's great industries. Countries which were Lancashire's customers in the nineteenth century now have their own mills, and some have become successful exporters of cheap cloth.

Table 5.2. *Consumption of raw cotton (million lbs)*

	World	U.K.	% (U.K./World)
1790	25	25	100
1829–31	420	240	57
1882–4	4,000	1,480	37
1910–13	10,500	2,100	20
1926–8	12,200	1,470	12
1936–8	14,000	1,320	9
1949–51	14,200	1,000	7
1953–5	16,800	820	5

Source: R. Robson, *The Cotton Industry in Britain* (London, 1957, p. 2).

This account covers most of the ground, except it leaves out the role of protectionism in the development of the Japanese[4] and Indian[5] textile industries, and it totally ignores the commitment by both capitalists and workers to archaic labour relations and techniques. Table 5.2 shows graphically the decline in the consumption of raw cotton.

However, these figures tend to suggest that all was well with the cotton industry prior to 1914, but Ronald Smith (1954) has presented powerful evidence that the difficulties of the inter-war years were rooted in the last quarter of the nineteenth century. There was, in this period, a 'noticeable slowing down in the pace of expansion' (Smith, p. 694) and, technologically, a period of 'marked time'. The impression given by Smith is of Lancashire expanding slowly on the basis of the strong position built up in the 1850's and 1860's but taking a decreasing share of an expanding world market. Towards the end of the nineteenth century, the U.S. and Asia were overhauling the U.K. lead, helped by protectionist policies and there was a continuous decline in the prices of sold goods. With Lancashire strongly tied to export markets (81% in 1910–13, according to Robson, 1957, p. 2) the world events after 1914 were crucial and extremely damaging. During the First World War there was an increasing tendency for countries like India and Egypt to substitute home production for British cottons and also, given strong demand at home in Britain and shipping difficulties, a tendency for Japan to penetrate traditional British Asian markets. After 1918, there was the brief boom of reconstruction that proved so damaging for British staple industries since it produced a situation of over-capitalization in the ensuing depressed markets after

1920.[6] In addition, the policy of putting sterling back at its pre-1914 convertability, whilst good for City morale, led to a severe over-pricing of cotton exports. Lancashire's markets sagged further in the depressed and protectionist 1930's. The history after 1945 makes even more sombre reading. After a short post-war boom, remarkably similar in its consequences to that of 1918–20, the cotton industry began to collapse totally in the years after 1952. Asian competition led to a massive penetration of the home market as a result of Britain's commitment to international free trade. This collapse prompted intervention by the central state apparatus in the form of the Cotton Industry Act, 1960, which had two main aims: firstly to reduce the size of the industry and secondly to stimulate modernization by the offer of subsidies for re-equipment.

The first aspect was a spectacular success: 49% of spindles and 40% of looms (Freeman *et al.*, 1966, p. 123) were scrapped and many factories closed down. The modernization programme had more mixed results, with the spinning sector, rather belatedly, abandoning its traditional mule production, but with weaving still far behind its international competitors in terms of investment and productivity. Rochdale itself escaped better than other textile towns in the vicinity from the fullest impact of this shattering post-war collapse, since two of its specialities – heavy textiles for industrial uses and the finishing trade – had both stood up much better traditionally than the weaving section, as is revealed in the fact that between 1952 and 1958 Rochdale only lost 5% employment in the cotton mills, whereas in the Burnley area employment in cotton fell by 24% and in Blackburn by 21%.

The engineering industry in Rochdale, or in Lancashire as a whole, has not been the subject of previous empirical research. Nevertheless, from discussions with local inhabitants and from an examination of local newspapers[7] and lists of industrial firms,[8] a general portrait can be drawn. The early engineering industry in Rochdale was almost entirely connected, not surprisingly, with the production of textile machinery. These firms, the most prominent of which include Tweedales & Smalley Limited, William Tatham Limited, Thomas Holt Limited, Petrie and McNaught Limited, and Tomlinsons Limited, were all family businesses during the period covered by this research. All of these concerns developed in the mid-nineteenth century and were carried forward on the wave of expanding cotton.

The other main engineering firms, despite more distant origins in some cases, only became significant in size during the 1890's and 1900's. John Holroyd and Company Limited, the machine tool making firm, moved to Rochdale between 1896 and 1906, and the growth of spring manufacture – which is strongly centred in Rochdale – also dates from this period. Consequently, there emerges a picture of increasing diversification and differentiation within the Rochdale engineering sector and, as illustrated by the figures in Table 5.1, of the increasing importance of engineering as a major source of employment during the twentieth century, especially for men.

As can be seen from this brief industrial history, Rochdale has been a major centre for cotton and engineering production during the period between the 1850's and the 1960's. Research in Rochdale will, therefore, permit an examination of the Lancashire cotton industry which, with the overall secular decline of the British textile industry, has been a neglected area for empirical sociological research. Of even more importance, it will permit research into the social structure of a medium-sized town: an area which has been an empirical lacuna in traditional sociological accounts of community structures. Both Frankenberg's (1966) and Lockwood's (1966) models contain such a gap. Frankenberg's 'morphological continuum' of community structures deals with rural areas, small towns like Glossop and Banbury, but from these locations it jumps to metropolitan areas such as Bethnal Green and then to new housing estates. Lockwood's typology of the working class also fails to draw upon evidence from medium-sized towns but rather deals with small towns like Banbury (the epitome of traditional deference) or isolated communities like coal mining villages (the exemplar for traditional proletarianism). It is only in relation to post-1945 affluence that Lockwood shifts his attention to those medium-sized towns, like Luton, that constitute such important centres of population during the period under review. The main reason for the absence of medium-sized towns from Frankenberg's and Lockwood's models derives from the lack of empirical research conducted by social scientists into such environments: a major purpose of this research is to rectify this situation, by an examination of one such town, Rochdale. Clearly, this renders any answer to the question of the typicality of the results of the research into the processes of class structuration problematic. No claim is being made that Rochdale is either a typical or prototypical community. What will be claimed is that the processes discovered are of a general kind and are *likely* to be general in effect. However, this is ultimately an empirical question. All that can be mounted in defence of such a study is that some empirical knowledge is better than none and that perhaps a certain possible loss of typicality will be outweighed by the gains derived from a combination of specific and detailed primary data.

The data

The reason for choosing Rochdale rather than any other similar location lies in the availability of good records for the examination of structuration within the manual working class during the period between the 1850's and the 1960's. As will be seen in the next two chapters, Rochdale has good records on wages and earnings within the manual working class and adequate records about the general framework of trade unions. More importantly, Rochdale possesses the best data on intermarriage in the whole of the region. Given the problems connected with obtaining a sample, which will be discussed in considerable detail below, Rochdale's strong Anglican[9] tradition became of paramount importance for this research.

Since 1837, marriages have been conducted either in authorized religious establishments or in the civil registry offices. An 'ideal' sample of marriage records aimed at discovering patterns of class endogamy would include both sources of information. However, this is an impossibility owing to the present position taken by the General Register Office. As I discovered in my correspondence with the G.R.O. and my discussions with the Rochdale Superintendent Registrar, 'No public right to consult the original entries is given under the Act', and I must re-echo the frustration of Schofield *et al.*, who write that: 'Unless something is done to make the vital registration returns and the post-1861 census schedules accessible, a great deal of potentially valuable research work in the fields of demographic, local, social and economic history will be frustrated. We shall find ourselves in the paradoxical situation that the establishment of the General Register Office in 1836 has in some respects actually hindered the study of this country's population' (*Local Population Studies*, 3, 1969, pp. 4–6).

Since it proved impossible to obtain a sample of marriages from the civil registers, it was necessary to generate the sample from authorized religious establishments. However, prior to 1900 only Anglican churches in Rochdale were registered for marriage.[10] There are no official records of marriages in other than Anglican churches before the period 1907–1910. Nevertheless, this is not a serious disadvantage because in 1900 Anglican churches accounted for 67.8%[11] of all marriages in England and Wales as a whole, and the Anglican Church in Rochdale was much more powerful than in neighbouring towns. The strength of the Anglican tradition derives from the fact that Rochdale Parish Church, St Chad's, was a very powerful and wealthy living in the eighteenth and early nineteenth centuries and, as a consequence, a series of Rochdale vicars ensured that churches were built all over the town to provide the burgeoning population with church places.[12] The array of large churches that cover Rochdale is a testament to their success. Roman Catholicism has never been strong in Rochdale, mainly because there was little Irish immigration into the town during the nineteenth century. Indeed, the records of the two Roman Catholic churches suggest only a small number of marriages and since these records are unofficial and do not provide information on the occupations of the contracting partners, such marriages do not feature in this research. After 1900 there is information from Methodist and other non-conformist churches which could, in principle, permit a comparison with Anglican marriages. However, the absolute numbers of such non-Anglican marriages proved to be so small, despite attempts to 'over-sample' them, that such comparisons proved illusory in practice.

Civil marriages have risen as a proportion of all marriages throughout the period of this research. In England and Wales, civil marriages represented 10.5% of the whole in 1874. 15.0% in 1899 and 28.0% in 1957.[13] However, we know nothing about the biases involved with the sample collected in Rochdale since little is known in detail or with precision about the occupational distributions of civil, Roman Catholic or other non-registered religious marriages. Without access to the complete civil registers, it would seem unlikely that sensible estimates of bias can be made.

The sample itself was drawn from a series of ten-year spans: 1856–1865, 1875–1884, 1900–1909, 1920–1929,[14] and 1955–1964. These were chosen so as to cover the period of the research (1856–1964) and to reflect possible developments associated either with economic change or with the two World Wars. A selection of Anglican churches that covered all areas of Rochdale was included in the sample, as were all available non-Anglican churches and chapels.[15] A two-tier systematic stratified random sample was drawn from the records of the churches selected. The sample was stratified upon the basis of bridegroom's occupation in order to ensure that sufficient non-manual occupations were included in the sample. The standard procedure was to include information from every tenth marriage of manual grooms and every third entry for non-manual grooms.[16] There were five kinds of exception to this standard procedure.[17] All deviations were dictated by the difficulties encountered in gaining access to the marriage records and by the need to make rapid decisions about the sampling frame on the spot. Three of the kinds of exceptions involved over-sampling the non-conformist records. This was done in order to try and compensate for the low number of registrations in such churches. The general low level of marriages solemnized in non-conformist churches in the twentieth century caused considerable surprise, since secondary materials and popular mythology have represented Rochdale as a strong centre for non-conformity. Given this surprising lack of marriages in non-conformist churches and chapels, the strong Anglican presence in the town was extremely useful. The other two 'exceptions' relate to Rochdale Parish Church, St Chad's. They relate to the years 1856 and 1857 and to the entire decennial period from 1875 to 1884. The reason for these deviations relates to specific difficulties in gaining access to the marriage records and to the fact that St Chad's was the first church to be visited. It proved impossible to return there. However, none of the five kinds of exceptions should bias the decennial samples significantly, apart from perhaps the first period, between 1856 and 1865. This is because the over-sampling of non-conformist churches proved nugatory since their absolute numbers were so small when compared with marriages in Anglican churches. Indeed, the numbers in the samples from non-conformist churches proved so low that no meaningful comparisons proved possible.

It is also worth pointing out that the ratio between the total number of marriages in Rochdale and the number of marriages in the churches investigated remained at about 25%[18] throughout the entire span of the research. The proportion of marriages in the sample as a percentage of the total number of marriages in the churches investigated rises from 11% in the period 1856–1865 to 25% in the period between 1955 and 1964.[19] More specific features of the sample will be discussed when the data are analysed in chapters 11 and 12. However, this chapter ends with an explanation of the dates that constitute the beginning and the end of the research period. 1856 was chosen as a convenient starting-point because, as was argued earlier in this chapter, this was the date when the town of Rochdale officially came into being. More importantly, by the mid-1850's Rochdale was clearly an industrialized community with a 'mature' class structure. By starting in 1856 an analysis of the 'longue durée' of the industrial-capitalist class structure could be mounted. The reason for stopping in the mid-1960's rather than more recently was dictated by problems of gaining access to the relevant data. In particular, the clergymen of Rochdale were not keen for their most recent marriage records to be examined for reasons of privacy and confidentiality. At one stage it appeared as if no post-war records would be supplied for inspection. However, in the event, a compromise was settled upon which limited my investigations to finishing in the mid-1960's.

PART II

The economic structuration of class

6

The trade union structure in the Rochdale cotton and engineering industries

This chapter investigates the internal structuration of the manual working class in Rochdale from the perspective of trade union organization. As will be shown in the next two chapters, such workplace organization is central to, and crucial for, an understanding of trends in economic differentials associated with skill within the manual working class. The purpose of this chapter is to ascertain the degree of union organization around the axis of skill. In other words, this chapter will discuss the extent to which the manual working class has been organized at work upon the basis of sectional, occupation skill rather than upon a class basis. Given the model of rhythms of working class sectionalism outlined at the end of chapter 3, particular interest will focus on changes in trade union organization and the extent to which the model captures the essential cadences of working class development.

The first important point to note in the analysis of the trade union structure in Rochdale over the last hundred years is the problem of source materials. Many trade union records have been lost and all material from the local Trades Council has disappeared. In addition, there is the difficulty that those union records that survive have not been kept with academic inquiry in mind and often prove uninformative over key areas of explanation. Furthermore, there are difficulties associated with the cotton unions in as much as their localized, de-centralized structure has facilitated a mode of organization that, from the perspective of written evidence, has indeed been sparse. As a consequence of such difficulties, the basic contours of the union organizations have been reconstructed from secondary sources[1] and supplemented by appropriate inquiries to local unions[2] in order to verify and enlarge upon these secondary accounts. This chapter will focus exclusively on cotton and engineering since, as was shown in the preceding chapter, these industries have dominated employment in Rochdale and no useful records exist for any other industrial sectors.

The cotton industry

Mule spinning

1850–1914

The period after 1850 forms a natural watershed in cotton trade union development. As Turner (1962, pp. 114–15) has shown: 'no modern cotton union can trace a continuous history before 1850 – this, despite the existence of labour combinations in the industry over a preceding century'. The 1850's also present themselves as the first modern decade of cotton unionism in that the major problems of the previous two decades, from the perspective of labour – the demise of handloom weaving and the conflict between hand-mule and automatic mule spinning – had been resolved in favour of the fullest expansion of non-handicraft production, undertaken in the large new factories. However, the trade unions of the 1850's and 1860's were locally based and not connected one with another in any systematic fashion. The major federations or 'Amalgamations' were formed in the 1870's and 1880's.[3]

The stimulus for Amalgamation was not simply economic rationality – improved organization for wage bargaining by the operatives – but also the need felt increasingly for stronger alliances to promote the political demands of cotton labour against the employers in Parliament. However, the key point to emphasize is that the union structure for industrial bargaining had been formed in the previous 'local era' of mid-Victorian prosperity. This can be seen from the continuity of union workplace strategy between the two phases of unionization. The Spinners' Union throughout the period concentrated on three aspects of workshop relations with a view to, as Chapman (1900, p. 467) points out laconically, 'making their remuneration as large as possible', and also to maintaining their skilled status. These involved the stipulation of the number of minders and piecers to each self-acting mule, payment in the form of a piece-rate for the minders and time-rates for the 'big' and 'little' piecers and the organization of the piecers into the Spinners' Union in order to pre-empt any threat of a rival piecers' union. All these aims were pursued by an aggressive policy of industrial relations, whose cost required a high weekly individual contribution.[4] Each area of policy was successfully undertaken during this period. The number of men-to-machines in the Rochdale district was agreed at two piecers to help one minder maintain production over two machines. The piece-rate system was formalized and subject to the Oldham List[5] in 1876 and after the 1893 lock-out, to the requirements of the Brooklands Agreement.[6] Despite the impression of collusion with management that these appeared to reveal, what was being pursued in fact was a policy of gaining the maximum benefits from a given technological system. Smith (1954) has provided a thorough analysis of the cost of such activities: the Oldham District spent £298,000 between 1871 and 1896 on 'Dispute and Breakdown Pay' and also between 1879 and 1896 it contributed £320,000 to the Amalgamation itself for more generalized disputes. Indeed, between 1883 and 1893, there were 3,005 separate disputes in Oldham. All this supports the contention of Thomas Ashton, Oldham District Secretary of the Spinners' Union, who said in his Monthly Report of May 1873 that 'no Trade Union in the U.K. has had to spend so much money in keeping up wages and fighting for reasonable labour conditions as this Association'. Unfortunately, the Rochdale District records do not permit a parallel analysis of the costs of industrial disputes, but it is reasonable to assume that very similar efforts were involved. If the costs were high, the rewards were commensurate, as can be readily seen in the Appendix on 'Wages in the Cotton Industry' which reveals a continued wage bonanza during this period for the minders, if not for the piecers.

This leads us to the third element in the Spinners' strategy, the absorption of the piecers into the Spinners' own organization. The success of this can be seen from this lengthy quote from Chapman's article on 'Some Policies of the Cotton Spinners' Trade Unions', which summarizes the position before the First World War:

> The piecers have never had a successful organization. It is true that they have been members of the spinners' clubs from the earliest times . . . But in these clubs, it has been asserted, they are organised in great part against themselves. They have no share in the management, and never had. Consequently in 1890 some Bolton socialists separately organised the piecers; but according to the 'Cotton Factory Times' (24 Nov 1893), the spinners induced the piecers to give up their new-born club. We may well ask here, but why did the piecers consent, why have they since not revolted, and why had they no clubs of their own before? The reasons are not far to seek. The piecers all hope to become spinners soon, and find it hard to fight against their future bread and butter. Moreover, the ablest, who would make unionism a success, are as a rule the first to be promoted; again those who made themselves prominent in organising their fellows would run the risk of never putting off the piecer and becoming the complete spinner. (1900, p. 470).

The key aspect of the relationship between spinner and piecer lay in the sub-contracting between spinner and management. As Jewkes and Gray (1935, p. 166) put it, in relation to the inter-war period, 'the piecer is, for all practical purposes, the employee of the spinner'. Evidence from Catling's (1969) study of *The Spinning Mule* reveals that the spinner combined the functions of supervisor with that of co-worker but the sub-contracting role extended this to the wage packet as well. In certain areas, like Oldham and Bolton, it would appear that the official piece lists controlled the total amount to be paid for piecing but not the proportions for each piecer. In other districts, and it appears that Rochdale followed this pattern, the piecers' wages were a matter of the discretion of the minder. This sub-contracting relationship involved the exclusion of management from two important areas of control. Firstly, they were excluded from direct supervision of the labour process and, secondly, they were prevented from engaging in direct wage negotiations with piecers – who comprised a majority of workers in many spinning mills. The sub-contracting system has often been seen[7] as a pre-industrial capitalist form of labour organization or, at the very least, transitional; but the evidence on the Spinners' Union suggests that it can be inserted successfully within the industrialized form of capitalist production and, provided with the right structural supports, can continue for lengthy periods. Indeed, the recent works of More (1980), Littler (1982) and Holbrook-Jones (1982) demonstrate that sub-contracting was an extensive type of industrial relations system in the second half of the nineteenth century. It was the conflict between sub-contracting and integrated factory production that appears to have been central to managerial assaults rather than any incompatibility between sub-contracting and capitalism *per se*.

The inter-war years

Essentially, the inter-war years present a variation on the same theme as before the First World War. The Spinners' Union maintained its strategic aims and was generally successful. In 1920 piecers were accepted as full members of the union but this seems to have had no impact in changing their relative position. Jewkes and Gray (1935, p. 168) summarize their status accordingly: 'The piecers, although members of the local association and, through it, of the Amalgamation, are never in a position to exercise any effective influence over the policy of the association. For the most part, the districts and provinces are controlled by executive committees to which piecers are not appointed.'

The spinners maintained their control over bargaining as embodied in their sub-contracting role. Jenkins, a local activist, remembers the period as one when 'in the late 1920's and early 1930's the conditions of young cotton workers were terribly bad' (1972, p. 52). He describes the conflicts of sub-contracting clearly (p. 52): 'Under this system the boss paid the spinner for the total work done and the spinner paid his piecers. The less the piecer received, the more the spinner had for himself. It also meant that the boss could side with the spinners against the piecers and occasionally could set the piecers against the spinners.' It was this last point that was crucial in the reaction of the Spinners' Union to the two major attempts to break their monopoly over wage bargaining. The first, in 1920, was an attempt by Moran to create a viable organization for piecers. It failed, partly as a result of the structural experiences catalogued earlier by Chapman but also, more crucially, by being cold-shouldered by the Employers' Association. The other attempt, in 1932, was sponsored by Communist Party members and likewise floundered on the rocks of violent opposition from the Spinners. During the inter-war period, sub-contracting in spinning supported increasing wage differentials and also provided the basis for the mainten-ance of the skilled status of the minders. These issues will be discussed further in the next two chapters.

The post-1945 period

In many ways the post-1945 period presents the ironic situation of fundamental changes in the relationship of spinners and piecers whilst automatic mule production as a whole was being almost completely extinguished in Lancashire. The practice of spinners directly paying piecers was discontinued as a result of the progressive implementation of the 1949 'Evershed' Commission proposals which established the twin principles of direct payment by the employer to the piecer and a piece list for spinners that did not require the spinner to pay his piecers out of his own earnings.[8] However, it is not possible to conclude very much about internal social relations in spinning from the results of these changes, since the post-1952 collapse of cotton in Lancashire meant that what spinning remained was almost exclusively of the ring form, a type of activity always disdained by the Spinners' Union and involving quite a different set of social relations, more akin to those in weaving than those in mule-spinning.

The cardroom

If the industrial organization of the Spinners has proved of continued fascination for historians and economists, other areas of cotton labour have received scant attention. This can be seen most clearly in the case of the National Association of Card, Blowing and Ring Room Operatives, evidence for which can only be assembled by a compilation of odd phrases and paragraphs in secondary sources.[9]

The 'Card Union' came into existence in 1886. Prior to that date, there were a few local branches but until the mid-1880's these contained only a few thousand members. The formation of the Union was prompted by the Oldham lock-out of 1885. Whenever there had been a dispute between the Spinners' Union and the employers that led to strike action or a lock-out, all workers prior to the weaving stage were placed out of work, including the cardroom workers. In view of this and the extent of the Oldham dispute, the cardroom workers felt a strong need for a co-ordinated organization and this led to the foundation of the Association in 1886. No doubt, part of the impetus was the changing ethos of labour relations in Britain in the 1880's and certainly the new Association was quickly involved in a large number of strikes.[10]

The Cardroom Association has been an open, non-exclusive union, involved in the standard primary activities of direct wage bargaining for cardroom workers rather than supporting sub-contracting like the Spinners' Union. However, the Cardroom Association has contained within its ranks a small group, the strippers-and-grinders, who have been the major exception to the solidity of the skilled/non-skilled divide in Rochdale since the 1850's.

The rise to 'skill' by the stripper-and-grinder can only be sketched since much of the evidence is lacking; indeed, this account relies heavily on Turner's definitive study of the cotton trade unions. The strippers-and-grinders underwent a serious decline in skill during the period of the transition to factory production and up until the 1870's. Their occupational function was progressively differentiated from their early position as mechanics and supervisors within the cardroom, by the elimination of their supervisory and the sub-division of their machine-tending functions. As Turner (1962, p. 165) puts it, 'by the 1850's their position differed little from that of general labourers ... in the mid-'70's their wages were actually falling when those of every other class of cotton operatives were still moving up'. Entry to the occupation was entirely 'free' and the employers kept their position depressed by the use of a permanent surplus of cardroom labourers. However, by the 1920's the position had changed dramatically. By 1903 they had secured agreements that stipulated the proportion of men to machines and by 1914 they had erected an 'apprenticeship' barrier around the job.[11] As a consequence of these increasing restrictions, the wage rates paid to strippers-and-grinders rose between the 1880's and the post-1945 era, with the result that they eventually reached parity with the highest-paid group traditionally – the mule-spinners. How was this achieved? It would appear as if there was a systematic attempt by strippers-and-grinders to exploit technical change in order to extend their control over machinery.[12] However, an important point to grasp about the strippers-and-grinders' rise to 'skill' is that it was achieved partly through the medium of their monopolization of trade union offices in the Cardroom Amalgamation. The strippers-and-grinders were instrumental in the formation of the Amalgamation and whilst conducting its policies for the predominantly female membership in a non-exclusive manner, this occupational group used its control of trade union offices to elevate its position from non-skilled to skilled by means of an increase in the breadth of their occupational role and by tight restrictions on entry into the job.

Weaving

The major union in the weaving section is the Amalgamated Weavers' Association. The source material for this union is relatively comprehensive. There is a history of the Amalgamation itself (E. Hopwood, 1969) and also a history of the Rochdale Branch,[13] as well as Gray's (1937) study of the *Weaver's Wage* and Turner's classic. However, the content of these histories is mixed and consequently we are still left with a fragmented picture of the union's structure and development.

The first Amalgamation was founded in 1858 and its rules exhibit the classic form of an 'open' or non-skilled union. They were:

(1) To maintain as far as possible a uniform rate of wages upon as high a standard as possible, consistent with the true interests of trade as affecting operatives.
(2) To protect its members from illegal or unjust stoppages, or unjust treatment of whatever nature that unscrupulous employers may endeavour to subject them to.
(3) To render assistance to its members in case of fines, failures and breakdowns.
(4) To ensure the respectable interment of its members by the payment at death of an allowance to their relatives or friends. (cited in Hopwood, 1969, pp. 50–1).

The second Amalgamation (the present) was based upon the first, and was founded in 1884 with very similar rules. The Rochdale branches of these Amalgamations are more difficult to trace but there was certainly a branch in existence by 1861 and there were about 500 members in 1884. The major rationale for both Amalgamations was to ensure the implementation of the piece-lists that had governed wages in the weaving section since the 1853 Blackburn strike and subsequent List. As the Webbs (1920) correctly noted, these Lists were extremely important for the characteristics of labour relations in the industry:

It is difficult to convey to the general reader any adequate idea of the important effect which these elaborate 'Lists' have had upon the Trade Union Movement in Lancashire. The universal satisfaction with, and even preference for, the piecework system among the Lancashire cotton operatives is entirely due to the existence of these definitely fixed and published statements. An even more important result has been the creation of a peculiar type of Trade Union official. For although the lists are elaborately worked out in detail ... the intricacy of the calculations is such as to be beyond the comprehension not only of the ordinary operative or manufacturer, but even of the investigating mathematician without a very minute knowledge of the technical detail. Yet the week's earnings of every one of the tens of thousands of operatives are computed by an exact and often a separate calculation under these lists. And when an alteration of the list is in question the standard wage of a whole district may depend upon the quickness and accuracy with which the operatives' negotiator apprehends the precise effect of each projected change in any of the numerous factors in the calculation. It will be obvious that for work of this nature the successful organiser or 'born orator' was quite unfit. There grew up, therefore, both among the weavers and the spinners a system of selection of new secretaries by competitive examination... the first secretary to undergo this ordeal was Thomas Birtwistle, who, in 1861, began his 30 years' honourable and successful service of the Lancashire weavers. Within a few years he was reinforced by other officials selected for the same characteristics. (S. Webb and B. Webb, 1920, pp. 308–9).

In general structure the Weavers' Amalgamation is similar in many ways to the Cardroom Association. Both unions are open, non-exclusive and almost completely concerned with questions of wage determination in a direct sense. Most disputes in weaving have centred around wage increases or decreases and related issues like time-cribbing, the slate system, driving and humbugging and more recently the 'more-looms' system.[14] The first, time-cribbing, related to the tendency of employers to circumvent the Factory Acts by starting their machines before the official time, thereby increasing productivity! The slate system and humbugging were both forms of 'driving'. The drivers in question were the overlookers, who besides maintaining the looms mechanically also acted as supervisors of the weavers and received a wage based upon the output of the weavers under their command. Slating involved a method of driving the weavers by publishing their wages on a slate exhibited in the weaving shed. Humbugging appears to have been the practice of overlookers discussing their wages (or more appropriately an alleged wage, rather less than the truth) with the weavers under them. The Amalgamation fought both these attacks on the weaver's wage around the turn of the century and was prompted to address this call to all operatives on the subject of 'Driving and Humbugging in weaving sheds'.

Fellow Operatives,

In consequence of the obnoxious system of driving and humbugging operatives in weaving sheds, practised by some overlookers, it has become absolutely necessary that some protection be made against your mental depression, which we believe in some instances had ended in the destruction of life. This being so, we propose trying the following method as a means of improving your present position:

Should any overlooker speak to a weaver about his earnings at any time or place, or speak unjustly when fetched to tackle a loom, we request such weaver at once to report the same to a member of the Weavers' Committee, and if such a tackler be found guilty of doing so, action will be taken against him ...

Yours faithfully
The Executive Council
The Northern Counties Weavers' Amalgamation. (cited in Hopwood, 1962, p. 62)

The 'more-looms' dispute that occurred in the inter-war period was essentially an attempt to improve productivity on existing machinery: in other words, to get the weavers to work 8 looms instead of the normal 6 for a small wage increase. This precipitated massive industrial conflict in Lancashire, particularly between 1929 and 1932, which was resolved more or less on the employers' terms.

All this evidence, despite its patchiness, demonstrates that the Weavers' Amalgamation was a non-sectional union, concerned predominantly with the primary problem of direct wage determination and not with secondary tactics of social exclusion. This cannot be said of the two skilled unions for which there is some evidence in the weaving section: the Overlookers[15] and the Tapesizers.[16] The Overlookers and the Tapesizers both placed rigid emphasis on two modes of restriction: firstly, the regulation of the 'acceptance' of learners and, secondly, the regulation of the ratio between men and machines. The regulation of the acceptance of learners by the Overlookers involves the election of prospective members into the union prior to their being sent for training by management. The Tapesizers do not seem to have such a 'masonic' method, instead engaging in informal negotiation with management over the subject. The regulation of the number of machines per man was a restriction engaged in quite deliberately by the Tapesizers, for their 1882 Rules stated that: 'No member shall attempt to work more than one machine under any circumstance.'

The differentiation of the roles of the Overlooker into maintenance mechanic and supervisor is the major exception to the structural continuity amongst the unions in the weaving section throughout our period. The loss of the supervisory task was the direct result of the progressive adoption of the automatic loom in the 1920's. The former Lancashire loom was a relatively easy machine to 'tune' and the Overlookers found little difficulty in supervising the weavers. The Overlooker was responsible to management for the quality of the cloth produced and his wage was determined by a combination of the amount and the quality of woven cloth. However, with the adoption of the more complex automatic loom, the tuning became a more difficult process. The loom Overlooker had less time to supervise the weavers and this responsibility became the prerogative of the 'Boss Tackler' or 'Weaving Foreman', who was originally an overlooker. The Overlookers became the equivalent of maintenance engineers in the 1920's, a situation which has persisted until the present day.

What then can be concluded from this general material from secondary sources on the cotton industry about trends in trade union organization within the manual working class in Rochdale around the axis of skill? It is clear that the cotton unions have been organized upon an industrial sectoral basis. This is because union organization from the outset has been powerfully rooted in the factory. Amalgamations have followed the path of associations of unions from industrial sectors like weaving, spinning or carding. *However, within each sector there have been internal occupational organizations upon the basis of skill.* Indeed, skill and occupational union organization appear inextricably linked. This theme will be discussed in considerable detail in chapter 8, when the social bases of skill are analysed. However, the present task centres around examining trends in occupational sectionalism over time, and specifically, the extent to which the model outlined at the end of chapter 3 captures the rhythms of change. It should be clear that developments in each of the three sectors – spinning, weaving and carding – do not reveal identical or even similar patterns of change. Perhaps the most salient feature from all three sectors is one of *marked and persistent structural stability in the relationship between skilled and non-skilled unions rather than endemic change.* Nevertheless, those changes discussed *do not follow similar chronologies.* The main changes in the spinning sector occurred in the post-1945 era with decreasing sectionalism associated with the ending of sub-contracting. In weaving, sectionalism was transformed but not transcended in the 1920's, with the differentiation of the overlooker's role. In the cardroom, sectionalism was re-established between the 1880's and 1920's by the recomposition of the job of the stripper-and-grinder. Clearly, the fact that each of the above occupations discussed – mule spinner, overlooker and stripper-and-grinder – is 'skilled' is of considerable interest, but the disparate chronologies suggest that the general model of working class sectionalism outlined in chapter 3 fails to correspond with the evidence from the cotton industry in Rochdale. The next question is whether the model fits the engineering industry in Rochdale any better.

The engineering industry

1850–1880

The emergence of the engineering industry was one of the major consequences of the Industrial Revolution. The construction of the machinery and steam engines used to propel other industries into the factory era of industrial capitalism provided the basis for the development of expertise in engineering. In the period before 1820, most of the machines constructed were 'one-off' jobs and were made by itinerant millwrights, who were both highly skilled and very scarce. The millwrights possessed their own tools and moved from mill to mill to build the machinery. Entry into the occupation was limited by means of apprenticeship and the artisan had to develop a wide range of skills in order to be able to handle the different requirements presented by each new job. After around 1820 the first major transformation of the workforce began with the expansion of the industry into factories. The basis for this move was the massive increase in demand for steam engines, which could be produced in larger numbers, more efficiently, by standardized work processes in factories. For the millwrights this represented a major attack on their status as skilled craftsmen but, in fact, despite the development of factory production incorporating new machinery like Maudslay's improved lathe, the new factories required a workforce of engineers with considerable skills. However, if the transition to factory production involved little change in the overall skills required by engineering workers, it was, nevertheless, a major shift in social and industrial relations, since most of the tools required for production became fixed-plant machinery and ceased, therefore, to be the property of the workman. Indeed, a major theme of the history of the subsequent hundred years revolves around the successive attempts by the employers and management to develop machinery and sub-divide tasks in order to eradicate the need for skilled craftsmen.

The early trade unions in the engineering industry were small, localized, sectional units that were uninterested, as a rule, in the broad movements of protest against industrialization like the Owenite Grand National Consolidated Trade Union and Chartism. Nor were the machine-makers particularly sympathetic to Luddite-type machine smashing and most of their organized efforts seem to have concentrated on maintaining apprenticeship restrictions and providing Friendly benefits. However, despite evidence of continuous combination by engineering workers, the story is very fragmented until the establishment of the Amalgamated Society of Engineers in 1851. The Amalgamation did not envelop all the small craft societies in the engineering industry, and despite successive incorporation of the smaller societies, the Engineering Union remains today, as it was in the mid-nineteenth century, the dominant but not the sole representative of workers in the industry.[17] However, in Rochdale the A.S.E. (Amalgamated Society of Engineers) and its successor, the A.U.E.W. have encountered little in the way of small sectional craft societies, and have been the predominant organization of metal workers in the town.

The main aim of the A.S.E., according to William Newton, one of its founders, was 'to destroy the redundancy in the labour market'. The leaders of the union regarded over-supply of labour as the major threat to their skilled position and advocated its elimination as a means of achieving satisfactory wages and conditions. They advocated two policies to this end, the reduction of hours worked and the foundation of workshops by the Society. Of the latter, not much resulted but the former, reduction of hours, provided one of the main factors precipitating the first major confrontation between the A.S.E. and the employers: the Lock-out of 1852.[18]

In the period around 1850 the local branches of the Society were pursuing four policies to achieve a reduction in excess labour. They opposed systematic overtime, more than one apprentice to four journeymen, 'illegal' (i.e. non-apprenticed) men and piecework. At Hibbert and Platt's in Oldham, the largest engineering works in Britain (employing 1,500 men), the local union opposed systematic overtime, piecework and the employment of 'illegal' men. Platt, the local Liberal Party chairman and subsequently Liberal M.P. for Oldham, opposed the union and managed to organize the Central Association of Employers of Operative Engineers. The ensuing confrontation led to a national lock-out in January 1852, which included men from Rochdale. After a lengthy struggle, the A.S.E. was defeated completely. Men returning to work were confronted by 'the Document' which they had to sign as a condition of employment and which forbade the membership of a trade union. As a direct result of the defeat, a Delegate Meeting at Glasgow expunged the rules seeking to abolish piecework and overtime and those attempting to regulate the number of apprentices. However, the main aim of the Society remained the limitation of the number of workers available for employment in the industry by attacks on overtime, piecework, 'illegal' men and too many apprentices. Their objection to systematic overtime was that it enabled the employers to achieve high production levels without engaging unemployed engineers, whilst the apprenticeship rules were aimed at reducing and ultimately eliminating the numbers who were unemployed. The objection to piecework, amongst others, was that it involved 'speed-up' of production and required less labour as a productive input. 'Illegal' or non-apprentice served men were disliked because they weakened the bargaining position of the Engineers by increasing the overall pool of available operatives. From the employers' perspective, the large overhead costs of the machinery used for production required them to economize on labour as much as possible, and all the methods described had that as their major aim. This divergence of interests was recognized by William Allan, General Secretary of the A.S.E., in his evidence to the 1867 Commission on Trades Unions:

> Every day of the week I hear that the interests [of employer and employed] are identical. I scarcely see how they can be while we are in a state of

society which recognizes the principle of buying in the cheapest and selling in the dearest market. It is in their interest to get the labour done at as low a rate as possible and it is ours to get as high rate of wages as possible and you can never reconcile these two things.

However, as a consequence of the seriousness of the defeat in 1852, the A.S.E. did not engage in much strike activity for the next twenty years. Rather, they attempted to implement their unwritten aims by means of direct local negotiation or by 'passive resistance', a tactic which involved members of the Society picking off obnoxious employers one-by-one. If the employer proved recalcitrant, the members were instructed to 'black' his factory. The first major strike was in 1871 on the Tyne. Here, the local A.S.E. District achieved the 54-hour week under the leadership of John Burnett.[19] In response, a local employer, Armstrong, convened a meeting of engineering employers from other areas of Britain, and helped to form the Iron Trade Employers' Federation. Ironically, the Tyneside employers withdrew soon afterwards, since they had found it impossible to reconcile their interests with those of other regions.[20] The North-East again provided the location of a major dispute in Sunderland between 1883 and 1885 over the apprenticeship rules.[21] However, the major grievances increasingly centred around the growth of payment-by-result systems.

A major objection to piece rates was that they failed to secure the earnings of workers during the troughs of the trade cycle. With the increasing levels of unemployment after 1873 during the period of the 'Great Depression' this objection grew in strength. There was an additional bone of contention in that most payment-by-result systems involved sub-contracting, whereby the employer engaged a 'piece-master' or taskmaster who was responsible for completion of the job. Under this system, the distribution of the total wage costs was in the exclusive hands of the sub-contractor, which resulted in many grievances between taskmasters and workers. Some piece-masters, according to Jefferys (1945, pp. 63–4), 'were in the habit of engaging men for about six weeks and then discharging them in order to avoid sharing the piece-money with them . . . and men were discharged if they made any enquiry about the piece-money'. In some cases, often where the A.S.E. was strongly organized in the workshops, the employers paid the men directly and the piece-master co-ordinated efficient production, yet he still claimed between 5% and 10% of the price of the job for his fee.

By the beginning of the 1880's, engineering craftsmen had successfully achieved the transition from handicraft production to the production of machinery by means of machinery. This transformation of the labour process had not eliminated industrial skills but changed their content. The A.S.E. was an archetypal craft union, sectional and exclusive. Indeed, exclusion took two distinct forms: the exclusion of non-skilled labour from membership and from performing work regarded as proper only for the Engineers and also the exclusion of the other craft unions, notably the Boilermakers and Shipwrights, by means of demarcation rules. However, the Society had suffered a serious defeat in 1852, followed by the failure of the Sunderland apprentice battle in 1883, and had failed to organize even 10%[22] of the labour force in the industry. The precarious balance between exclusion and the strength of the Society was to a large extent obscured in the golden years of the 1860's and early 1870's when Britain was 'the Workshop of the World'. In the subsequent half a century after 1873, the chilly winds of foreign competition and technological revolution demonstrated the weaknesses of the A.S.E.

1880–1897

The period after 1880 witnessed a fundamental change in the British engineering industry. Growth continued, both of production (especially exports of machinery)[23] and of employment.[24] Moreover, the range of products developed swiftly. In the 1850's, most engineering production was concentrated in three areas: textile machinery, locomotives and steam engines. The 1880's and 1890's saw the continuation of these products, but also the addition of new commodities like armaments, agricultural machinery, cycles and, as a direct result of the 'Second Industrial Revolution',[25] electrical engineering. Furthermore, this growth was accompanied by increasing foreign competition, particularly from Germany and the U.S.A.[26] This stimulated increased concentration in the industry, itself facilitated by the Limited Liability Acts of 1856 and 1862.

However, the most crucial result of foreign competition, increasing concentration and size of firms and the adoption of new technologies, amounted to what Jefferys (1945, p. 122) has called 'a revolution in the tools' New machines were introduced to supersede the centre lathe. These machines, the capstan and turret lathe, vertical borer, radial drill and universal milling machine were far more specialized than previous machinery and incorporated far more skill into the mechanisms than hitherto.[27] The main productive emphasis was on interchangeability of parts rather than dead accuracy. In addition, new metals like high-speed steel and new hand instruments like verniers and protractors made for standardized production. In this context of increased rationalization of production, there was a sharp movement towards payment by piecework and bonus systems, which reached their apogee in Taylorism: the 'perfect' embodiment of the principles of mass production.[28] The crucial result of all these processes for change, as far as workshop relations in the engineering industry were concerned, was the growth of semi-skilled machine operatives. Clearly, this was a threat far more serious than the four major issues of the mid-century: systematic overtime, piecework, apprentices and 'illegal' men. Semi-skilled 'handymen' could be seen as an example of the latter, but in fact they were a threat to the entire position of skilled men in engineering, since their existence constituted a denial of any rationale for widespread social exclusion and suggested a potentially new form of the division of manual labour within the industry, involving the wholesale removal of skilled men from routine production.

In the 1890's, the conflict between the demands of the A.S.E. to control the establishment of the new machinery and the 'power to manage' claimed by the engineering employers reached flash-point. The period as a whole was one of increasing militancy by labour. The success of the London match-girls' strike, followed by the achievement of the dockers' 'tanner' (sixpence), both strongly supported by the nascent socialist movement, was followed by a legal assault on trade unions by the High Court Judges that culminated in the Taff Vale and Osborne decisions. The concomitant rise of the Independent Labour Party and subsequent foundation of the Labour Party all contributed to the rising militancy amongst the workers.[29] In this situation, the growing use of capstan and turret lathes and of milling and grinding machines, particularly in the armaments factories helped to radicalize the engineering workers. Throughout the 1890's there were many examples of radical engineers facilitating the development of trade unions amongst such trades as shop assistants, carters and navvies.[30] George Barnes, General Secretary of the A.S.E. during the 1897 lock-out, stood as I.L.P. (Independent Labour Party) candidate for Rochdale in 1895, although failing to secure election.[31] Indeed, the Rochdale engineering workers established links with socialist political parties of the working class that produced the result in the 1920's that many of the local Labour Party Officers and Trades Council members belonged to the A.E.U.[32] and most of the Parliamentary candidates were officials of the Engineering Union.[33]

The A.S.E. itself was reorganized in 1892 and the number of permanent officials was increased. More significantly, the union organization became far less centred on London. In addition, new occupations became eligible for membership, notably electrical engineers, roll turners and machinemen. The new strength given by the union organization to the Districts of the union quickly led to renewed and bitter hostilities between the A.S.E. and the employers. In 1895, the Clyde employers intervened to support their Belfast counterparts in their dispute with their local A.S.E. District by locking-out the Glasgow men. This was followed in 1896 by the formation of the Federation of Engineering Employers' Associations, prompted mainly by the armaments producers, especially Armstrong's of Newcastle.[34] Early in 1897, the men founded an 8-Hours Committee for engineering workers, which provided the pretext for a test of strength between the rejuvenated A.S.E. and the newly formed Employers' Federation.

The ostensible cause of the 1897 Lock-out was a conflict over the 8-hour day, which the employers were unwillng to concede. They claimed that the new machines required longer, not shorter, hours to cover the overhead capital costs of their installation. This claim appeared somewhat specious to the union in the face of profits like Armstrong's, which were £358,000 net in 1896.[35] However, the main aim of the employers was to 'smash the union', which was made explicit by Siemen, President of the (newly formed) London branch of the Federation, who stated publicly that the goal of the Lock-out was 'to get rid of trade unionism altogether'.[36] The employers fought for thirty weeks, with the aid of the Free Labour Association's blacklegs,[37] and forced a virtual unconditional capitulation by the A.S.E. Jeffreys (pp. 147–8) states that 'the longer purses of the employers had won', a point of view criticized by Clarke (1957, p. 135), who claimed that 'the reasons for the defeat were not primarily financial'. However, a summary reading of *The Engineering Trade Lock-out* (1898) reveals the error in Clarke's assessment. Whilst not denying the success of the employers in the propaganda battle in the press and for wider influential opinion (Alfred Marshall wrote 'I want these people to be beaten at all costs'),[38] a major factor in the defeat *was* financial. The cost of the Lock-out to the A.S.E. rose to almost £30,000 a week, which reveals the fragility of the union's funds at the end of the struggle which stood at £134,000.[39] Nevertheless, money alone was not the whole story. A crucial weakness was the failure of the A.S.E. to secure the co-operation of the other sectional unions in the engineering industry, notably the Boilermakers. This was the direct result of the hostility between the two unions, particularly in the North-East, over demarcation in the shipbuilding industry. This hostility was intensified by the failure of the A.S.E. to join the Federation of Engineering and Shipbuilding Trades in 1891. The belief held by Robert Knight, General Secretary of the Boilermakers, that the conflict was unnecessary was also subscribed to by the T.U.C., (Trades Union Council) whose support was at best lukewarm. The A.S.E. also failed to gain the support of the non-skilled, many of whom continued at work during the Lock-out.[40] This failure to secure co-ordination amongst the institutions of organized labour was as important as the financial constraints in the defeat of the A.S.E. It also further embittered relations between the A.S.E. and the other craft societies, and led directly to withdrawal from the T.U.C. by the Society.[41]

1897–1922

The enormity of the defeat suffered by the A.S.E. can be seen from the 'Terms of Settlement' it was forced to sign with the employers in 1898. This is reproduced in full in Appendix F. It represented a major defeat for the principles of craft control, as can be seen from the statement of the 'General Principle of Freedom to Employers in the Management of Their Works'. In addition to the 'acceptance' of the managerial prerogative of control over the manning of new machinery, the union also conceded all the other major aims it had fought for over the previous half century such as limitation of apprentices and rejection of piecework and overtime. In addition, the new 'Procedure for Disputes' initiated a national framework for wage bargaining that was designed to prevent the A.S.E. relying on the same tactics as it had used after the previous defeat in 1852. Following that Lock-out, the very success of the employers led to the collapse of the employers' organization and facilitated the re-establishment of craft controls by means of picking-off individual employers. The Employers' Federation after 1898 did not collapse, for it did not over-reach itself, restricting its combination solely to matters of labour relations and not attempting to build up a major cartel in the industry, which still retained a highly competitive structure.

However, despite co-operation between the Executive of the A.S.E. and the Engineering Employers' Federation at a national level, the A.S.E. membership as a whole did not accept the radical change in power embodied in the 1898 'Terms of Settlement'. At first isolated local workshop tactics involving a general refusal by craftsmen either to train handymen (semi-skilled machinists) or to rectify ('follow') a handyman's 'bodged' job were the Engineers' response. Subsequently, the District Committees on the Clyde (in 1903) and on the Tyne (1908) defied the National Executive of the A.S.E. and forced increasing decentralization of power towards the District and local shop stewards.[42] This bifurcated structure of the Engineering Union, always present in embryo since the foundation of the A.S.E., was to become crucial in the period after 1914.

Nationally, there was considerable variation in the success achieved by these local actions. Jefferys (1945, p. 129) provides evidence that by 1914 46% of fitters and 37% of turners were on piece-rates, which is an indication of declining craft control. However, in Rochdale, as can be seen from Table 5 of Appendix D on wages in engineering, only 15% of fitters and 25% of moulders were on payment-by-result systems in 1914. Nevertheless, 38% of turners were on such piece-rate payment systems. However, without sustained investigation beyond the scope of this research, it is impossible to state how such proportions came about. Clearly, the strength of the A.S.E.

in Rochdale, and the competitive position amongst the engineering employers helped facilitate such results, but without detailed evidence, which is lacking for Rochdale, it is not possible to investigate the precise workshop tactics empirically. These issues will be discussed more fully in the conclusions of this section.

Demarcation disputes, particularly in shipbuilding, continued with the Society constantly on the look out for 'the pilfering propensities of other trades'. Most seriously, from the perspective of future disputes and the real possibilities of blacklegging by the semi-skilled, demonstrated in the 1897 Lock-out, the A.S.E. retained its craft exclusiveness and failed to organize such non-skilled grades. Furthermore, new labour organizations were prepared to fill this increasing area of employment. In 1898, the Workers' Union[43] (one of the principal founders of the Transport and General Workers' Union in 1922) was founded and began recruiting substantially amongst non-skilled engineering workers, and even, in the Midlands, amongst skilled men. The same year saw the formation of the National Amalgamated Union of Labour (originally the Tyneside and General Labourers' Union) which was one of the major components of the General and Municipal Workers' Union amalgamation in 1924.[44] Both these general unions had made substantial inroads into the union organization of engineering workers by 1918. However, despite the strong dominance of the Employers' Federation at a national level[45] in industrial relations, which was increasingly being challenged in the burgeoning social unrest[46] of the pre-1914 crisis, the local Districts were relatively successful in controlling manning of the new machines. This involved what was called 'following the machine',[47] and entailed the recognition by the employers that special regard should be given to the employment of redundant skilled engineers at the craft rate, despite the nature of the tasks involved.

The First World War transformed the situation swiftly. It was a war fought with the aid of military hardware that required the total mobilization of the British engineering industry for victory. Many skilled engineering craftsmen volunteered for military service and were decimated in the disastrous campaigns of the early war. This loss of manpower exacerbated the labour shortages resulting from expanded production, particularly of munitions. In this context, the traditional issues once more came to the fore: new entrants, piecework and manning of machinery. The Government[48] demanded the sacrifice of all customs and practices that inhibited maximum output, thereby attacking at a stroke all the mechanisms of exclusion that preceding generations of skilled engineering workers had built up to defend their position in the labour process. The national officers of the A.S.E. made a voluntary declaration in March 1915, that lifted shop restrictions. However, this proved insufficient in practice, mainly because the rank-and-file objected to its abuse by the employers, under whose control labour relations remained in the enterprises, but also because of the progressive divorce of the union leadership from the rank-and-file in the pre-war era, symbolized by the growing influence of syndicalist views amongst the workforce. As a result of the failure of munitions production to match Government expectations, they set up the National Advisory Committee on Output on 17 March 1915. This was promptly followed by the 'Treasury Agreement' of 25 March 1915, between Government, employers and unions.[49] By this agreement the unions:

> gave up the right to strike, agreed to relax all customs which restricted the output of munitions, and permitted dilution on government work. As safeguards the promise was obtained that these measures would be operated solely in firms on war work, that they were to be only for the duration of the war, that dilutees would get the rate for the job, and that profits of firms on such work would be limited. (Jefferys, 1945, p. 175).

Later in 1915 the Ministry of Munitions was set up under the leadership of Lloyd George and the voluntary Treasury Agreement, against the wishes of the A.S.E. leadership, was made statutory by the Munitions Act. This was generally regarded as an oppressive measure by engineering craftsmen and they particularly objected to Section VII, whereby managements could dismiss a worker and blacken his name on the leaving certificate which was required for presentation to prospective employers, whilst the worker himself could not leave his employment without permission. These features were remarkably similar to the Inquiry Note which the Iron Trades' Employers' Association had attempted, with some success, to instigate in the 1870's. Indeed, it was the evident one-sidedness of social arrangements that proved to be so explosive. As food prices rose sharply and rents rocketed, profits increased dramatically. These factors precipitated the first major struggle by engineering workers in Glasgow, where the Clyde Workers' Committee remained powerful throughout most of 1915 and 1916 until its suppression by the Government.[50]

Traditional grievances increased. The dilutees, generally women working on machinery previously the prerogative of A.S.E. men, were paid on piece-rates and, as a consequence of extensive overtime, they were often earning as much as, if not more than, the skilled craftsmen, paid on an hourly rate. The *Report of the Committee on Labour Embargoes* in 1918 stated the problem clearly: 'a striking difference exists in many cases between the earnings of certain sections of skilled time-workers and those men and women employed on systems of payment by results who entered their occupations since the beginning of the war as dilutees.'

The grievances of skilled engineering craftsmen over wages and the social effects of rationalization of production provided the underlying factors upon which the massive increase of hostility in the industry during 1917 and 1918 developed. The first major incident occurred in the munitions centre of Sheffield. The pretext was the exemption of skilled men from conscription. As Jefferys (1945, p. 181) puts it:

> In the autumn of 1916, feeling was running high over the mounting number of instances where recruiting officers were forcibly enrolling skilled men in the army, despite the Government's pledge that men who volunteered for munitions work and received badges to show they had done so, would not be called up. The call-up of Leonard Hargreaves, a skilled fitter employed at Vickers, Brightside, Sheffield in November 1916, while dilutees remained in the works, brought matters to a head.

Immediate action by the Shop Stewards' Committee in Sheffield involving strike action led to the release of Hargreaves[51] and prompted the Government to accept a Trade Card issued by the A.S.E. for craftsmen who volunteered for munitions work as constituting a valid exemption from conscription. However, in April 1917, the Government withdrew the Trade Card Scheme and also proposed the extension of dilution to private work. This confirmed the worst fears of the men as to the real intentions behind dilution, the elimination of all craft controls from British engineering. The largest area of private engineering work was textile engineering concentrated in Lancashire, and it was scarcely surprising that the first dispute occurred there. Interestingly enough, it involved the Rochdale firm of Tweedale and Smalley's. The Rochdale conflict sparked off major strike action, led by the shop stewards, against the new rules. The ferocity of the reaction severely shook the Government, particularly that redoubtable class warrior Winston Churchill, Minister of Munitions, and the extension of dilution was dropped, along with the leaving certificates. In June, as a consequence of the May action, the National Administrative Council of Shop Stewards was formed and was closely involved in the continued militancy in the industry throughout the last eighteen months of the war and beyond.

Indeed, it is worth noting, and this issue will be scrutinized in detail in chapter 8, that metal workers were in the vanguard of conflicts in most European capitalist societies during and after the First World War.[52] Moreover, it appears as if there might be more than a national contradiction between the militant socialism espoused by the Shop Stewards Movement and the craft exclusiveness pursued by the membership. Hinton (1973) has subjected the 'ambiguities' of the British Shop Stewards Movement to caustic analysis, demonstrating convincingly the inner tensions of the movement. The reason behind the engineering crafts-men's hostility to the 'managerial prerogative' was their desire to exclude management from control over the labour process in order to preserve craft privileges such as wage differentials and autonomy in the workplace. This involved also the exclusion of non-skilled, non-members of the A.S.E. from the same processes since they represented the instrument whereby manage-ment could eliminate such privileges. This stance involved a rejection of the fullest rationality of the capitalist productive system and in this hostility to the capitalist employers the mass of craftsmen were at one with their revolutionary, syndicalist leadership. However, their approach could scarcely be regarded as the epitome of egalitarian socialism, for they had no great interest in the dilutees. Indeed, the rank-and-file shared this indifference with the A.S.E. leadership who spent the war period evolving a *modus vivendi* with the general unions in the engineering industry, whereby the latter were cajoled into acceptance of the restoration of a pre-1914 status quo.

The ambiguities and contradictions within the Shop Stewards Move-ment are illustrated by this quotation from Hinton's admirable and extensive study:

> ...and it has been argued that the demand for workers' control arose solely out of the ideological inheritance of those revolutionaries to whom the craftsmen turned for leadership when the traditional props of their economic security were apparently knocked away by wartime dilution. After all, the formal acceptance of a remote revolutionary goal was a small price to pay for the leadership of revolutionary socialists who were needed for the much more immediate practical reason that only these leaders had the audacity required to challenge established trade union practices to the degree that seemed necessary. The revolutionary goal of workers' control is thus seen as being artificially tacked on to rank-and-file aspirations of a quite different order. It does, however, seem unlikely that so clear a distinction can be drawn between the consciousness of the leaders and that of the rank-and-file. The 'militant craftsman' and the 'revolutionary engineer' certainly describe categorically different states of consciousness; but both states may well have co-existed, and interacted, in the same head. 'Our policy', wrote Gallacher and Paton in 1917, 'is that of invaders of our native province of industry, now in the hands of an arrogant and tyrannical usurper, and what we win in our advance we control exclusively and independently.' It is impossible to distinguish in this between the revolutionary engineer's hostility to capitalist parasitism on industry, on the one hand, and the militant craftsman's resistance to the 'arrogant and tyrannical' encroachments of managerial prerogative. The two states of consciousness are fused in a unified rhetoric, each reinforcing the other. Within the wartime shop stewards' movement an

>interaction was taking place between syndicalist doctrines of workers'
>control and the non-instrumental aspects of the tradition of craft control.
>(Hinton, 1973, pp. 334–5)

The end of conflicts on the Continent in November 1918 was not matched
by similar pacific behaviour on the home front. Indeed, there was increased
militancy by many sections of the labour movement. On the industrial
front, the triple alliance of miners, railwaymen and transport workers was
involved in two major confrontations, whilst there were big strikes in the
cotton industry. On the political front, labour organized to prevent any
major military intervention against Russia. Indeed, the Bolshevik
Revolution had a profound effect on social relations in Britain, as
elsewhere in Europe, and certainly provided part of the ideological support
for militancy. However, the material basis for the massive wave of strikes
and wage claims was the immediate post-war boom of reconstruction.

The onset of the depression in late 1920 coincided with a 6d per hour
wage claim by the newly formed Amalgamated Engineering Union. The
Employers' Federation, after some delay, during which the signs of the
severity of the slump became more and more apparent, responded with the
demand for a major cut in wages in order to restore international
competitiveness which was reluctantly conceded. Despite the new organizational strength of the A.E.U., it was in a weak position since there was
growing unemployment amongst its members and the Federation itself had
increased its own membership to over 2,000 affiliated firms.

However, the real issue of contention between the employers and the
unions centred on the perennial problem of managerial functions. The
unions had managed to limit these in practice by 'following the machine'
and by the strength of shop-floor shop stewards' organization and,
furthermore, the A.S.E. had withdrawn from the 1898 terms of settlement
in 1913. What occurred in 1922[53] was remarkably similar, in essence, to the
previous major conflict of 1897–8. The issue that precipitated the conflict
was whether management should have the sole prerogative to decide when
overtime should be performed. The A.E.U. believed that the Overtime
Agreement of 1920 provided that overtime should only be worked when
both sides agreed. A major limitation to any local agreement was the
number of engineering workers unemployed in the area, and several
Districts banned overtime completely. The employers disagreed fundamentally, claiming, with some justification, that the Agreement provided for no
such limits. The A.E.U. stated that 'It is not reasonable or humane to insist
that overtime should be worked by some if, instead, more men could be
employed', but the Employers, realizing the severe financial strain that
unemployment was causing the A.E.U., forced the union to agree to the
following memorandum:

I. General

1. The trade union shall not interfere with the right of the employers to exercise managerial functions in their establishments and the Federation shall not interfere with the proper functions of the trade union.
2. In the exercise of these functions, the parties shall have regard to the provisions for avoiding disputes of April 17, 1914, which are amplified by the Shop Stewards and Works Committee Agreement of May 20, 1919, and to the terms of other national and local agreements between the parties.
3. Instructions of the management shall be observed pending any question in connection therewith being discussed with the provisions referred to.

II. Overtime

It is agreed that in terms of the Overtime and Night Shift Agreement of 29 and 30 September, 1920, the employers have the right to decide when overtime is necessary, the workpeople or their representatives being entitled to bring forward under the provisions referred to any cases of overtime they desire discussed. Meantime, the overtime required shall be proceeded with.

However, despite an official recommendation for acceptance of this memorandum as a result of the weakness of the union, the membership rejected it in a ballot by 50,240 votes to 35,525.[54]

As a result, the Employers gave notice of a general lock-out. As Wigham states bluntly (1973, p. 121), 'This was not, like the lock-out of 1897, a battle of equals. Victory for the employers was certain from the beginning.' With around 25% of its membership unemployed, coupled with the drain of funds throughout 1921 in unemployment benefits, the A.E.U. was in no state to resist. After three months of struggle, the membership capitulated and the following Agreement was accepted: 'The employers have the right to manage their establishments and the trade unions have the right to exercise their functions.' At the end of the conflict, the A.E.U., which held resources of £3.25 million at its inception in July 1920, was left with only £35,572 in the general fund[55] and had been forced to suspend all its benefits apart from sickness and superannuation.

1922–1964

The defeat for the A.E.U. was enormous. Indeed, the 1922 defeat prompted a series of structural changes in the A.E.U. that appeared to change it from a craft union to an industrial union catering for all grades of engineering workers, including the non-skilled. The first step was taken in October 1922, when sheetmetal workers, pipe fitters, motor mechanics and pipe benders were allowed entry to the union. However, the major step was

Table 6.1. *The proportion of skilled, semi-skilled and unskilled workers in firms belonging to the Engineering Employers' Federation*

	Skilled %	Semi-Skilled %	Unskilled %
1914	60	20	20
1921	50	30	20
1926	40	45	15
1933	32	57	11

Source: J. Jefferys, *The Story of the Engineers* (1945, p. 207).

taken in 1926 when the union was opened to all ranks of male engineering workers. Recruitment was slow before 1939, with only 145,577 men joining, but it accelerated dramatically during the Second World War to 335,224. During the Second World War, the final exclusion was removed with acceptance of women engineering workers into the A.E.U. from January 1943, and 138,717 women were recruited during that year alone.[56]

The development of superficial industrial unionism ran parallel to the progressive collapse of the privileged position of skilled engineering workers. By 1938, the erosion of apprenticeship had grown considerably, and a union inquiry of that year discovered that only 16% of firms engaged apprentices.[57] Walter Greenwood's *Love on the Dole* gave a vivid portrait of the inter-war realities of apprenticeships. The exploitation of apprentices as cheap labour which he described accompanied a general increase in the proportion of semi-skilled operatives in the industry, as progressive rationalization, often under the auspices of 'scientific management' reduced many tasks to routine machine operations. The relative decline of skilled men (mainly fitters and turners) can be seen in Table 6.1. The importance of these figures is that they demonstrate the complexity of the inter-relationships between technology and 'skill', for the rate of increase of semi-skilled operatives was faster between 1921 and 1926 (a period of depressed demand and low investment) than between 1914 and 1921 (a period of expanding demand and massive investment). Clearly, the tendency towards an eradication of skilled engineering manual workers was prompted more by the balance of advantages in industrial conflict within engineering than by any simple technological determinism.

However, if the national picture for skilled engineering craftsmen was bleak, the position in Rochdale was considerably better for such apprentice time-served men. As can be seen from Appendix D on earnings in the engineering industry, 51.3% of all workers paid by E.E.F. (Engineering Employers Federation) members in Rochdale were skilled in 1964; a proportion little different from the 57.0% in 1935. Indeed, in 1930, 71.3% of such engineering workers were classified as skilled, a figure slightly *higher* than the 69.6% in 1914. Several difficulties surround the interpretation of these figures. Firstly, there is a lack of information available about non-unionized or alternatively organized engineering workers in Rochdale. However, the Census material described in Table 5.1 shows that there were 4,265 employed in engineering in 1931 and 5,632 in 1911. If it is assumed that about 30% of these are non-manual occupations (which, as will be seen in succeeding chapters, is unlikely to be an over-estimation) it is clear that the earnings material for Rochdale covers less than half of all manual engineering workers in both Census years. Unfortunately, actual membership figures for the local A.E.U. or A.S.E. are lacking for 1930 or 1914. Secondly, it is also unclear what proportions of skilled men would exist amongst non-Federated engineering employers or the numbers of non-Engineering Union engineering workers. Nor is it absolutely clear if all A.E.U. engineering workers employed by the Rochdale E.E.F. are included or only selected categories.[58] Nonetheless, despite such problems, it is clear that the proportions of skilled engineering workers in Rochdale appear significantly higher than the E.E.F. national averages reported by Jefferys and reproduced in Table 6.1. It is also evident that the national patterns of change are not reproduced in the Rochdale data. Far from there being, in Rochdale, evidence of a secular 'de-skilling' of engineering workers, there is a remarkable consistency in the skilled : non-skilled ratios. Indeed, two pieces of recent evidence suggest that the 'de-skilling' pundits have misunderstood actual empirical trends in skilled engineering work during the first two-thirds of the twentieth century. There is still a large number of skilled engineering workers in Britain. The Donovan Commission stated that 'in engineering and electrical goods manufacture nearly 580,000 skilled men are employed'.[59] In December 1972, there were 290,580 Section 1 (apprentice-served) members of the A.U.E.W. out of a total of 1,146,087.[60] The upsurge of wage militancy in the Leyland Toolroom and amongst skilled maintenance engineers at Heathrow Airport in the Spring of 1977, mentioned earlier, suggests that skilled engineering workers are still very much in evidence.

Two features of the engineering industry help to explain the continued strength of skilled manual workers. Firstly, there is a structural bifurcation within the A.U.E.W. itself, whereby national minimum rates are negotiated by the national union leadership and the Engineering Employers' Federation. Secondly, as a result of competition with the T.G.W.U. and G.M.W.U. for the organization of the non-skilled, the A.U.E.W. negotiates national minimum rates for all grades of work. It is these rates which led Knowles (1951) and Turner (1952) to argue that there was occurring a progressive collapse of differentials within the engineering industry. Unfortunately, as will be shown in the next chapter, the proportion of engineering earnings made up by the national minimum rate has progressively declined since 1918. A larger and larger proportion of engineering earnings are made up by special piece and bonus rates, all of which are determined by either local officials or, more often, shop stewards. Herein lies the rub. Local union negotiators are drawn overwhelmingly from the ranks of apprentice-trained skilled engineering workers. It would appear, therefore, that just as after the 1852 and 1897 Lock-outs a national defeat for the union was retrieved through local action against local employers, the 1922 defeat again promoted such action. The seriousness of the defeat was indicated in the growth of non-skilled work in engineering, yet the skilled men in Rochdale, through local action, succeeded in retrieving considerable ground after the early 1920's and maintaining their relative position throughout the period between 1930 and 1964.

In Rochdale, considerable successes in local conflicts with management were revealed in the 1920's. The proportion of time-paid skilled men was 70% in 1925,[61] and it was only the massive decline in employment associated with the Depression between 1929 and 1933 that led to the relative growth of semi-skilled work and payment-by-result systems. Also, as was shown earlier, the number of skilled men as a percentage of all engineering workers paid by the local E.E.F. actually rose during the 1920's and only declined in the early 1930's. Again, however, data sources that could provide more information on these issues are lacking.

What, then, of management? Why have they tolerated such a situation? Why have they not de-skilled the entire labour force? Again, however, there is a lack of concrete evidence and the investigator is forced to infer the likely forces at work. Of crucial significance are the complex inter-relationships of supply and demand within the local labour market suggested in chapter 4. Management in Rochdale requires skilled engineering workers to perform various tasks in the enterprise, mainly of either a maintenance or of a 'setting-up' kind. The A.U.E.W. in places like Rochdale controls the supply of such men whom it insists must monopolize certain tasks and certain types of machinery. Management in places like Rochdale is in a competitive situation for such labour, competing with other employers and hence it cannot say 'take it or leave it' to local officials and shop stewards of the engineering union. Furthermore, the nature of the local product market and the forms of producing enhance the relative power of skilled labour within the Rochdale engineering labour market. A great deal of production (for instance, spring-making) requires considerable changing of the machinery in order to accommodate batch-production and, consequently, given the relative power of organized skilled engineering labour, forms of production have evolved which support the operation and continuous changing of machinery by skilled craftsmen rather than by semi-skilled machinists. As Blackburn and Mann (1979) have demonstrated in their analysis of the labour market for non-skilled workers in Peterborough, employers value reliability and responsibility above all other characteristics in their labour force. Given these structural features, it is not surprising that, firstly, employers are prepared to accept a degree of skilled work on processes that *technically* could be performed by non-skilled men; and, secondly, that the local nature of such bargaining procedures means that the nature of 'skilled' work varies from locality to locality. We may hypothesize that the greater the salience of engineering employment in a local labour market and the greater the competition between firms within that market, the higher will be the proportion of skilled engineering workers.

Clearly, much of the argument in this section is fragmentary and sketchy. Lack of or inaccessibility of union and employers' records is compounded by the kinds of issues involved. The structure of power in a local labour market is not always the subject of discussion by participants, either verbally or in written records. Often, it would appear as if these structures are seen as external, immutable and scarcely worthy of comment. Indeed, informal discussions with management suggest that 'capitalist rationality' is often situationally specific rather than the embodiment of deep, underlying economic tendencies like 'de-skilling'. Obviously, a great deal more research is needed, from a sociological point of view, on the structures that govern labour market behaviour. Nevertheless, the model in chapter 4 does serve as a useful point of departure for the analysis of labour market structuration in Rochdale.

The most salient features of the labour market in Rochdale over the period examined have been the strong organization of skilled manual workers and the competitive relations between local employers. Engineering workers have been organized strongly into a union expressing the sectional interests of the skilled. Such interests involve differentials over the non-skilled as a reward for apprenticeships and also the employment of all skilled engineers, despite encroachments by the non-skilled. The local engineering firms were, for the duration of the research period, small or medium sized employers and, in the main, family-owned concerns.[62] This reflects the general structure of the engineering industry in the period between the 1850's and 1960's, which was relatively small-scale and competitive.

The cotton industry and, in particular, spinning (which has long been the major strength of Rochdale textile production) also revealed a highly competitive structure, at least until the early 1960's. It is possible to suggest three phases of this continued structure. The first lasted from 1850 to 1914, and may be regarded as the 'golden' period of Lancashire cotton. In the 1890's, Schulze-Gaevernitz (1895) demonstrated the high levels of efficiency exhibited by British mule spinners during this era. He showed that three spinners (i.e. a minder and two piecers) could attend 1,000 spindles in 1887 in Britain, whilst it needed 5.8 in Alsace, 6.2 in Switzerland, and 7.2 in Saxony. In Britain, the distance travelled by the carriage and the speed of the self-actor were both considerably greater than those achieved on the Continent. Consequently, higher wages and shorter hours in Britain did not prevent British competitiveness, and Tyson (1968, p. 121) has argued that 'this supremacy over Continental countries was maintained until 1913'.

The second phase, from 1914 to 1945, can be regarded as the period of decline in the industry. This was the result of a series of factors: severe foreign competition from low wages, high efficiency countries like Japan and India, an over-valued currency after 1925 which devastated the export trade and, perhaps most significantly in the long run, the over-capitalization of the industry in the immediate post-war boom of 1918 to 1920.[63] This meant that investment lagged behind foreign competitors and that massive debt charges inhibited take-overs or rationalization of the industry. Ashton (1926) has shown that the Oldham District had 201 textile firms in 1884, 208 by 1914 and still 203 in 1924. The various trade directories[64] suggest a similar picture for Rochdale. This highly competitive structure of cotton capital persisted throughout the 1930's despite attempts made by the State to rationalize the industry.[65]

The third phase, from the end of the Second World War, witnessed the mass destruction of the Lancashire cotton industry. There is a considerable lack of useful research[66] on this period from the point of view of labour relations and capital structure, but what appears to have happened is that the relatively small firms that characterized phases one and two generally went into liquidation. Some were incorporated by take-overs into the large man-made fibre[67] conglomerates that now dominate what is left of the British textile industry. However, little can be said about labour relations in this period as evidence about them is, as yet, lacking.

Consequently, for the duration of the period between the 1850's and 1960's the cotton industry, like the engineering industry in Rochdale, was competitive in structure. This means that the occupational divisions that have formed the basis of unionization in all sectors of the cotton industry have confronted a competitive structure of buyers in the labour market. The most powerfully organized skilled unions in cotton have used this structure to preserve their own position within that labour market. In the first phase, such labour organizations often enhanced productivity as can be seen from Schulze-Gaevernitz's figures cited above. In the second and third phases, low rates of return on capital and entrenched labour relations inhibited radical restructuring. It is the contention of this chapter that the relative stability of union organization around the axis of skill throughout our period in Rochdale has been facilitated by the competitive structure of buyers in the local labour market. Consequently, the entire Rochdale cotton and engineering industries can be seen as inhabiting one of the four 'boxes' outlined in the model at the end of chapter 4. The box in question is the one where strongly organized skilled unions confront a competitive structure of employers. These issues will be returned to in chapter 8.

However, it is now necessary to consider the degree to which either cotton textile or engineering workers' trade union organizations around the axis of skill correspond to the general model of the labour aristocracy outlined in chapter 3. In other words, does the evidence analysed in this chapter embody the rhythms of 'homogenization' and 'sectionalization' suggested by that model? The evidence in the previous section on cotton failed to show any such cadences. Patterns of continuity and change in cotton, as far as the evidence permitted, did not follow a path parallel to, or congruous with, the general model of sectionalism outlined in chapter 3. Neither did the evidence on engineering. Trade union organization of manual workers in the engineering industry has always been strongly structured and divided around the axis of skill. There has also been a long tradition of hostility between the various sectional skilled union organizations in the British metal industry, as is witnessed by the history of demarcation disputes, especially between the A.E.U. and the Boilermakers' Union.[68] These inter-skill rivalries have not featured strongly in Rochdale, since the predominant metal manufacturing has been in textile machinery and spring-making – neither of which is organized by skilled manual unions other than the A.E.U.

There has been persistent conflict with the employers over skill and its structural supports – apprenticeship and regulations governing the manning of machinery. Three great lock-outs have been fought over these issues, and three times the result has gone overwhelmingly to the employers. Three times, local action has been undertaken to retrieve these national defeats. Localized action has taken place since 1922 in Rochdale, but no decisive documents have been located to support this. Only informal remarks by engineering workers and employers support this view.

Lack of direct data from employers and trade unions might appear to make further corroboration a hopeless task. However, powerful empirical support would be provided to the thesis that local action by the skilled within the framework of a national industrial union continued if evidence could be produced that showed a persistence of skilled earnings differentials throughout the period from 1922 to 1964. If such evidence materialized, the central contention of this chapter about trade union structuration in the engineering industry – that the skilled divide has existed continuously despite formal changes in the national structure – would appear far more plausible. It is to these issues that this research now turns.

7

The course of wage differentials in Rochdale during the period 1856–1964

The nature of the evidence

This chapter investigates empirical material on wage differentials between skilled and non-skilled manual workers in Rochdale during the period between 1856 and 1964. The evidence pertains to the engineering and cotton industries which are by far the largest employment sectors in the town, as was demonstrated in chapter 5. The data are presented in their original form in Appendices D and E. Before proceeding with their analysis, it is necessary to describe certain of their features in some detail.

The sources for the tables on wages in the engineering and cotton industries are very similar prior to 1914. The figures for 1859 and 1877 on engineering derive from the *Return of Wages 1830–1886*,[1] which were assembled to provide an historical background to the first national wage census in 1886. In both years the evidence relates to 'Manchester and Neighbourhood' and gives the wage rate per week. Both features present problems for this research. Firstly, it is not clear whether the area 'Manchester and Neighbourhood' includes Rochdale. Even if it did not, it is unlikely that the rates would differ very much from those presented, since Rochdale was certainly within the close economic hinterland of Manchester.[2] Any difference would probably be in the order of a few pence per week and would not significantly affect the overall averages constructed. Secondly, information in the form of a weekly wage rate presents the first major conceptual difficulty in the analysis of differentials since the weekly wage rate does not necessarily correspond to weekly earnings because it does not include 'extra' payments like bonuses and overtime.[3] However, this difficulty, which, as will be seen, has severely handicapped many recent attempts to examine the course of twentieth century differentials in engineering, is not a major problem in the nineteenth century engineering industry, since, as Hart and MacKay have pointed out, 'wage rates accounted for the bulk of earnings up to 1914' (1975, p. 33).

The evidence for the cotton industry in 1859 and 1877 derives from the *Returns of Wages, 1830–1886*,[4] which themselves were transcripts from previous Government statistics on wages.[5] However, there is a divergence between the 1887 compendium volume and Bowley's (1900) analysis of wages in the cotton industry which is also derived from the same original sources. It would appear as if Bowley introduced data from hand-mule spinning in the construction of his average for spinners on fine counts and also evidence for 'little' and 'big' piecers which are not included in the statistical sources which he cites.[6] I have followed the 1887 compendium data, as does G.H. Wood (1910) in his own analysis of wages in the spinning sector, in the construction of Tables 1 and 2 of Appendix E.

The evidence for 1886 for both industries derives from the comprehensive wage census of that year[7] and presents data on average weekly wage rates. The material on cotton is presented for 'Rochdale, Heywood and Neighbourhood' and that on engineering for 'South Lancashire (excluding Manchester)'. Since the material also gives the precise number of people employed during the census period, I have presented the unweighted and weighted averages for the different levels of skill. The weighted average allows for the different size of certain occupational categories and is the average used where available in this investigation. The 1906 wage census[8] was the most comprehensive ever taken nationally. It gives information for both the cotton and engineering industries on numbers employed, forms of payment (piece-rate versus time-rate) and average earnings.

In the period from 1906 onward, the evidence for the two industries becomes separate and the major sources become the respective employers' organizations. The material for the engineering industry has been collected by the Engineering Employers' Federation and relates to the Rochdale district of the Federation. The evidence is collected for the purposes of wage negotiations and is regarded as very accurate. Hart and MacKay present evidence on the relationship between E.E.F. results and those produced by the Ministry of Labour in the mid-1960's and declare that 'It is clear that there is extremely close agreement between these two returns. The difference of the . . . estimates lie within the very narrow range of 0.0 to + 4.4%' (Hart and MacKay, 1975, p. 35). I have collected evidence for the years 1914, 1918, 1925, 1930, 1935, 1955 and 1964, which gives, overall, a series of eleven points in time from which to construct the picture of wage differentials within the engineering industry.

Unfortunately, the material on cotton is not so rich. A major reason for the gaps was the loss of many records held by the Textile Employers' Federation in wartime air-raids, including the inter-war wage inquiries. However, some useful information, itself derived from the destroyed records concerning the 1930's, is contained in Jewkes and Gray (1935) (see Appendix E, Table 5) and Gray (1937) (see Table 6). The difficulties in assembling adequate post-1945 evidence lie in the lack of relevant data, which is partly the result of the dramatic decline of the industry and the subsequent demoralization of industrial relations. There is some material in the Evershed Commission Report,[9] but it is not very thorough, and consequently I have relied exclusively on data furnished privately to me by the U.K. Textile Manufacturers Association.

Although the data are of mixed quality, with variations in the areas covered and the type of information, they are also extremely powerful. What has been collected is a unique series of precise evidence on wage differentials within the working class over the last hundred years, which is both industrially and geographically specific. The averages of wages for different skills permit an accurate answer to the question of long-term trends in differentials and, more importantly, it makes possible an explanation that is rooted in concrete social relations rather than mysterious historical forces like egalitarianism or modernization. In addition, the strength of the material on wages permits a critique of previous accounts and explanations of the course of wage differentials in Britain over the last century.

Previous analyses of the course of skill differentials in Britain[10]

The issue of declining differentials between skilled and non-skilled workers has been a long-standing feature of British industrial relations, most notably in the engineering industry. From the First World War, through the immediate post-1945 era of austerity,[11] to the more recent difficulties in the Leyland toolroom[12] and at Heathrow Airport,[13] the claim that wage differentials within the working class are on the decline, or even more dramatically, that they no longer exist, has been a persistent feature of British society. Evidence provided for such assertions is often either rudimentary or non-existent, but has received some support from two of the three major sets of inquiries into differentials within the British manual working class conducted by economists in the post-1945 period.

The Oxford articles

The first attempt to describe the course of wage differentials in Britain and to provide an interpretation revolved around the efforts of Professor K.G.J.C. Knowles at the Oxford Institute of Statistics. Of the four articles produced, the first on 'Differences between the Wages of Skilled and Unskilled Workers, 1880-1950'[14] became the accepted orthodoxy. In this article, Knowles and Robertson assembled data on skill

Table 7.1. *Skill differentials in four industries (time rate of unskilled as % of skilled)*

	Building	Shipbuilding	Engineering	Railways
1880	63.9	54	60	—
1890	65.6	51	59	—
1900	66.7	52	58	—
1910	65.2	—	—	—
1914	66.5	55.2	58.6	54.3
1920	81.0	77.2	78.9	81.2
1925	75.6	68.8	70.9	69.4
1930	74.5	68.5	71.2	63.9
1935	74.9	68.3	71.9	61.1
1940	77.9	75.3	77.2	64.7
1945	80.8	81.0	81.9	76.0
1950	84.1	81.7	84.7	77.4

Source: Knowles and Robertson, 'Differences between the Wages of Skilled and Unskilled Workers, 1880–1950', *Bulletin of the Oxford University Institute of Statistics*, 13, April 1951, p. 111.

differentials in four industries: building, shipbuilding, engineering and the railways. The trend appeared unmistakable, as can be seen from my shortened version of their table in Table 7.1.

From this table it is clear that the overall trend supports the view that 'in general, skill differentials have been narrowing for a long time'. Indeed, it is difficult on the basis of this table to argue with Knowles and Robertson's historical interpretation that:

> The table shows considerable stability in all industries up to 1914. Thenceforward there was a sharp movement upwards, until the breaking of the post-war boom. The subsequent fall stopped well short of the pre-war level, and a further period of stability lasted until the late 1930's. With the onset of the second World War there was a further rise, albeit rather less steep ... throughout the period there is a clear tendency for skill differentials in the different industries to approach each other. (1951, p. 110)

Based upon this evidence, Knowles and Robertson attempted to provide an explanation. They concluded that unemployment was not a major factor in the change of differentials since:

> During the depression of the early 1930's, unemployment was very high in shipbuilding, high in engineering, and low on the railways. Yet, of these,

railways was the only industry which showed a widening of the differential, and this was because flat-rate changes in railwaymen's wages were made in accordance with changes in the cost-of-living index. (1951, pp. 113–14)

They accept a correlation between trends in differentials and general movements in the cost-of-living (i.e. inflation). This they attribute to the practice of granting flat-rate increases in order to combat rising prices, a procedure which during an inflationary period must produce decreasing differentials; unfortunately, they have little to say about the converse, the association of differentials and general reductions in prices (i.e. deflation). This is not perhaps surprising since their own data would not support such a relationship, as can be seen in the early 1930's, where their evidence fails to show any inverse relation between deflation and differentials.

Unfortunately, evidence from time-rates provides a totally inaccurate picture for the real trends in wage differentials in both the engineering and shipbuilding industries, since there has been a progressive divorce of time-rates from actual earnings since the First World War. As Hart and MacKay have shown convincingly:

> in the engineering industry there was, over 1914–68, a widening gap between rates and earnings. Hence, whereas wage rates accounted for the bulk of wage earnings up to 1914, they steadily dropped to only just over 50 per cent of total earnings by the end of our time period. (Hart and MacKay, 1975, p. 33)

Knowles and Robertson were let down badly by the nature of their sources, which all refer to changes in wage rates. Their second article, 'Earnings in Engineering, 1926–1948',[15] attempted to rectify this mistake by means of new data on earnings provided by the E.E.F., whilst retaining their overall conclusions and concomitant explanation. They concluded that:

> The skill differentials (for fitters and labourers) based on rates and earnings did not follow the same course in pre-war years – that on rates was generally lower than that on earnings. However, the skill differential based on earnings has narrowed considerably, so that both now stand at about the same level. (1951, p. 196)

However, their figures pertain to the period 1926 to 1948 and whilst the earlier years are well represented (1926, 1928, 1931, 1934, 1935, 1936, 1937, 1938, 1939), for some inexplicable reason, subsequent figures are only given for 1942 and January 1948. This could have been the result of a reluctance by the E.E.F. to disclose more modern figures because of the sensitivity surrounding wage negotiations at that period,[16] but the effect is to isolate one month, January 1948, at one end of the series and to project a trend backwards. However, as will become apparent from the Rochdale earnings material, January 1948 was all too likely an exceptional point in time and consequently a very poor month upon which to base an historical time-series.[17]

Knowles and Robertson's short third article[18] on the subject of engineering earnings did not add very much to their previous analyses, but the final article by Knowles and Hill[19] demonstrated a greater subtlety than hitherto. They concluded that:

> Between 1926 and 1953, the skill differential based on the effective rates of fitters and labourers narrowed by 16 points. This narrowing has caused increasing concern to the A.E.U.: Mr. Jack Tanner has recently opposed further flat-rate increases on the grounds that 'it would not be in the best interests of the industry were the gap between the skilled and the unskilled rates to narrow still further...' But in terms of average earnings the skill differential has not closed very much. (Knowles and Hill, 1954, p. 299)

It becomes apparent that the Knowles interpretation of the trend of wage differentials had almost turned full circle from a clear acceptance of declining differentials to an announcement that they were not declining 'very much'. Much of the confusion derived from the initial reliance on inadequate data, since the notional time-rates bore increasingly less relationship to actual trends in earnings over the periods analysed by Knowles and his colleagues. Unfortunately, the first article – the most inaccurate – contains the main explanations and it is this article and its explanations that became the orthodoxy for many post-war labour economists.

The Turner thesis

Turner's analysis of wage differentials was orginally presented in his article 'Trade Unions, Differentials and the Levelling of Wages'.[20] However, this account was presented subsequently in a more succinct form in an article on the relationships between inflation and wage differentials in Britain,[21] and it is to this briefer presentation that this critique will mainly address itself.

Turner (1964), basing his evidence exclusively on the Knowles articles discussed in the previous section, stated that skill differentials had generally been 'narrowing' since the early twentieth century. He countered the popular view that this had been caused by increased levels of education or by technical change, by arguing that:

> These things have certainly contributed to the reduction of particular differentials. But there is no obvious correlation between the rate of technical and educational progress and the general movement of differentials. Relative skill differentials, for instance, were pretty constant in

Britain during the latter nineteenth century and up to the first World War. Then they declined sharply, but were partly restored in the inter-war period. The narrowing, however, was resumed with the coming of the second World War and has continued to the present day. There is, therefore, a certain inverse connection between the general level of employment and that of relative differentials. (Turner, 1964, pp. 131–2)

Turner's reliance on Knowles *et al.* is pronounced, as is a certain asymmetry of interpretation, since it can be observed easily from Table 7.1 that during the inter-war period differentials widened by around 5% to 10% in the 1920's but remained almost constant from 1930 to 1935, the period of most savage unemployment.

Turner's overall explanation of declining wage differentials can be presented in the form of four propositions:

1) narrowing differentials have been associated with periods of rapidly rising prices, and with the growth of mass unionism;
2) mass trade unions prefer to demand equal 'flat-rate' increases for their members;
3) in a period of inflation, 'flat-rate' increases must, of necessity, decrease percentage differentials;
4) the choice of 'flat-rate' demands in situations where mass and sectional unions both confront employers jointly for the purposes of industrial bargaining is 'dictated by the numerical preponderance of the less skilled workers'.

It is immediately apparent that there is a certain asymmetry involved in proposition 4, even on Turner's own account; for, as he showed earlier in the same article:

> If the group secures a percentage advantage, its lower-paid members may complain that the skilled workers' cash advantage has been unfairly increased; if the advance is uniform in cash, the skilled workers protest that their differential has been relatively diminished. (Turner, 1964, p. 125)

Yet, despite the fact that the form of wage increase (or decrease) means that the interests of skilled and non-skilled operate in different directions, we are left to believe by Turner that in every wage demand by the A.E.U. between 1917 and 1952, the interests of the skilled were systematically ignored in favour of uniform cash advances. Turner elaborates his model by reference to the exceptions: those unions that consistently demand percentage increases, thereby preserving proportional differentials and enlarging absolute cash relativities in earnings. These unions, most notably the Spinners and those organizing workers in heavy steel,[22] have:

> no apprenticeship system, and entry to the better paid jobs is by promotion from the less skilled workers. In these cases it seems that the

lower paid have been reconciled to the maintenance of abnormal differentials by the chance of ultimately enjoying them. (Turner, 1964, p. 133)

Nevertheless, the overall picture is clear: differentials have declined since 1914 and the major factor involved in this secular trend has been the bargaining strategies conducted by skilled and non-skilled trade unions.

Routh's account of differentials

Guy Routh's *Occupation and Pay in Great Britain, 1906–60* (1965) is the major secondary source for the course of occupational pay in Britain in the twentieth century. However, it is a very difficult book to comprehend, since there is a lack of clarity about the sources and mode of generation of many of the tables included. For instance, Table 46 on the 'Median earnings for occupational classes 4 and 5, 6 and 7 in various industries, 1906 and 1960' (Routh, 1965, p. 102) presents the data on differentials in terms of unskilled (7), semi-skilled (6) but combines skilled (5) with foremen, supervisors and inspectors (4) for no apparent reason. His data certainly provide little comfort for either Turner or Knowles *et al.*, for as he states clearly:

> For men as between classes 4 and 5 (taken together) and 7 there has, on this evidence, been a general narrowing of differentials for four out of the six industrial groups. But the narrowing in these groups is cancelled by the widening in the others, so that the percentage relationship of the averages is the same in the two years.
>
> Between the semi-skilled and classes 4 and 5, the data show an actual widening of differentials between the two years, substantial in textiles and, in other groups, small but general. (p. 102)

In Table 48, 'Occupational class averages as percentages of the average for all occupational classes, men and women, 1913/4, 1922/4, 1935/6, 1955/6 and 1960', Routh (1965, p. 107) provides figures, shown in Table 7.2, from which no dramatic shifts in intra-class economic relationships can be inferred. Indeed, Routh himself emphasizes the continuity of national wages structures, whilst accepting short-run fluctuations in differentials associated with the general level of prices. However, his acceptance of Jaques (1956) theory of an intuitive notion of a 'fair wage' and of Wootton's (1954) emphasis on conservatism in wage bargaining is insufficient to explain the remarkable continuities uncovered, for conservatism *per se* never achieved much in industrial conflict, as the experience of the handloom weavers demonstrated. Nor can we accept notions of 'fair wages', either intuitive or acquired through social experience, as determining the structure of wage differentials, since one man's idea of a fair wage is another's idea of an insupportable burden.

Table 7.2. *Skill differentials of men in selected years as a percentage of total employed population (N.B. women in a separate sub-table)*

	1913/4	1922/4	1935/6	1955/6	1960
Skilled	124	115	121	117	117
Semi-skilled	86	80	83	88	85
Unskilled	79	82	80	82	79

Source: G. Routh, *Occupation and Pay in Great Britain, 1906–60* (1965, p. 107).

It would appear, therefore, from an examination of the arguments of Knowles, Turner and Routh about trends in wage differentials within the manual working class in Britain, that there is no agreement amongst investigators. Turner believes strongly in declining differentials, Knowles oscillates and Routh finds little evidence for any decline. The empirical material collected on differentials in Rochdale will throw considerable light on this debate and also provide evidence with which to assess the general model of working class sectionalism outlined at the end of chapter 3, since one of the main indicators of such sectionalism in the literature has been earnings differentials.

Differentials in Rochdale

In order to facilitate the exposition, the analysis of intra-class wage differentials in Rochdale will be divided into two separate sections, dealing in succession with the engineering and cotton industries.

Engineering

The information on skill differentials in Rochdale is presented in Table 7.3. The columns give information, where available, for each of the eleven years selected for investigation. The rows give the actual monetary wage for averages of skilled, semi-skilled and unskilled engineering workers in the town, and also the percentages represented by the semi-skilled and unskilled averages as a proportion of the skilled average (100%). The final row gives the differential of unskilled to skilled as a decimal to two figures. It can be seen that the rise in actual wages for the skilled average from 31s 11d to 367s 1d[23] over the period has not been accompanied by similar dramatic shifts in relativities. The maximum unskilled:skilled differential was 0.52 in 1859 and the minimum 0.75 in 1918.

Money wages rose slowly in the second half of the nineteenth century,

Table 7.3. *Average wages in the Rochdale engineering industry by skill for selected years*

	1859	1877	1886	1906	1914	1918	1925	1930	1935	1955	1964
Average wage skilled	31s 11d	31s 10½d	30s 7½d	36s 8d	37s 8½d	74s 10½d	61s 6½d	57s 7d	66s 9½d	239s 11d	367s 1d
%	100	100	100	100	100	100	100	100	100	100	100
Average wage semi-skilled	19s 1d	24s 0d	21s 6d	27s 11½d	—	—	—	—	54s 1¼d	203s 8d	306s 8d
%	59.77	75.28	70.22	76.25	—	—	—	—	81.00	84.89	83.54
Average wage unskilled	16s 9d	19s 0d	17s 8d	21s 3d	22s 10d	56s 2¾d	43s 1½d	38s 5d	46s 4d	172s 3¼d	267s 5d
%	52.47	59.60	57.67	57.95	60.56	75.09	70.07	66.72	69.37	71.80	72.85
Differential skilled/ unskilled	0.52	0.60	0.58	0.58	0.61	0.75	0.70	0.67	0.69	0.72	0.73

Source: Appendix D.

with an acceleration of growth towards 1914. However, the two most dramatic jumps in money wages occurred during the two world wars. Wages doubled in the First World War and almost quadrupled between 1935 and 1955. However, this latter increase also involved the effects of post-war inflation, associated with full employment, as is revealed by the continued rise in money wages between 1955 and 1964 – an increase of around 50%. Wages fell in monetary terms after the 1920 collapse of the reconstruction boom, from their high point around 1920, until the period after 1933. However, these falls were nothing like as dramatic as the increases in the years associated with inflation.

The trend in the differential between skilled and unskilled engineering workers, the most widely used indicator of relativities by previous analysts, reveals long periods of stability, with two shifts in the secular trend. Both changes involved a diminution in the differential enjoyed by skilled engineering craftsmen over unskilled labourers. The first occurred during the third quarter of the nineteenth century and the second, and more dramatic, took place during the First World War. The differential between 1877 and 1914 stood close to the ratio of 5:3 for skilled men in relation to the unskilled. Despite the severity of the depression in 1886 and the boom conditions of 1914, the relativity remained more or less constant. This evidence on the nineteenth century is the first surprising result, for the shift in the relativity from 0.52 to around 0.60 between 1859 and the last quarter of the nineteenth century predates both the development of general unionism in engineering and the increasing influence of socialist egalitarianism. My own interpretation, which, in view of the lack of suitable materials with which to substantiate the point, must remain conjectural, is that the change between 1859 and 1877 reflects the development of the industry described in Table 5.1. For in 1859 the engineering industry was in its earliest period of development and skilled engineering craftsmen, particularly, were in short supply in Rochdale and consequently enjoyed high differentials over the unskilled labourers. The third quarter of the nineteenth century witnessed the establishment of the industry in the town, and led to a diminution of scarcity amongst skilled craftsmen.

However, there is less difficulty in explaining the changes in trends during and after the First World War. As can be seen from Table 7.3, the differential narrowed from around 0.60 to 0.75 between 1914 and 1918 in Rochdale, returning to around 0.70 in 1925, a position from which it had scarcely moved between then and 1964. Clearly, the period between 1914 and 1925 is of major interest in the analysis of wage differentials. This eleven year interval contained the First World War and its concomitant acceleration of inflation and also the third great Lock-out in the engineering trade and subsequent transformation of the nature of the

A.E.U. from craft to a form of industrial unionism. Material, particularly on the social and economic effects of wartime inflation,[24] is abundant and provides the means of explaining the dramatic collapse of differentials between 1914 and 1920 and their subsequent reversal. However, the standard interpretations of this era, with regard to intra-manual working class relationships, are often ambiguous as can be seen in the volumes produced on the *Economic and Social History of the World War*,[25] especially those by the labour historian G.D.H. Cole.

Cole, as a Marxist, believed that the war had accelerated trends, immanent within capitalist development, towards the elimination of skilled manual work and the homogenization of the working class. As he stated clearly (1923b, pp. 3–4):

> the change which has come about in the relations between skilled and less skilled workers, although it has an economic phase, and is important in its economic content, is fundamentally a psychological change. What really makes it a change vitally affecting the future of industry and society is that it consists, above all, in a modification of the attitude of the different grades of workers one to another. The skilled worker can no longer think of the less skilled workers quite as he was apt to think of them before the War, and the less skilled worker will no longer be conscious of the same subordination to the skilled workers.

However, there are considerable ambiguities in the evidence that Cole furnished for homogenization; namely, trade union growth amongst the semi-skilled and rapidly declining wage differentials. For Cole himself in the same study showed quite clearly the hostility between the A.S.E. and the general labour unions (principally the Workers' Union and National Union of Gasworkers and General Labourers) over the issue of dilution. As Cole put it in his conclusions to *Trade Unionism and Munitions*:

> Many skilled Trade Unionists... greatly preferred the introduction of women under dilution schemes, even at lower wage rates, to that of less skilled men, because they held and felt that women were likely to be less powerful competitors after the war... The position would, of course, be greatly changed if the 'Industrial Unionists' got their way, and skilled and less skilled were effectively combined in a single organization based on the principle of 'Union by Industry'... (1923a, p. 219)

It would appear that Cole's political commitment to industrial unionism led him to over-emphasize the social transformations between skilled and non-skilled engineering workers. The explanation for his over-accentuation of the evidence on declining wage differentials lay in his restriction, quite legitimately for the main purposes of his study, of his analysis to the period between 1914 and 1920. As can be seen from Tables

Table 7.4a. *Advances in time wage rates in engineering 1914–1920*

	Cost of living index	Skilled		Unskilled		% differential	Cash differential
		Amount[a] s d	Rate[a] s d	Amount[a] s d	Rate[a] s d		s d
1914	100	—	39 11	—	21 10	55	18 1
1917: up to April[b]	170	7 0	46 11	7 0	28 10	61	18 1
April	170	5 0	51 11	5 0	33 10	65	18 1
August	180	3 0	54 11	3 0	36 10	67	18 1
October	180	6 10	61 9	4 7	41 5	67	20 4
December	185	5 8	67 4	5 8	47 1	70	20 3
1918: August	210	3 11	71 4	3 11	50 11	71	20 5
December	220	5 8	76 11	5 8	56 7	74	20 4
1919: December	225	5 8	82 7	5 8	62 2	75	20 5
1920: March	232	3 5	85 11	3 5	65 7	76	20 4
May	250	3 5+ 11[c]	90 2	3 5+ 1 1[c]	70 7	78	19 5

Source: R.S. Spicer, *British Engineering Wages* (1928, p. 43).

[a] to the nearest 1d.

[b] consolidation of previous wartime District negotiations.

[c] being average advances between 1917 and 1920 awarded in Special District Cases.

Table 7.4b. *Reductions in time wage rates in engineering 1921–1922*

	Cost of living index	Skilled		Unskilled		% differential	Cash differential
		Amount s d	Rate s d	Amount s d	Rate s d		s d
1921: July	222	3 5	86 10	3 5	67 2	77	19 8
August	220	3 5	83 5	3 5	63 10	77	19 7
November	203	3 1	80 4	2 4	61 6	77	18 8
December	199	3 1	77 3	2 4	59 1	76	18 2
1922: January	192	3 1	74 2	2 4	56 9[a]	76	17 5
July	181	5 6	68 8	5 6	51 3	75	17 5
August	179	5 6	63 2	5 6	45 9	72	17 3
September	178	5 6	57 8	5 6	40 3	70	17 5

Source: R.S. Spicer, *British Engineering Wages* (1928, p. 43).
[a]Spicer gives the amount as 56s 0d but this is a mistake, the correct figure is 56s 9d.

7.4a and 7.4b, this limits the picture to the period of inflation and declining differentials whilst having the effect of ignoring the subsequent onset of deflation and the re-establishment of increased differentials in earnings by skilled engineering workers. The reason for the rise and fall of differentials in wage rates and earnings between skilled and unskilled engineering workers lay in the form of increases granted during the inflationary period to compensate workers for rising prices. As Spicer (1928, p. 45) puts it: 'This was of course simply due to the fact that flat advances were usually given to the various grades on the grounds that a man was equally affected by an increased cost of living whether he were skilled or not.'

The fact that a similar process of flat-rate reductions was set in motion during the deflation in 1921 and 1922 was the major reason why relativities expanded once more. However, the differential did not widen to its old pre-1914 level, which reflected the difficulties of the A.E.U. in the face of the severities of the capitalist trade cycle and the weaknesses of craft organizations in engineering after the 1922 Lock-out that were discussed in the preceding chapter. However, the major problem in the analysis of this period lies not in the mechanisms whereby changes in differentials occurred, but in the reasons behind the mechanisms themselves. Trends in rates and earnings ran parallel during this period, mainly because rates formed the predominant content of earnings and also because opportunities for piecework expanded approximately at a similar pace. As rates between skilled and unskilled narrowed, so did earnings, both in Rochdale and throughout British engineering, as is revealed by Table 7.5. However, this raises the immediate question of why flat-rate changes were acceptable to the negotiating parties in engineering, particularly the A.S.E. and the general unions.

An answer to this problem is exceedingly difficult, given the sparsity of information on the subject, but the main reason seems to lie in the fact that the A.S.E. had put most of its efforts, in the pre-war period, into securing basic rates in its Districts and into negotiating simple additions to the rate by means of small increases of a few pence on both the skilled and unskilled rates. The effect on differentials was very small in a period of approximate wage stability, and such disadvantages were far outweighed by the simplicity of flat-rate pence increases for District bargaining in such a complex industry as engineering.[26] It would seem that the A.S.E. continued with such bargaining formulae into the war period, scarcely expecting the dramatic inflation that accompanied hostilities. The industrial militancy in 1916 and 1917 forced Government control of wages until the end of the war[27] and this machinery simply took over the traditional practices. The general unions happily supported this until 1920, whilst the A.S.E., itself strongly influenced by industrial unionism and

Table 7.5. *A comparison of figures for Rochdale differentials between earnings of skilled and unskilled in engineering with Spicer's national time-rate differentials*

	Rochdale (earnings) differential			Spicer (time-rates) differential		
	%	Cash s	d	%	Cash s	d
1914	61	15	11	55	18	1
1918	75	18	8	71	20	5
1925	70	18	5	70	17	5

Sources: Appendix D and Tables 7.4a and 7.4b.

wartime egalitarianism, seemed to accept the rough justice of flat-rate increases. However, in 1920 and 1921, the newly-formed A.E.U. began to regain the relative position of skilled men by negotiating flat-rate decreases. There is certainly some plausibility in Turner's (1962) suggestion that competition between the A.E.U. and the general unions for members amongst non-skilled engineering workers prompted the continuance of this practice after 1922 and prevented the re-establishment of differentials as wide as those in 1914. However, it would seem that the problems are more complex than Turner appears to suggest, for although there has been a persistent commitment by the A.E.U. to flat-rate increases at a national level for all grades of skill, which as Knowles has demonstrated (cf. Table 7.1) led to the long-term collapse of the time-rate differential, the Rochdale evidence shows clearly that this has not been paralleled by any equivalent collapse in the earnings relativity of skilled engineering workers, at least not before 1964. This divergence between earnings and wage-rates was the result of two major factors. Firstly, the growth of piecework amongst skilled workers in engineering in Rochdale (see Table 7.6) has meant that an increasing proportion of earnings is derived from various bonus payment schemes. Secondly, and most crucially, the negotiation of rates and of earnings reflects a structural bifurcation in the A.E.U. itself.[28] The national officers negotiate the time-rates with the E.E.F. and they generally prefer flat-rate increases all across the skilled board. The District officials and factory shop stewards negotiate the local piecework and bonus systems and it is clear that skilled craftsmen dominate District and local bargaining procedures. These men, often unreconciled to the erosion of wages and status involved in national bargaining, have fought a sustained and, as far as the material examined here shows, a successful campaign to maintain relativities between skilled and unskilled in their local areas.

Hence, the stability of differentials between the earnings of skilled and unskilled Rochdale engineering workers between 1923 and 1964 bears little or no relation to levels of employment, inflation, social democratic egalitarianism or even (except in a remote sense)[29] to technological change. The crucial variable has been the form of industrial bargaining prevalent in the determination of earnings – District and factory based negotiations with individual employers over piecework rates. The results of this bargaining structure are clear enough in terms of the ensuing differentials. However, what is lacking is precise data on the strategies conducted at the point of production. Union and employer records in Rochdale do not facilitate such an enterprise; perhaps better records exist elsewhere which will throw more light on this subject.

However, the differential between skilled and unskilled is not the only measure of intra-class relativities within the engineering industry in Rochdale, since there are also the differentials associated with semi-skilled work. For the purposes of this research, only the differential between skilled and semi-skilled will be examined, but it would not appear from Table 7.3 that there has been any great change in the relationship between unskilled and semi-skilled engineering workers over the last sixty years. A serious problem in the examination of semi-skilled engineering workers lies in the paucity of available data; indeed, neither Knowles nor Turner have anything at all to say about this problem.[30] This hiatus in information is particularly unfortunate since, from the perspective of declining differentials, it might be thought that this particular line of division could be more flexible, given the rapid increase of semi-skilled production as a result of persistent technological rationalization in the engineering industry. Furthermore, the success of skilled craftsmen in maintaining their relative position *vis-à-vis* labourers since 1925 was won at the expense of increased payment-by-results systems, themselves predominant features of semi-skilled work in engineering since the beginning of the twentieth century (see Table 7.6). The evidence from Rochdale, which covers the years 1859, 1877, 1886, 1906, 1935, 1955 and 1964, does not support the hypothesis of an overlap of skilled and semi-skilled earnings nor of a rapid decline in relativities. Since 1877, the semi-skilled/skilled differential has varied from 75.3% in 1877 to 83.5% in 1964. The differential appears very stable between 1935 and 1964, with a small but persistent secular rise from 1877 to 1935, apart from 1886, which, given the severity of the depression when the wage census was taken, is explicable in terms of reduced earnings as a direct consequence of low orders. Admittedly, the data on the semi-skilled in engineering relate only to members of the A.E.U., but despite the absence

Table 7.6. *The growth of piecework in the Rochdale engineering industry, 1906–1964 (percentage on piecework)*

	1906	1914	1918	1925	1930	1935	1955	1964
Fitter	44.3 ⎱ₐ 0.0	14.6	38.8	26.9	44.0	41.6	62.3 ⎱d 16.5	35.4 ⎱e 0.0
Turners (skilled)	69.6 ⎱b 0.0	38.1	56.8	22.0	43.5	36.3	53.6	44.6
Patternmaker	0.0	0.0	23.1	56.4	87.5	87.2	38.5	45.5
Moulder	45.4 ⎱c 0.0	24.6	17.7	49.5	37.6	33.0	59.7	63.9
Sheetmetal worker	—	—	—	4.9	37.1	30.4	61.3	61.0
Coppersmith	—	—	—	60.0	—	85.7	—	—
Turners and machinemen etc. (semi-skilled)	65.9	—	—	—	—	—	83.2	76.1
Labourer	52.2	4.3	15.3	14.3	7.8	—	18.0	22.5

Source: Appendix D.

a 44.3% = Fitters, erectors, and millwrights in textile machinery production; 0% = those in general engineering.
b 69.6% = Turners (other than brass) in textile machinery production; 0% = those in general engineering.
c 45.4% = Moulders in iron and steel; 0% = moulders in brass.
d 16.5% = Toolroom fitters; 62.3% = other fitters.
e 0% = Toolroom fitters; 33.4% = other fitters.

of similar concrete evidence from the general unions in Rochdale, it is unlikely that there would have been any significant divergence between semi-skilled earnings in the various unions.

Summary of differentials in engineering in Rochdale

The relative earnings of skilled and non-skilled engineering workers have not declined significantly since the mid-1920's, contrary to the arguments of Knowles *et al.* and Turner. The major change in the trend of differentials occurred during the First World War. The stability of proportional earnings has been achieved by judicious manipulation of piecework and other bonuses negotiated at the local level by the skilled craftsmen who still dominate District offices in the union and also provide most of the shop stewards. The success of skilled engineering workers in retaining their differential in earnings over the non-skilled has been the direct result of their local control over bargaining with the employers that was outlined in the preceding chapter and which is such an important feature of British industrial relations.[31] The A.E.U. over this period was essentially an industrial union at the centre, but often a craft union in the localities, especially with regard to its direct bargaining practices with individual employers. It is this structural bifurcation within the A.E.U. that has maintained skilled differentials in earnings in the first two-thirds of the twentieth century. Turner was clearly correct to emphasize trade union bargaining strategies for an understanding of trends in such differentials, but his inadequate data led him to mis-identify the real processes at work in the industry. Of the three positions outlined earlier, Routh's view that differentials have not altered much in the twentieth century is closest to the evidence, although Routh's precise chronology is dubious.

Cotton

As was discussed earlier in this chapter, the evidence on earnings in the Rochdale cotton industry is less exhaustive than that pertaining to engineering. However, all the available material is presented, in full, in Appendix E, and it is from there that the tables generated for this section derive. The major weaknesses lie in the absence of evidence on the earnings of overlookers, tapesizers and strippers-and-grinders in the twentieth century. Another weakness lies in the poor quality of the post-1945 material.[32] Nevertheless, it is possible to make some use of the data to enlarge upon the account constructed for the engineering industry in the previous section. In particular, the main internal skilled differential in spinning between the minder and the piecers can be examined.

The figures on average earnings in the spinning section in Rochdale (Table 7.7) reveal the crucial importance of the form of labour organization

Table 7.7. *Average earnings in the Rochdale self-acting mule spinning industry, 1859–1932*

		1859	1877	1886	1906	1920	1932
Minder	Earnings	21s 0d	32s 10d	31s 3d	40s 10d	112s 10d	87s 0d
	Differential	100%	100%	100%	100%	100%	100%
Big piecer	Earnings	10s 0d[a]	13s 8d[a]	14s 11d	19s 7d	52s 9d	36s 4d
	Differential	47.62	41.65	47.74%	47.95%	46.75%	41.75%
Little piecer	Earnings			9s 11d	12s $11\frac{1}{2}$d	38s 0d	26s 6d
	Differential			31.74%	31.74%	33.67%	30.45%

Source: Appendix E.

[a] As was discussed in note 6 the evidence only relates to 'piecers' in 1859 and 1877. It is highly probable that 'piecers' in these contexts referred to 'big' piecers, as Bowley assumed in his estimates, but there is no certainty of this.

Table 7.8. *Differential between minders' and skilled engineering workers' earnings in Rochdale, 1859–1932*

	1859	1877	1886	1906	1920	1932
Minder	21s 0d	32s 10d	31s 3d	40s 10d	112s 10d	87s 0d
Average skilled engineer	31s 11d	31s 10d	30s 7d	36s 8d	90s 2d[a]	57s 7d[b]
% differential: minder/engineer	65.79	103.14	102.19	111.34	125.10	151.09

Source: Appendices D and E.

[a] 90s 2d = minimum rate for skilled men in engineering in 1920. This may under-represent actual earnings by around 6d to 9d at this time.

[b] 57s 7d = average earnings in Rochdale for 1930. Given the depth of depression in 1932, it may well be that this figure over-estimates the average for 1932 by a few pence.

amongst spinning operatives. It can be seen that the differential between the minder and the big piecer probably never was less than 2:1 in the period between 1859 and 1932. The differential for the little piecer was even greater, and both differentials reveal the strong impact of sub-contracting and piecework on wage relativities within the spinning industry. It is clear that the minders' commitment to sub-contracting, piecework and the systematic 'disorganization' of the piecers, which was analysed in the preceding chapter, produced substantial economic rewards for the minders. Indeed, the size of minders' earnings gives strong support to Chapman's argument that it was the prospect of such ultimate 'glittering prizes' that helped to accommodate the piecer to his positition (Chapman, 1899).

What is even more remarkable is the widening of the differential between the minder and piecers in the period between 1920 and 1932, which demonstrates the importance of the practices of sub-contracting for differentials in spinning. Between 1886 and 1920 there was a virtual stasis in differentials, after they had narrowed somewhat with the progressive implementation of the 1876 Oldham piece-list.[33] This stability in rela-tivities was achieved despite the severity of the depression in 1886 and the economic effects of the First World War and subsequent reconstruction boom. The differential expanded by fully 5% between 1920 and 1932. What appears to have happened is that the minders' strong controls over the labour process, including the remuneration of their assistants, enabled them to offset some of the effects of the inter-war depression in cotton by reducing the proportion paid to the piecers out of the total earnings of the

Table 7.9 *Average earnings in certain occupations in the Rochdale cotton industry, 1859–1937*

	1859	1877	1886	1906	1937
Minder	21s 0d	32s 10d	31s 3d	40s 10d	87s 0d
%	100	100	100	100	100
Ring Spinner	9s 0d	17s 6d	12s 2d	15s 10d	—
%	42.86	53.32	38.91	38.82	—
Winder	9s 0d	14s 2d	12s 2d	15s 4d	29s 5d
%	42.86	43.17	38.98	37.55	33.82
Weaver (average looms)	(3 looms) 15s 6d	(3 looms) 18s 6d	(3 looms, women) 14s 9d	(females, 3, 4 looms) 19s 6d	39s 3d
%	73.81	56.37	47.2	47.76	45.11

Source: Appendix E.

machine. Such an interpretation is further supported by the material on the differential between minders and skilled engineering workers in Rochdale between 1859 and 1932 in Table 7.8. It is clear from this table that, despite the limitations of the evidence on engineering for 1920 and 1932, differentials between minders and skilled engineers expanded during the 1920's. Indeed, the evidence in Table 7.9 on average earnings in cotton reveals a similar pattern for the differential between minders on the one hand and winders and weavers on the other.

Summary of differentials in cotton in Rochdale

The trends in earnings between skilled and non-skilled workers in the spinning section of the cotton industry reveal marked continuities over long periods of time. The differentials between minders and piecers have been remarkably constant and demonstrate the crucial importance of the form of labour organization within the spinning sector. This becomes startlingly clear in the inter-war years when the differential between minders, on the one hand, and on the other, piecers, winders, weavers and skilled engineers, respectively, all widened. This was made possible by the control exercised by the minders over the earnings of their assistants by virtue of their sub-contracting role with the employers. Unfortunately, there is insufficient evidence with which to probe the earnings differentials of overlookers, tapesizers and strippers-and-grinders, all of whom were discussed in the preceding chapter. However, the evidence produced on differentials within the spinning section in Rochdale permits a comparison with the relationships in engineering and an answer, albeit provisional, to the trends in wage differentials between the skilled and non-skilled between the mid-nineteenth century and the mid-1960's.

Conclusions

The task of this research is to investigate whether the general model outlined in chapter 3 captures the rhythms of internal working class structuration around the axis of skill. This chapter has analysed wage differentials between skilled and non-skilled manual workers which are a main index of economic structuration. The analysis has focused on Rochdale and specifically upon the cotton and engineering industries that have dominated employment and production in the town since the mid-nineteenth century. As far as the available data permit, the following conclusions emerge.

Firstly, *there has been no unilinear trend in the behaviour of earnings relativities between skilled and either semi-skilled or unskilled workers in cotton or engineering*. It is not possible to talk meaningfully in this context about *the* historical trend in skill differentials. Nevertheless, long periods of stability in intra-class wage differentials have been apparent within specific industrial sectors. In cotton, the differential between minders, big piecers and little piecers has been in the ratio of around 100:45:32 for most of the period; certainly between 1886 and 1920. The two shifts in trend, neither of them dramatic, occurred in the late 1870's and in the 1920's. On the first occasion, relativities narrowed to the figures described above, as the result of the progressive implementation of the 1876 Oldham piece-list, which regularized earnings in spinning in Rochdale. The 1920's witnessed a widening of the differential almost to the old mid-nineteenth century ratio, as a direct result of the spinners' attempt to offset the effects of the inter-war depression on to their assistants by means of reducing their assistants' relative earnings.

In engineering, similar long periods of stable relative earnings have been apparent, with the first major shift occurring during the 1860's and the second during the period of oscillation between 1914 and 1925, when the differentials in engineering between skilled, semi-skilled and unskilled shifted from a ratio of around 100:75:60 in the pre-1914 period to 100:82:70 in the post-1925 era.[34]

None of this evidence on trends in wages differentials between skilled and non-skilled manual workers corresponds to the general model of skilled manual workers outlined at the end of chapter 3. The industrial revolution created a factory-based manual working class which possessed clear economic differentials. These differentials persisted in both the cotton and engineering industries right up to 1914. Differentials between the skilled and unskilled in engineering narrowed between 1859 and 1877 when, according to the tenets of the general model of the labour aristocracy, they should have expanded. From 1877 to 1914, the skilled differential remained approximately the same when, again according to the model, it should have narrowed considerably. In the spinning section of cotton, differentials were wider than in engineering as a result of the internal contract between minders and piecers. They narrowed somewhat after 1877 as a result of the implementation of the Oldham piece-list. However, they remained more or less constant from the 1880's until the 1920's.

Nor is there any evidence from these data on wages to support the idea that internal economic structuration associated with skill either declined in the inter-war years or expanded after 1945. Indeed, powerful evidence from the spinning sector suggests that the opposite is true for the skilled differential between the minders and the piecers. Evidence from the engineering industry shows that, despite a declining differential skilled *rate* between 1914 and the 1950's and 1960's, *earnings* differentials between skilled and non-skilled engineering workers remained approximately proportional throughout the period.

Such conclusions throw considerable doubt on the reality of popular conceptions of 'squeezed' differentials in the post-1945 era and upon the interpretations associated with Turner and Knowles. These data also strongly support the view suggested at the end of the last chapter that the A.E.U. remains structured around the axis of skill despite its formal industrial unionism.

All these points demonstrate the crucial significance of trade union organizations, strategies and tactics for the analysis of the relationships between skilled and non-skilled manual workers. The stability of re-lativities has been closely allied to the local nature of industrial bargaining in both the cotton and engineering industries in Rochdale. These results vindicate the local nature of this research, for aggregate analysis of differentials can easily misunderstand the causal mechanisms in their generation, which are local rather than national. However, given the overwhelming concentration of the cotton industry in Lancashire[35] and the marked specializations of different types of production in certain localities of the county, the cotton trade unions combine industrial and local organization in one unit, whereas the amorphous nature of the engineering industry permits a structural bifurcation within the A.E.U. between the national centre and the local peripheries. The stability of differentials in both cotton and engineering reflect the strengths of both the A.E.U. and the Spinners' Union in local wage bargaining. The differences in the parameters of the structures of relativities reflect the stronger power of the Spinners historically, deriving from their role as sub-contractors. Indeed, evidence from the iron industry[36] on wide earnings differentials between skilled and non-skilled supports the hypothesis that sub-contracting permits wider sets of relativities than more orthodox work processes.

Hence, *there has been no unilinear trend towards the elimination of differentials in earnings between skilled and non-skilled workers in Rochdale between 1856 and 1964. There have been movements towards a widening of the gap (sectionalization) and movements reversing such changes (homogenization).* However, *the key component in all the trends has been the persistent and generally successful attempt by local groups of skilled manual workers to preserve their higher levels of earnings.* Neither unemployment, mass-unionism, socialist ideologies, nor technological change have proved particularly important, in general terms, in the history of wage differentials. The major change has been the elimination of automatic mule spinning, and more recently most of the textile industry in Lancashire, by means of foreign competition. Indeed, this may be one of the most important conclusions of this research, namely that economic relationships within the working class may well only be transformed by the destruction of the industries within which they are located. Nevertheless, when it comes to understanding the course of economic differentials within the manual working class in Rochdale, local bargaining structures appear crucial. It is to these issues that this research will now turn.

8

Skilled manual workers in the labour process

In chapter 1 it was argued that it is important to investigate the structure of the working class and not to assume it. It was suggested in chapter 4 that one way of achieving that aim would be through an analysis of the forms and types of labour markets which characterize the essential nature of capitalist social relations. The purpose of this chapter is to summarize and reflect upon the general significance of the empirical material presented in the previous two chapters on the internal structuration of the Rochdale working class, in order to assess the utility of the model developed in chapter 4. However, the first task is to ascertain whether the general model of working class sectionalism presented in chapter 3 is accurate. That model presented a five-point chronology of the rhythms of working class sectionalism and homogeneity. It suggested that the industrial revolution created a relatively homogeneous manual working class. After 1848, this homogeneity disintegrated amid the prosperity of the mid-Victorian era. However, the 1880's and 1890's witnessed a renewed tide of homogenization which was maintained until the end of the Second World War. The post-1945 period, again according to the model, has seen a further period of increased differentiation within the manual working class.

The initial assertion that the industrial revolution created a homogeneous working class is itself highly dubious. Asa Briggs (1960) supports the view of homogeneity with evidence to suggest that the very concept of 'class' is coterminous with the period of industrial revolution and the emergence of factory production. However, the emergence of concepts is not an infallible guide to the nature of social structure. The notion of 'class' emerged in the realms of polemic and its meaning for social actors has long remained ambiguous. The entry of a concept into the historical arena *is* significant, but not necessarily as a simple reflection of social relationships. It is not possible to assume a homogeneous manual working class simply upon the basis of the emergence of the concept of 'class'. Similarly, E.P. Thompson's profound vision of the 'making of the English working class'

117

(1963), with its emphasis on class consciousness and attitudes, should not blind social scientists to the very significant divisions between sections of the manual working class in the period of industrialization between 1790 and 1850. Fong (1930) has used Census material and Government reports to demonstrate the heterogeneity of the British manual working class in the 1840's. In particular, he has shown the strength of sub-contracting relations or 'internal contracts' between groups of workers. As Musson,[1] amongst others, has shown, little support can be given to the idea that the conditions of life of skilled manual workers, as compared with the non-skilled, were at all similar in the 1840's and 1850's. Earnings differentials[2] were large, often maintained by authority relations between artisan and labourer that produced a synthesis of market relations and those at the point of production. Factory production, of itself, did not change many of these structures dramatically. This is not to minimize the important social and psychological changes associated with factory production,[3] but to reiterate the point that, in Britain, factory organization often *preceded* widespread mechanization of production. From this latter observation it is possible to develop a more plausible model of the inter-relationships between skill and the labour process during the period of industrialization and, as a consequence, a more accurate conception of the complex economic structuration of the manual working class than the imagery of homogeneity suggested by the model for the period prior to 1850 – the moment when the main empirical content of this research commences.

The 'orthodox' view[4] of the developments of the labour process and their effects on skill can be presented in the form of a three-stage model:

Competitive pre-industrial
The labour process under this stage can be labelled *artisan production*. The skills involved are derived from long apprenticeships. There is no separation of mental and manual functions in the work process and no separation of the direct producers from the means of production. There is a large degree of self-employment and consequently most Journeymen hope to become Masters. Conflict between Masters and Journeymen is sporadic and limited to wages and wage-related issues such as the overall number of Journeymen and apprentices. Examples of such artisans would be masons, shoemakers and millwrights.

Competitive industrial
The labour process here can be termed *craftsman production*. There is a separation of the direct producers from the means of production but an incomplete separation of conception and execution. Hence, there still remain mechanized skills. Conflict between craftsmen and

Diagram 8.1. *Skill and the labour process during the period of industrialization in Britain*

	'Skilled' route	'Non-skilled' route
Forms of transition to industrial capitalism	1. Artisan production	A. Artisan, domestic production
	↓	
	2. Factory production	
	↓	
	3. Automatic production → in factories (with existing labour)	B. Automatic factory production (with new labour force)
Examples	Engineers	Weavers
	Mule spinners	Cardroom workers

employers is endemic and centres around craft controls over machinery. Examples of such craftsmen would be turners, printers and carpenters.

Oligopolistic industrial[5]

The labour process can now be termed '*de-skilled*'. Manual work has become completely routinized as a result of the total separation of conception and execution promoted by 'scientific management'. Examples of such de-skilled workers would be assembly-line workers and machinists.

The general argument in this developmental model is that increased technological development produces decreased 'skill' in a unilinear fashion. Clearly, such a viewpoint is technologically deterministic and extremely mechanistic, and consequently it is highly misleading since it leaves out of the model a crucial factor mediating the relationships between technological development and skill in the labour process, namely, organized resistance by occupational groupings within the manual working class. *It was the differences in forms of worker organisation and worker resistance during the transition to highly mechanised factory production in Rochdale that strongly affected whether specific groups of workers were skilled by the 1850's.* This is illustrated in Diagram 8.1.

The main difference between the two routes shown in the diagram is that in the case of the 'skilled' route, factory production preceded automation,[6] whereas in the case of the 'non-skilled' route the two occurred simultaneously. The vital difference between mule spinners and engineers on the one hand and weavers and cardroom workers on the other is determined by the insertion of the former groups (spinners and engineers) into factories prior to automation. What this effectively meant was that both spinners and engineers were able to maintain the structural supports of their skills through organized resistance to managerial attempts to restructure work processes during the period of automation. The entry of skilled engineers and skilled spinners into factories facilitated the development of collective forms of resistance to managerial strategies that attempted to break these structural supports. The workers who were utilized for automatic factory production in spinning and engineering were the same as already existed within the factories, and the exclusive structures that were developed during the transition to automatic factory production in spinning and in engineering involved strong elements from the previous modes of collective organization.

However, Lazonick (1979) has recently argued that the continuity of the sub-contracting exclusive mechanisms in mule spinning between the early and later nineteenth century was not the result of the power of the minders' union, but rather the consequence of supervisory exigencies associated with the transition from hand mule to automatic mule production. Lazonick argues that Turner (1962) failed to produce evidence to support the view that the minders' union fought strongly in favour of sub-contracting. Lazonick's counter-claims are equally based upon scant evidence. Cuca (1977) has shown the strength of the Spinners' Union in the first quarter of the nineteenth century and demonstrates convincingly the well-organized collective solidarity of the spinning factory workforces. If the Spinners were perceived as over-powerful and burdensome by the employers, as Lazonick himself concedes,[7] one might reasonably have expected that the capitalist owners would have attempted to break this power when they re-equipped with self-acting machinery. Certainly, there is no doubt that the exclusive mechanisms associated with sub-contracting were transmitted or that the Spinners were highly militant and effective in their labour relations, both in the 1820's and 1830's and in the second half of the nineteenth century. Lazonick emphasizes the advantages to capitalists with scarce managerial resources of sub-contracting but given the long history of conflict in this sector of cotton, it would seem remarkable, to say the least, if the period between 1838 and 1844 (which Lazonick dates as the crucial period of transition) was one when the interests of owners and minders achieved harmony. Without more empirical research and *direct* evidence to the contrary, it would appear more plausible to argue that organized skilled workers' strategies and tactics were crucial in the transmission of sub-contracting into the 'automatic' period of mule spinning. Given that both hand mule and automatic mule production co-existed[8] well into the third quarter of the nineteenth century (often in the same factory) and that hand mule and self-acting minders formed united unions,[9] it would seem reasonable to believe that the continuity of exclusive structures was imposed on capitalists rather than welcomed with open arms.

The 'non-skilled' route involved a radical disjunction between the pre-factory and factory workforces. The domestic production of the weavers could produce no effective *collective* resistance and certainly no organized craft trade unionism because of the individuated, petty bourgeois structure of domestic hand loom weaving.[10] The workforces that entered the mechanized weaving sheds and cardrooms were *not* the pre-existing artisans but a new workforce (predominantly female) with no antecedent craft forms of resistance. Furthermore, the high degree of automation of the new weaving machinery made the re-establishment of craft controls extremely difficult. What, then, were these craft forms of resistance? What were the structural supports of craft skill in the labour process that were successfully transmitted to the new mechanized factory environments? My argument is that they centre around mechanisms of *social exclusion*. More precisely, skilled manual workers in mechanized factory milieux are defined by their high degree of *social control over the operation and utilization of machinery*. These *exclusive controls* involve a double exclusion, both of *management* from direct or complete control over the labour process and of *other workers* who offer a potential threat to such controls.[11]

Clearly, such an interpretation of the nature and structuration of the Victorian manual working class provides no empirical support for any notion of an homogeneous working class in the period before 1850. How could those social historians associated with notions of the 'labour aristocracy' have been misled on this point? My view is that such historians, mainly Marxist in persuasion, have constantly collapsed a whole series of factors about the manual working class into an 'essentialist' model. It is the contention of this research that such approaches are totally unjustified empirically and have no status theoretically. However, I shall return to these points later in this and subsequent chapters. Suffice it to say that it would appear as if social historians, like Hobsbawm, Thompson and Foster, confuse the rhythms of the political development of the manual working class with those evident at work and in the community. For example, the rise of the Chartist movement, in itself, no more suggests a unilinear tendency towards working class unity than does its collapse portend a reaction in the opposite direction towards increased section-alism. The rhythms of the workplace, the community and the polity are not necessarily identical and their axial principles may be dissimilar.

The main component of the empirical material presented in this research commences in the period immediately after 1848. Does it support the general model of working class sectionalism in chapter 3? If the focus is concentrated firstly on the cotton industry, there would appear to be little evidence to support the contention that the workforce was becoming *increasingly* divided in the period after 1850. The spinning workforce was *already divided* by the mechanisms of sub-contracting in 1850. This remained a constant feature of social relations within the spinning sector until the 1950's. Indeed, it can be argued that the abolition of the sub-contracting relationship between minder and piecers portended an increasing homogeneity of the spinning workforce. However, one should not be led too far in this direction, for despite the rapid collapse of the cotton industry and the destruction of mule spinning – for minders and piecers alike – the minders still clung on to their 'skilled' differential until the bitter end.[12]

Contrary to popular notions of the inter-war years that are embodied in the model of working class sectionalism in chapter 3, that period of massive economic depression did not engender an increasing similarity of condition amongst manual workers but much more, in spinning at least, a tendency towards *sauve qui peut*. This was demonstrated powerfully in the evidence on internal earnings differentials in the spinning sector which *widened* during the massive depression in the 1920's and 1930's (see chapter 7, Table 7.7). Nor does such a picture confirm the imagery of the homogeneous traditional working class in the inter-war years put forward by most of the authors discussed in chapter 2. In textiles, as a whole, there was a general tendency throughout the period between 1856 and 1964 towards a differentiation of functions[13] within the manual workforce. This was part of a general feature of capitalism after the 1880's which witnessed a persistent and concerted attempt by capitalist management to assert increasing control over the labour process. These attempts have been most clearly analysed in the United States with studies by Braverman (1974), Nelson (1975), and Edwards (1979) being the most notable. The evidence presented earlier on the changing relations between overlookers and weavers suggests that the assertion of the 'managerial prerogative' to control work practices was part of a general process in Britain, the United States and also in France,[14] Germany [15] and Italy[16] during the period from 1890 to 1940.

However, if there was a tendency in textiles towards an increasing attempt to establish managerial hegemony in the workplace and, as a corollary, a tendency for all manual workers to become alike in their relations to management, this did not necessarily involve profound changes in the internal relations between different sections of workers. Overlookers, tapesizers, strippers-and-grinders and minders still preserved many of the exclusive practices associated with 'skill' in the 1950's and 1960's. Their success is revealed in the material presented on earnings differentials in Table 7 of Appendix E on the 'Average weekly earnings in the weaving and ancillary sections of the cotton industry and the man-made fibre industry', which suggests that earnings differentials in textiles between the skilled and non-skilled remained more or less constant up to the period when this research ends in the mid-1960's.[17]

When the focus is shifted to the engineering industry, a complex picture emerges of developments in economic structuration within the workforce. The industrial revolution created new skills in the metal industries. But these artisan skills were incorporated into factory production before massive mechanization. Consequently the continuous efforts by management since the 1880's to enforce its 'prerogatives' have been matched by a highly organized, defensive, skilled craft, manual workforce. Persistent efforts to reduce the discretionary controls of skilled manual workers have been met with permanent localized resistance. Nevertheless, the cumulative effects of the rationalization of production have produced a general weakening of the power of skilled manual workers. However, despite the arguments of Braverman (1974) and Nelson (1975), who suggest the elimination of skilled manual work in twentieth century America, it is clear that skilled manual workers in Britain still continue the fight to preserve their position in the workplace. By means of the virtual monopolization of trade union and shop steward offices achieved by apprentice-served men in the engineering section of the A.U.E.W. a whole series of tactics continues to be employed to preserve the relative power of skilled manual workers. Dilution agreements still contain clauses which require employers to dismiss or downgrade dilutees if a time-served man seeks employment.[18] This can lead to a situation in a period of high unemployment (like the present) where a man without an apprenticeship who has been doing a job classified as appropriate for an apprentice-served man and consequently is being paid at the full craft rate, must be removed from that job to make way for a younger, less experienced, apprentice-served man. Similarly, the A.U.E.W. is very careful about the employment of men trained in engineering skills at Government Training Centres. They may never achieve Grade 1 membership of the A.U.E.W. and in Rochdale, like other Lancashire engineering centres, they find it difficult to gain employment because of informal pressures on management by the A.U.E.W. The battle for 'skill' has always centred on manning arrangements, and the most important conclusion to be drawn from this discussion must be that the strategies of social exclusion which constitute 'skill' also reproduce a structural division within the manual working class between the skilled and non-skilled.

Differentials in earnings in the engineering industry have followed a path similar in some respects but dissimilar in others to those in textiles. From the mid-nineteenth century until 1918, there was a slight erosion of the

differentials between the skilled and non-skilled in the engineering industry
in Rochdale. However, this erosion was concentrated in the period between
1859 and 1877; thereafter, there was stability in skilled differentials up to
1914. A considerable erosion of differentials was associated with the
implementation of the Oldham List in 1876 in cotton spinning, but again
there was stability in differentials until the outbreak of the First World
War. During the war differentials in engineering contracted, and then
expanded once more in the early 1920's. In cotton spinning, there was no
change in earnings relativities during this period. In the 1920's, there was a
continued expansion of the differential between skilled and non-skilled
engineering workers which was paralleled by a similar development in
spinning.

After the Second World War, the differential between the skilled and
unskilled in engineering remained approximately constant but diminished
slightly between the skilled and the semi-skilled. On the other hand, what
limited evidence there is on the textile industry suggests no significant
changes in earnings differentials. Clearly, the evidence is only on average
earnings, but despite such problems it does suggest that trends in earnings
differentials are complex and often specific to particular industries. To talk
of *the* differential between skilled and non-skilled workers in general is not
always illuminating.

What is suggested, nonetheless, is that the general model constructed in
chapter 3 is not an accurate portrayal of the structuration of the Rochdale
manual working class around the axis of skill. There is a very poor 'fit'
between the sequences suggested by that model and the developments of
trade union structures and earnings differentials. While the strength of the
theory of the labour aristocracy lies in its emphasis on the significance of
the 'skilled' divide within the British manual working class, its weakness is
that it is inaccurate and for that reason must be discarded. Nor are the
varied versions of the traditional working class discussed in chapter 2 of
any greater empirical validity.

What sort of an explanation should be put in its place? Clearly *any
alternative must embody an emphasis on the centrality of 'skill' within the
British manual working class*. However, as was argued in chapter 1, there is
an alternative conception of the structural position of skilled workers
associated with the notion of the 'militant craftsman'. This conception has
been put forward for Britain by Hinton (1973), for the United States of
America by Montgomery (1976) and by a series of writers[19] for France.
Unfortunately, there is considerable flexibility of usage: for Hinton, the
militant craftsman describes the reaction of a skilled factory workforce to
radical changes in work practices associated with increased automatic
production, whereas Montgomery is referring to conflicts by skilled

workers associated with the implementation of mechanization itself. In the French literature, what are often at issue are the reactions made by independent, petty bourgeois, artisan producers to competition from factories themselves. In each case, radicalism is the response but the social relationships embodied in terms like 'artisan', 'craftsman' or 'skilled worker' and the concomitant forms of reactions to technological changes differ significantly.

Bearing such differences in usage in mind, it is possible, nonetheless, to contrast the tradition of 'militant craftsman' studies with the labour aristocracy corpus. For proponents of the latter thesis, there is a strong relationship between manual skill and political conservatism and quiescence, whereas advocates of the 'militant craftsman' emphasize the association between manual skills, technological change and radicalism. It would appear that both theories reflect a part of the reality in Britain. Skilled manual workers have possessed a dialectical position within the British class structure since the 1850's: a position that can be seen partly as a result of the articulation of craft and mass forms of production in the development of British capitalism.

Skilled manual workers have at certain moments been in the vanguard of British socialism. In Rochdale, the militancy of engineering workers before, during and after the First World War was noted in chapter 6. Further, the A.E.U. was a powerful element in the emerging Labour Party. During the period between 1918 and 1931 all the Labour parliamentary candidates were Engineering Union officials;[20] both skilled craftsmen and socialist in their political persuasion. Yet, the very mechanisms of exclusion used to reproduce craft in the labour process meant that these same workers were suspicious of other elements in organized labour and often were involved in practices focused in the workplace that maintained their power at the expense of the less skilled. Manning arrangements whereby skilled union negotiators acquired the right for craftsmen to operate machinery that could have been worked by the non-skilled are clear examples of this. How can such a paradox be explained? The answer lies in the articulation of craft and mass production. Craft forms of production allow considerable scope for workers' control over manning and the mode of producing. Considerable discretion is permitted. The metal-working craftsman operates machinery that requires him to transmit his intentions to the machine by means of handles, levers and knobs.[21] Feedback and control are achieved through his sensory apparatus – sight, feel and sound. The introduction of various automatic devices like mechanical cams and automatic feeds did not alter this essential relationship of man to machine. Even the use of these machines by the non-skilled to cut out many identical parts still required their 'setting up' by skilled craftsmen.

However, craft factory production denies capitalist management full control over the mode and forms of work. The fullest 'rationality' of production, according to the 'logic' of capitalism, requires that labour be predictable, uniform and controllable. It demands the establishment of complete managerial authority. Craft factory production stands diametrically opposed to such a system of production. Craftsmen stand opposed to modern capitalist management and their utilization of technical change to increase their social control over production,[22] and furthermore, for skilled craftsmen, the non-skilled represent the likely future if managerial 'prerogatives' are uncontested. Herein lies the dilemma of skilled manual workers; they are highly organized yet defensive, requiring an ideology with which to combat capitalist management. Socialism, with its explicit rejection of capitalism and its ideological commitment to more humanized forms of production, has offered such a value system since the 1880's. Socialism also stands for the unity of labour and for a belief in equality. Clearly then, there are contradictory pressures for skilled craftsmen involved in a commitment to socialism. Furthermore, the functional[23] congruence of certain elements in socialist ideology for skilled manual workers does not necessitate either their adoption or the particular type of socialism taken up. Any notion of a simple technological determination of workers' ideology must be rejected.[24]

Nevertheless, it is possible to suggest an hypothesis about the dialectics of skill and socialism. It would appear that it is in periods when widespread technical change is envisaged and being implemented by capitalist management that socialism seems most attractive. The anti-capitalist ideological[25] elements would seem to outweigh or facilitate a 'selecting out' of the negative[26] egalitarian implications of socialism. Such a process finds its expression in the 'militant craftsman' tradition outlined in chapter 1 and embodied in the works of authors like Montgomery, Lucas, Comfort, Moss, Hinton and Williams. It would seem that in the situations discussed by these writers the image of a powerful common capitalist enemy 'masks' the difficulties associated with egalitarianism for the skilled.

This is not to deny the autonomous character of politics, nor to hide behind vague notions of 'relative autonomy', but to suggest a possible set of relationships between socialism and technological change in Britain mediated by the organizations of skilled labour built up during the craft period of industrial capitalist factory production. Other factors must also be taken into account apart from the dialectic of 'managerial strategies' and 'workers' militancy'.[27] If we examine the swing in support by skilled manual workers towards the Conservative Party[28] manifest in the 1979 British General Election, it would appear that Labour Government incomes policies, particularly as they affected the engineering industry, were a highly significant precipitating factor. Systematic analyses of such phenomena are, as yet, lacking, but it would appear as if these incomes policies, devised as they were by representatives of the general, non-skilled unions, made significant inroads into established relativities within the manual workforce. Clearly, the success of the skilled in preserving or widening differentials in the 1920's and 1930's was related to the organizational weaknesses of the general unions in the period after the collapse of the 1926 General Strike and the passing of the 1927 Trade Disputes Act. Nevertheless, it would appear as if, despite other significant variables like the relative power of skilled versus non-skilled unions, there is a strong positive correlation in the period between 1880 and 1980 between espousal of socialist ideology by skilled manual workers and managerial assaults on the exclusive controls maintained by such workers. During the 1890's, socialism gained ground rapidly amongst engineering workers (particularly their District Officials) in the period of 'the employers' offensive'. The First World War revealed a similar, if stronger, set of developments. The resurgence of militancy and the rise in strength of the left[29] within the A.U.E.W. in the late 1960's was also paralleled by managerial attacks on the power of the skilled under the aegis of productivity bargaining. We may hypothesize that the very same skilled elements who supported the rise of Thatcherism in 1979 will shift rapidly leftwards if the long-heralded micro-chip revolution begins to change significantly the established working practices of Britain's skilled engineering workers, most of whom work in relatively small workshops.[30] However, the main thrust of the preceding section has been to suggest a different image of British skilled manual workers than traditionally portrayed in either the labour aristocracy literature or as embodied in notions of 'militant craftsmen'. Skilled manual workers adopt contradictory positions, which are the result of their structural location within the British manual working class; positions which may be labelled both militant and conservative.

What, then, can one conclude about the relationship of the term 'skill' to manual work in Britain? Firstly, it should be noted that some skilled manual workers are inaccurately assigned in the classification of occupations devised by the Registrar General[31] (which is the basis of most sociological research).[32] The reasons for this derive from the history of the British Censuses and the attempts made to produce a useful delineation of different social categories. The basis for the first sub-division of the manual working class in the 1911 Census appears to have been a specific interest in the problem of infant mortality rates.[33] The divisions utilized were:

1) Upper
2) Intermediate
3) Skilled
4) Intermediate skill
5) Unskilled
6) Textile workers
7) Miners
8) Agricultural labourers[34]

The main heuristic behind this classification was the demonstration that in 1911 there was a clear, graded increase in rates of infant mortality from class 1 to class 5 and thereafter random variation. The purpose was to galvanize political action in Parliament and Whitehall to deal with preventable causes of infant mortality. However, it would appear that the industrial basis of the classification as embodied in 'classes' 6 to 8 has had a serious and damaging impact on subsequent classifications. What seems to have happened is that whole sub-divisions of the textile industry's occupational structure have been lumped together as either skilled or semi-skilled. The result is an entirely misleading classification of textile occupations. According to the Registrar General cotton weavers are defined as skilled and cotton spinners as semi-skilled. In terms of actual technical activity both jobs involve machine minding and the development of 'expertise' through practical experience. However, as has been shown, technical expertise *per se* is not always the basis of skilled work within the manual working class. Cotton weavers may be more or less 'skilled' in the sense of 'experienced' but they have never been regarded as skilled workers by people in Rochdale during the period of this research. Weavers do not possess and have not possessed since the mid-nineteenth century effective means of social exclusion at the point of production. Mule spinners present the opposite picture: they have maintained strong structural supports of exclusion to sustain their skilled status for a large part of the period under consideration. Spinners have always, at least since the 1850's, been regarded in Rochdale as skilled. In terms of expertise, there was often no difference between the minder and his 'big piecer' assistant, but the social and economic distinctions were always clear.

Given the inaccuracies of the Registrar General's classification of occupations, there was a need to construct a new classification for this research. In particular great care had to be taken to ensure that the skilled: non-skilled divide was accurately reflected in such a classification.[35] During this period of my research I discovered a remarkable consistency in usage and definition of skilled manual workers amongst three types of sources. Firstly, both local newspapers[36] and standard secondary works[37] on the cotton and engineering industries presented a very similar set of distinctions. These secondary materials were mirrored in my discussions with trade union officials.[38] In turn, ordinary workers (mainly elderly) presented memories and reminiscences that were often carbon copies of the other sources. What became readily apparent was that the social definitions of skilled and non-skilled manual work have remained remarkably stable since the mid-nineteenth century. Indeed, only one major exception was found to this pattern: the occupation of stripper-and-grinder. As was seen in chapter 6, this exception is highly significant and reinforces the general interpretation of what *is* skilled manual working during the period under investigation.

Skilled manual workers therefore do not *necessarily* embody a set of activities that are more difficult to perform or learn than the non-skilled, although objective difficulty of task may constitute the basis for skilled manual work. In one sense, the notion of 'skill' can be seen as a legitimating device for income differentials, but such differentials reflect the social determinants of 'skill' rather than act as their cause. Skilled manual work is a traditional category of British class society but, although tradition can be a powerful legitimating factor in wage negotiations, it cannot survive socially in a vacuum since it requires powerful supporting mechanisms if it is to persist in the face of attempts to eradicate it. *The central feature of skilled manual work is some form of social exclusion.*

What are these forms of exclusion? Despite appearances they do not refer to those exclusive devices which are intended to restrict entry into an occupation by means of particularistic, ascriptive criteria. Historically, these *have* been features of skilled work in printing and metal-working. *However, simply restricting entry into occupations to men of the same family or religion cannot suffice to maintain skill.* The example of the overlookers in Rochdale is a case in point. The members of the Association of Powerloom Overlookers vote in their Districts on whether to accept nominees by the management into their trade. If there is a positive vote then the individual concerned may enter the union by paying an entrance fee and thereby becoming eligible for training as an overlooker.[39] There has been a strong predisposition to restrict entry to the sons (or male relatives) of men already in the trade. However, this is not the mechanism that maintains 'skill'. Such particularistic criteria for entry can co-exist with semi-skilled or unskilled work, as has long been evident in the docks, notably in Liverpool.[40] What preserves the skill of the loom overlooker are those rules that exclude other workers, either weavers themselves or mechanics like members of the A.U.E.W., from maintaining automatic weaving looms. *These exclusive controls over the operation and utilization of machinery are crucial to the maintenance of manual skill.*

Exclusion has been seen classically in terms of apprenticeships. These involve the restriction of certain specific jobs and tasks to individuals who have spent a number of years training to perform them. Clearly an apprenticeship of, for example, five or seven years *can* be used to provide an extensive preparation in the technical skills required for a trade but there is a good deal of evidence to suggest that the maintenance of apprenticeships has often been used for the purpose of preserving a privileged market position for specific groups of workers. Evidence for this has been very strong in the engineering industry and can be seen most clearly in the dilution struggles in World War One. In the munitions factories the skilled unions agreed to drop all 'restrictive practices' involving demarcation between different trades and insistence on jobs being done by 'time served' men (i.e. journeymen). In this situation many jobs were performed by semi-skilled female workers who acquired their expertise in weeks rather than years. The militancy that arose amongst the skilled men on the shop-floor can be seen within a context of their trade union organizations abandoning the basis of their privileged position which was swiftly reflected in the relative decline of differentials within the engineering industry. What is lacking, however, is an analysis of how the traditional rules were re-established after the war, especially in the face of the inter-war depression and the incentive for the owners and management to eradicate traditional work practices and restrictions. However, despite the lack of research into such periods by labour historians, it is possible to provide some clues as to a possible explanation. It would seem that in the face of massive over-capitalization in the immediate post-war period (1918–1920) and the persistent depression in the staple, export-oriented industries as a result of Britain's lack of competitiveness in overseas markets, the employers, which included those in the engineering industry, found it more acceptable to hoist the unions by their own petard rather than radically alter work processes. The tactics used by the engineering employers have been described by Walter Greenwood in *Love on the Dole* where the employers made full use of the normal ratio of journeymen to apprentices stipulated by the A.E.U. only to sack the apprentices when they were qualified and hire a new batch of young boys straight from school. Greenwood summed this up in the following extract from his novel:

> 'You're part of a graft, Harry,' he said. 'All Marlowe's want is cheap labour; and the apprentice racket is one of their ways of getting it. Nobody'll teach you anything simply because there's so little to be learnt. You'll pick up all you require by asking questions and watching others work. You see, all this machinery's being more simplified year after year until all it wants is experienced machine feeders and watchers. Some of the new plant doesn't even need that. Look in the brass-finishing shop when

you're that way. Ask the foreman to show you that screw-making machine. That can work twenty-four hours a day without anybody going near it. Your apprenticeship's a swindle, Harry. The men they turn out think they're engineers same as they do at all the other places, but they're only machine minders. Don't you remember the women during the war?'

'What women?' Harry asked, troubled by what Larry had said.

'The women who took the places of the engineers who'd all served their time. The women picked up straightaway what Marlowe's and the others say it takes seven years' apprenticeship to learn', a wry smile: 'Still, if you want to be what everybody calls an "engineer", you've no choice but to serve your seven years. Oh, and you were lucky to be taken on as an apprentice. I hear that they're considering refusing to bind themselves in contracting to provide seven years' employment. There is a rumour about that there aren't to be any more apprentices. You see, Harry, if they don't bind themselves, as they have to do in the indentures, they can clear the shop of all surplus labour when times are bad. And things are shaping that way now,' a grin: 'You've no need to worry, though. You've seven years' employment, certain.'

Hum!

It chilled Harry, momentarily. (Greenwood, 1933, p. 47).

In the post-1945 period, the A.U.E.W. has portrayed a paradoxical attitude to the actual content of apprenticeships. As Liepman (1958) has argued, they often appear indifferent to the content of apprenticeships particularly at the local level, a response which derives from their major defensive interest that apprenticeships of some form are served, and that jobs are restricted to 'time-served' men. Nationally, the A.U.E.W. has shown considerable interest[41] in more sophisticated apprenticeships but this has had little local impact. In engineering centres like Rochdale the major effort made by skilled engineering workers continues to be the preservation of exclusive controls over the operation and utilization of machinery.

The other major method for maintaining skilled manual work involves social exclusion but of a different, more complex, kind. It takes the form of excluding certain workers from direct wage bargaining rights with the employers. These subordinate workers are paid by other workers who are in a sub-contracting relation with the employers. This takes its classic form in the cotton spinning industry, where the spinner or 'minder' contracted a price for a piece of work and then paid his two assistants, the 'big' and the 'little' piecers, out of the price contracted in the ratio (more or less) of $60:40:26\frac{2}{3}$.[42]

There has been considerable confusion over the nature of the divisions within the working class involved in sub-contracting. Stone (1973), in her analysis of the U.S. steel industry, has shown how the employers broke the control of the skilled steel workers over large areas of the labour process at the turn of the nineteenth century. She contrasts the results of the employers' offensive at that time with an idealized version of the traditional set of labour relations in the industry, writing in terms of the steel employers attempting to 'break down the basis for unity amongst the steel workers' (Stone, 1973 p. 20). Yet her own evidence on wage differentials between the skilled sub-contractor and his subordinate helpers of between $\frac{1}{6}$ and $\frac{1}{2}$ contradicts the allegation of a unified workforce. Similarly, Howard's (1973) analysis of the system of internal contract in the iron industry in the third quarter of the nineteenth century fails to emphasize that such a system formed the basis for a structural division between manual workers in the industry. Yet his own evidence on a five month strike in the industry demonstrates such a division: 'Two clergymen who intervened were threatened with assassination but the main anger was directed against non-unionists, particularly the underhands who were being used to break the strike' (Howard, 1973, p. 420). The implication is clear, as in the cotton spinning industry, the 'non-skilled' assistants of the 'skilled' sub-contractors acted as a permanent threat to 'skill' since in reality many of them were technically as competent as their superiors. Nevertheless, the spinners also made use of strong demarcation rules against other workers, notably engineers, to prevent them from servicing their mules. Consequently, the exclusive practices associated with sub-contracting can be seen as reinforcing these primary controls over the spinning machinery.

Essentially, what appears to be involved overall is a series of attempts by certain skilled sections of the manual working class to increase their market power as sellers of labour within the framework of the capitalist system of production. What is at stake is an attempt to restrict the power of capital and its management within the workplace. It is an attempt to modify certain aspects of the fundamentally asymmetrical relationship of power involved in capitalist production, yet it secures such alterations by controls over other manual workers. These involve indirect controls over the supply of labour and direct controls over other workers in production itself.

Most important of all, the various kinds of exclusion outlined above – apprenticeship and sub-contracting – are not, in themselves, constitutive of skill. What all methods share is that these 'secondary' exclusive mechanisms are used for the 'primary' purpose of restricting managerial controls over the manning of machinery. Clearly, management rarely encounters an industrial *tabula rasa* when it attempts to alter modes of producing. It confronts the organizations of labour and, in the case of skilled manual work, historically it comes up against the strategies of exclusion focused on manning arrangements that have been erected to maintain and, on occasion, even create 'skill'. Skill is to be seen as a function of strategies of social exclusion in the workplace which *succeed* in controlling the manning of machinery. Despite the strictures of David Lee in his article on 'Craft Unions and the Force of Tradition' (1979), this does not involve either a 'culturalist' or 'phenomenological' position, if by these terms he refers to a notion that social actors can simply 'define' skills.[43] The argument being presented is both more subtle and complex than this interpretation and one which suggests that 'successful' definitions by social actors occur in specific structural situations and that assumes that the tasks of social science involve illuminating, analysing and explaining these structural variations. In other words, it is *not* being suggested that skill is simply an arbitrary social definition. This is because *successful* exclusion is a function of the relative power of capital and labour. A complex interaction of factors is involved in the successful exclusion tactics of skilled manual workers in Rochdale, which can be analysed in terms of the relative local strengths of skilled manual labour and capitalist employers. Organization by skilled manual labour around the mechanisms of exclusion is clearly necessary; and sectional organization in factories prior to widespread mechanization has been of crucial historical significance in the early maintenance of exclusive practices in Rochdale, but such prior organization is not logically necessary. However, what is central to, and crucial for, the success of these sectional organizations of skilled manual workers in their struggles to preserve their exclusive controls over work processes has been their strong organization and the relatively weak (from the perspective of bargaining) structure of local capitalist employers or, in other words, the nature of the local labour market. In Rochdale, there has always been a relatively 'tight' labour market for engineering workers during the period under review. This is partly due to the large number of engineering firms in the town and the closeness of other industrial centres like Oldham and Bury which have had the effect of producing strong competition amongst engineering employers for certain types of labour, especially those skilled workers able to maintain and 'set up' the various machines. The 'tightness' of the local labour market has facilitated high levels of unionization amongst engineering workers. It is the conjunction of certain scarce skills and strong union organization that has enabled skilled workers to extend the boundaries of exclusion, and in particular to extend the degree of control over manning machinery. We may erect a model of jobs as seen by management or design engineers that distinguishes between 'skilled' and 'non-skilled' tasks in the following way:

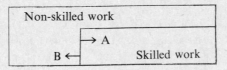

The two arrows suggest contradictory forces. Arrow A represents the tendency for management to rationalize work practices in order to extend its control over production and enhance predictability. Arrow B suggests an opposite force which is pursued by organized labour to extend the scope of skilled work. The empirical outcome in any specific case is determined by the forces described above. In Rochdale, the strength of the A.U.E.W., and the need for skilled engineering workers to fulfil certain tasks has led to a situation where the frontier of skill is pushed to the left of the diagram – towards a situation where skilled craftsmen control the performance of tasks undertaken by the non-skilled in other engineering centres.

The evidence for these arguments is fragmentary. It is partly based upon observation, but mainly upon discussion with the social actors involved. Unfortunately, stronger evidence for Rochdale proved impossible to locate. Trade union records do not deal with the everyday practices of control that sustain the structures outlined. Neither it would appear do management records. Employers shrug their shoulders and take it as a matter of course, which suggests that the forces at work are experienced as external and constraining. No doubt the shifting of the boundaries of skill in favour of engineering craftsmen is a small price to pay for relative industrial harmony.

In the cotton industry, the same factors appear to have determined the boundaries of 'skill'. For both skilled spinners and strippers-and-grinders used their powerful trade union organizations to confront management in a competitive industrial structure. The multiplicity of cotton firms and the 100% trade union organization of such occupational groups as mule spinners, overlookers, tapesizers and strippers-and-grinders meant that much the same forces were at work as in engineering. In the case of spinning the internal contract relations had a certain positive advantage for management: they were cheap administratively, involving the devolution on to labour of a whole series of managerial tasks.

However, part of the problem of analysing the evidence is that Rochdale lies in only one of the four boxes outlined in the model of managerial strategies at the end of chapter 4.[44] The organizational strength of labour and the competitive, atomized structure of capital have meant that there are strong structural pressures supporting the control over manning by organized skilled manual labour and little structurally to support managerial strategies that attempt to eradicate such modes of exclusion. Indeed, the lack of overt conflict has led to a dearth of empirical data. The argument presented in the last part of this chapter is therefore partly deductive and conjectural. Nevertheless, to limit social analysis to written data sources can lead to a failure to discuss interesting, if covert, sociological problems. In many respects we need more sociological research on the workings of local labour markets and the constraints that structure such phenomena. In particular, there is a need for detailed research on factory-based bargaining over skill. It is often argued today[45] that we need to orient sociological investigations towards the analysis of the intersection of objective, external structures and the reproduction of such structures through human agency. One method of dealing with these issues both empirically and in a theoretically-informed way would be through a more detailed examination of the structures analysed above.

As was argued in chapter 4, the content of manual jobs may have become less skilled during the last hundred years or so, although there is no definitive evidence. Certainly, as was shown in chapter 4, the lengths of apprenticeships in such industries as printing, engineering and building have been reduced. Indeed, the main variations in the lengths of contemporary apprenticeships can be explained to a considerable degree by variations in the relative organizational strength of skilled manual workers and the structure of the capitalist employers in these industries. Contemporary data from printing,[46] construction[47] and from the engineering industry,[48] all suggest that the battle for 'skill' remains central to industrial relations in these industries. More detailed research is required but the general picture is clear. Consequently, if 'de-skilling' is a theory about class structure and class relations in Britain rather than an argument about the technical content of manual jobs,[49] it must recognize the centrality of the social determinants of skill and the battle for their preservation in contemporary British society.

The picture that has emerged of workplace and market structuration of the manual working class around the axis of 'skill' is complicated. The rhythms of the two industries investigated – cotton and engineering – are not always parallel. Nevertheless, the interconnection of market advantage and workplace relations has been shown in the case of skilled manual workers. Their skilled differential is rooted in their exclusive controls over manning arrangements in the workshop. Little evidence was found to support the general model of trends in skill outlined in chapter 3. The 'militant craftsman' tradition explains the militancy of skilled workers, but ignores the active role of these exclusive tactics in the division of the British manual working class. A more complex historical model has been suggested. Certainly there is no evidence of a homogeneous manual working class *at any time* in Britain between the 1850's and the 1960's; a conclusion which offers no comfort to proponents of the 'traditional' working class. Nor is there any evidence that the British manual working class even shared a common set of economic interests since the battle for exclusion is a zero-sum game – the advantages of the skilled are gained at the expense of the non-skilled. Indeed, the voting behaviour of British skilled manual workers in 1979 strongly suggests that the skilled 'divide' remains a persistent and significant feature of the internal structuration of the British manual working class.

Nevertheless, it is necessary to avoid the impression that the analysis of class structuration should stop after a discussion of such factors as trade union structures and wage differentials. There is also the area of communal structuration that was suggested in chapter 1. The rest of this research will involve an examination of trends in marital endogamy between skilled and non-skilled manual workers. One central and basic assumption will be that it is unnecessary, indeed misleading, to adopt an 'essentialist' model of class structuration. The rhythms of workplace structuration may follow an identical trajectory to those of communal endogamy, but this is an empirical question amenable to critical scrutiny.

PART III

The social structuration of class

9

Classes, strata and occupations

This chapter is primarily definitional. It is a necessary interruption in the discussion of the empirical material on Rochdale since the concept of class is one of the most contentious in sociology. Nevertheless, this definitional task is oriented towards a specific research problem. As was made clear in chapter 5 and is evident from Appendix B, the historical analysis of the social structuration of the manual working class in Rochdale by means of looking at trends in marital endogamy produced a large sample of occupational data. As will become evident, this research classified these occupational data initially into seventeen categories and then collapsed these seventeen categories into seven strata. The seven strata were themselves condensed into three classes, which were taken to have been those central to the British class structure throughout the period under review. The purpose of this chapter is to explain these classificatory procedures as a necessary preliminary to the analysis of the data which will be undertaken in chapters 11 and 12.

The use of categories is indispensable for empirical research into class structuration. Without clear and precise rules for the determination of classes, class analysis cannot begin. The main debate centres, therefore, not around the need for categories *per se*, but the criteria used for categorization. However, the question of how to categorize classes cannot be discussed independently from the concept of class itself. Class has many meanings and nuances.[1] It is often used in popular parlance in either a general or a specific sense. Generally it can refer to a set of phenomena with common attributes or qualities, but specifically it connotes a set of shared economic, political and cultural attributes. Sociology and economics normally use the term 'class' to refer to certain kinds of shared characteristics which are essentially *economic*. Marxists, Weberians and many members of the general public concur with the view that the foundations of class lie in the economic realm. Indeed, this is the sense in which the class situation of skilled manual workers has been examined in chapters 6 and

7 – in terms of their economic position without the manual working class between 1856 and 1964. Two conclusions stand out from that analysis. Trade unions in Rochdale have been organized around the axis of skill during the period under review and these unions have been instrumental in the maintenance of skilled earnings differentials over the non-skilled and in the persistence of a skilled bifurcation within the working class.

However, in the literature on class analysis there is another aspect of class structuration – social structuration – which refers to the extent to which economic structuration is translated into social boundedness or, put in other words, into typical modes of social interaction. Social structuration analyses the degree to which structuration in the economic system – at work and in the market – is reproduced in the social sphere. Indeed, there is a strong presumption in the literature on skill that there will be such a relationship, as can be seen from the works of writers like Hobsbawm (1964), Foster (1974), Gray (1976) and Mackenzie (1973). This presumption is based upon an axiom of much Marxist social history, namely that the economic is determinant of the social. As was seen from the discussion of Lockwood – one of the major theorists in the 'conflict' tradition – such a model of causal primacy to economic phenomena is shared by other, non-Marxist forms of sociological analysis. The purpose of this third section of the book is to examine these assumptions *empirically* and *systematically* by means of an analysis of patterns of intermarriage in Rochdale since the mid-nineteenth century.

It is worth noting that this separation of the economic basis of class and the relationship to the social is *not* synonymous with the popular dichotomy of 'class' and 'status'. Status refers to the relative evaluation of positional roles and is, of necessity, built *into* any model of class hierarchy. This research will not examine the translation of 'class' into 'status' (often with an implicit assumption that class is somehow more virile than status) but rather the extent to which economic class statuses are translated into forms of social class statuses. (Literary style and Occam's razor dictate the relegation of the redundant term!)

In terms of its essential definition this means that class will not be taken to include either a 'political' or a 'social' component. Both these elements have been incorporated into the basic definition of class, but to the detriment of conceptual clarity. Marxists like Poulantzas (1975), Carchedi (1975), Wright (1976), Hindess (1977), Hirst (1977) and Hunt (1977) all include the political within the very core of their concepts of class. This has had the effect of collapsing the distinction between class-in-itself and class-for-itself and also of requiring a revision of the criteria for class identification when there is a change in the political climate. The clear tendency is for these contemporary Marxist writers to argue that political orientation and affiliation constitute the criteria for class identity, a position echoed by the conflict theorist, Dahrendorf. In his article in 1964 on 'Recent Changes in the Class Structure of European Societies', Dahrendorf argued that 'class involves a certain amount of class consciousness and political solidarity, if the term is to make any sense at all' (p. 251). Dahrendorf has persisted until the present (1980a and 1980b) with this political definition of class, arguing that the middle class 'are not a class in the strict sense of the term; their relation to power or even to property is ambiguous' (1980a, p. 7). However, as with contemporary Marxism, this serves to muddy conceptual clarity. It is far more appropriate to ask empirically about the extent to which class distinctions *stricto sensu* are translated into political action, 'collective solidarity' and 'class consciousness', than to introduce them into the definition of class at its inception. This same principle applies to the collapsing of economic and 'social' criteria within the concept of class. Stewart *et al.* (1973) have used friendship patterns to establish a continuum of social status which can function to categorize occupational data. It is unclear whether they wish to use this continuum for class purposes but, if they were so to do, it would clearly hinder class research, since it would collapse the economic bases of class with its social (or interactional) effects. As will be shown empirically in chapters 11 and 12, such interactional methods may well misrepresent the class structure in so far as the 'social' structuration of class is neither synonymous nor isomorphic with economic structuration. Similar arguments apply to the use of prestige studies to generate class categories. As Goldthorpe and Hope (1972) have argued, prestige studies tend to measure popular evaluations of the relative 'goodness' or 'desirability' of occupations and consequently introduce attitudes to class within the concept of class *ab initio*. Again, it would seem preferable, and certainly clearer in the long run, to ask empirically the degree to which the economic class structure is regarded by its members as the crucial indicator of moral worth rather than to assume congruence from the start. It is perhaps significant that Goldthorpe *et al.* (1980) have abandoned relative status in favour of shared economic attributes in their recent empirical analysis of the British class structure.

If it is accepted that class distinctions are rooted in the economic, then the next problem becomes *which* economic criteria are to count in distinguishing separate classes. There are two main contenders for the task: Marxism and Weberianism. Unfortunately, the differences between Marx and Weber have often been misunderstood, particularly the *alleged* difference between a Weberian emphasis on the market and a Marxist emphasis on productive relations as being *the* criterion for class identification.

Weber, in his notes in *Economy and Society* (1968) on class within capitalism, identified class as being constituted by two criteria, property and skill, of which the former is predominant but not exhaustive. The central point is that both property and labour of various qualitative kinds confront one another on the market. This is not to assume, as many Marxists appear to think, that Weber believes that a fundamental equality of exchange must occur since, as Giddens (1973) has shown, *for Weberians the market is a structure of relative power*. For Weber, the 'labour market' is a central defining characteristic of industrial capitalism. As he argues in the *General Economic History* in the discussion of 'the Meaning and Presuppositions of Modern Capitalism':

> The fifth feature [of present day capitalism] is free labour. Persons must be present who are not only legally in the position, but are also economically compelled, to sell their labour on the market without restriction. It is in contradiction to the essence of capitalism and the development of capitalism is impossible, if such a propertyless stratum is absent, a class compelled to sell its labour services to live; and it is likewise impossible if only unfree labour is at hand. (Weber, 1961, pp. 208–9)

The penetration of capital into the processes of production *per se* can be seen as a defining social characteristic of the industrial revolution for both Marx and Weber. Such an argument is a central theme of Marx's work, particularly *Capital*. Weber also accepts such an orientation when he argues in *Economy and Society* that:

> From a historical point of view, the expropriation of labour has arisen since the sixteenth century in an economy characterized by the progressive extensive and intensive expansion of the market system ... (p. 138)

The central criticism of Weber by Marxists like Binns (1977), Crompton and Gubbay (1977) and Therbörn (1976) is that Weber saw class as determined by 'superficial' market criteria, whilst Marx penetrated the 'appearances' or 'phenomenal forms' of capitalist society, and showed that classes are located in social relations of production. For Therbörn any acceptance of the market as the 'generic connotation of class' logically precludes a Marxist analysis since, put in a nutshell, Weber 'merely' focuses on exchange relations whereas Marx avoids such a vulgar approach and looks at the 'underlying' productive relations. Marxist critics of Weber appear to believe that the concept of 'exchange' in Marx is synonymous with Weber's notion of the 'market'. Nothing could be further from the truth! For Marx, the concept of 'exchange' is analytically distinct from those of 'production' and 'circulation', a view derived from his theory of the 'circuits of capital' and ultimately from his belief that production was the only arena for the creation of 'value'. This latter view is predicated upon the labour theory of value and is intimately tied to notions of 'productive' and 'unproductive' labour.

The 'market' does not perform the same role as 'exchange' in Weber's theoretical system. Weber rejects the 'production', 'circulation' and 'exchange' triad and sees the market as incorporating all aspects of economic activity in industrial capitalist societies.[2] Such a viewpoint is abundantly clear from even a cursory reading of his *General Economic History* or *Economy and Society*. For Weber, classes are constituted in the market but they are classes nonetheless. Weber provides a whole catalogue of social entities in the famous two fragments on 'Class, Status and Party'[3] in *Economy and Society*, which can be seen as classes or elements of classes. Weber does not ignore productive relations, but derives their essential nature in industrial capitalism from their market character. Consequently, when Therbörn argues that:

> The Weberian question for determining what class A belongs to is: How much does he have (i.e. of market resources)? Whereas Marx asks: What does he do? What is his position in the process of production? Weber's question of definition is in turn an answer to Weber's primary problem of class: How much is he likely to get (of 'provision with goods', 'external conditions of life' and 'subjective satisfaction or frustration')? But what Marx answers is: What is he likely to do (basically, to maintain the present society, or to change it)? (Therbörn, 1976, p. 8)

he has misread the fragments in *Economy and Society*. Indeed, he reproduces Runciman's (1968) misinterpretations of Weber's points in that he suggests that, for Weber, class is simply a scale of relative income. However, Weber does not ask 'how much' does A have but *'what'* does A have. He provides a long list of different kinds of capital and qualitatively different kinds of labour which possess no similarity with, or relevance for, the scaling of relative income, but from which an analysis of the empirical nature of industrial capitalist class structures can depart. Furthermore, it is important to grasp the underlying teleological assumptions and the explicit use of political criteria for the identification of classes that are so characteristic of Marxism, both of which underpin Therbörn's mistaken critique of Weber. For Therbörn, the capitalist class preserves 'present society' whereas the proletariat seeks to 'change it'. As was argued in chapter 1, such propositions lack either sound theoretical status or empirical plausibility.

The only reason for using Marx's complex architectonics as a conceptual framework for class analyses would be if they increased understanding of the phenomena involved. It is by no means clear that they do. The 'circuits of capital' out of which the Marxist concepts of 'production', 'circulation' and 'exchange' are generated are premised upon the labour theory of value. This theory of value is premised upon the quasi-Hegelian assumption that some underlying principle of 'equivalence' must govern exchange in capitalist societies. However, such an assumption is unnecessary and unwarranted as has been demonstrated by Cutler *et al.* (1977). The actual values that accrue to commodities in exchange are strictly arbitrary in the sense that no essential characteristics are incorporated in market exchanges. If the labour theory of value is dropped as both unnecessary and unhelpful, a whole array of derivative concepts may also be abandoned as irrelevant. Central amongst those are all theories premised upon notions of productive and unproductive labour, which make no sense once the labour theory of value has been abandoned. Indeed, many contemporary Marxists have rejected the notions of productive and unproductive labour[4] without recognizing that this implies a challenge to Marx's central theory for class analysis – the labour theory of value. The weakness of this theory,[5] which lies at the heart of Marxist class schemes, has led to a series of attempts to fill the conceptual terrain with the use of the notion of the 'labour aristocracy'. However, despite the fact that both Engels and Lenin used the term in a restricted sense (as was shown in chapter 3), the concept of the 'labour aristocracy' has been used increasingly to cover a multiplicity of diverse structural locations.[6] Any concept loses its power the wider its boundaries become and the extraordinary wide coverage of the term 'labour aristocracy' reveals the poverty of Marxist class analyses and the desperation that the loss of the labour theory of value provokes. Consequently, Marxism has been rejected as an adequate economic model for class categorizations in this research. Despite the rudimentary and, on occasions, contradictory nature of Weber's remarks in *Economy and Society*, this research accepts a broad Weberian definition of classes as sets of shared market positions.

Given this position, the next problem concerns the number of classes to be identified. This research identifies three main classes in British society since the 1850's – the capitalist class, the middle class and the working class. In so doing, it is in broad agreement with a longstanding tradition of conceptual work undertaken by contemporary neo-Weberian sociologists like Giddens (1973), Lockwood (1958), and Parkin (1971). All follow Weber in his rejection of the Marxist thesis that all labour will be de-skilled and that there would be a progressive homogenization of the proletariat and concomitant simplification of the class structure in industrial capitalist societies. Likewise, all three authors follow Weber in emphasizing differentiation within the category 'labour' and the need to move away from a simple capitalist/worker dichotomy in the theorization of industrial capitalist class structures, whilst still recognizing the existence of a dominant capitalist class itself. Giddens basic trichotomous scheme of 'upper', 'middle' and 'lower' or 'working' classes are determined in the following fashion:

'upper': 'ownership of property in the means of production'
'middle': 'possession of educational or technical qualifications'
'lower': 'possession of manual labour power' (Giddens, 1973, p. 107).

The rationale for these particular divisions is that each class epitomizes a different set of market and work situations. Giddens also holds that these economic classes are reproduced over generations by means of inter-generational closure: or, to put it in the language used subsequently in chapter 10 of this research, economic classes are translated into social classes by means of generational endogamy. However, the main problem with operationalizing Giddens' definitions for empirical research is that the possession of educational and technical qualifications of some sort characterizes a high proportion of the manual working class in countries like Britain, particularly the skilled and semi-skilled. This proves to have two unfortunate consequences for empirical research. Firstly, the 'lower' or 'working' class only comprises labourers and, as a consequence, the 'middle' class is in excess of 80% of the population and probably near to 90%. This defeats the main purpose of neo-Weberian sociology of class which is to get away from crude and undiscriminating models of the class structure of industrial capitalist societies in order to enhance explanatory power.

Lockwood (1958) also attempts to differentiate structurally within the broad category of the population in industrial capitalist societies that is forced to sell its labour power on the market. Lockwood emphasizes the analytical distinction between 'market' and 'work' situations. The two concepts 'work situation' and 'market situation' were devised to explain the differences in class position of clerical and manual labour. 'Work situation' is defined by Lockwood as 'the set of social relationships in which the individual is involved at work by virtue of his position in the division of labour' (p. 15). Lockwood has in mind such variable features as authority relations, immediacy of contact with employers and the degree of the sub-division or 'fragmentation' of tasks. Lockwood, following in the Weberian tradition, uses the term 'market situation' to refer to: 'economic position narrowly conceived, consisting of source and size of income, degree of job-security, and opportunity for upward occupational mobility'. For Lockwood, the crucial division of work situations under industrial capitalism comes between clerical and factory labour. He characterizes the work situation of the factory worker by means of this quotation from Michels:

> The mechanized factory and large-scale enterprise robbed the employer of his previous function as fellow-worker, overseer and adviser. Personal contact and conversational intimacy were also lost. Where the latter persisted it was not the expression of a working community but of class distinction and class distance. By the workers it was regarded as arrogance and insolence and answered in the same spirit, even occasionally by staging of strikes. Direct control over the work process was delegated to intermediaries. The employer became invisible to his employees. Shut away in closed, not always easily accessible offices, absorbed in matters of accounting, he became a stranger to his workers, with only the superficial ties of the labour contract to unite them. The relationship between employer and employee became unreal and impersonal. (cited in Lockwood, 1958, p. 78).

Lockwood sees clerical work on the other hand as involving quite different social processes:

> One consequence of such small, tightly knit work-groups is that the management of clerical work is not carried out with the same kind of impersonal discipline that is a common feature of factory organization; on the contrary it tends to be performed in a social context which must of necessity be fairly intimate in all but the very largest offices. (Lockwood, 1958, p. 78).

By contrasting the different work situations of clerical and factory labour, Lockwood in fact is emphasizing that the division between conventionally defined manual and non-manual workers is the crucial line of demarcation within the common positions of 'propertyless' labour. In this formulation, Lockwood has been followed by Parkin in his comparative analysis of stratification in industrial capitalist and state socialist societies (1971). As Parkin argues:

> Nevertheless, the fact that we do speak of a class system suggests that we can distinguish some significant 'break' in the reward hierarchy. In Western capitalist societies, the line of cleavage falls between the manual and non-manual occupational categories. (pp. 24–5)

However, more recently, Parkin (1974 and 1979) has provided a revised set of criteria for attempting to distinguish class categories within the broad majority of the population in capitalist societies. These criteria are defined in terms of different 'strategies of social closure', and there is more than a passing similarity between Parkin's revised criteria and Giddens' emphasis on structuration of mobility chances in the determination of social class discussed above. Nevertheless, the two concepts identified by Parkin do not necessarily require that Giddens' trichotomous class model be reproduced theoretically, or that the manual/non-manual division be retained as central. The two strategies are labelled by Parkin as 'exclusion' and 'solidarism'. Exclusion is defined as 'the attempt by a given social group to maintain or enhance its privileges by the process of subordination – i.e. the creation of another group or stratum of ineligibles beneath it' (1974, p. 4). Solidarism on the other hand 'may be regarded as collective responses of excluded groups which are themselves unable to maximize resources by exclusion practices' (p. 5). However, Parkin still wishes to retain 'the more conventional manual/non-manual schema' (p. 13) and simply tack these two strategies of closure onto it.

Unfortunately, as Parkin shows himself, major social groups at the manual/non-manual interface are characterized by dual strategies. Skilled manual workers:

> use certain exclusion techniques, such as the apprenticeship system, designed to restrict entry to skilled trades in combination with closure strategies of a purely solidaristic kind aimed at the re-allocation of resources between capital and labour. (Parkin, 1974, p. 13)

This 'ambiguity' in the class position of the upper stratum of the manual working class is mirrored by the situation for clerical workers. As Parkin argues again:

> The ambiguities in the class position of the 'white-collar proletariat' may similarly be understood in terms of their adoption of dual strategies. Here the reliance upon exclusion devices of a credentialist kind, epitomized by the efforts to attain professional status, is generally supplemented by the purely solidaristic tactics of organized labour. This resort to dual closure strategies is altogether characteristic of intermediate groups in the stratification order. (Parkin, 1974, p. 13)

Consequently, emphasis on strategies of closure does not vindicate any clear division within the category of propertyless labour and this research follows Lockwood and the 'early' Parkin in regarding the manual/non-manual line as the central divide within the non-capitalist class. Such a viewpoint is supported by the overwhelming majority of researchers into the empirical structuration of class. Investigators operating within the prestige and status tradition, like the Registrar-General[7] and Goldthorpe and Hope (1974), and also those more concerned with the economic determination of class categories, like Goldthorpe (1980) and the Department of Employment,[8] all consider the manual/non-manual clea-vage to be the most salient division within the non-capitalist class. Empirical research by Wedderburn and Craig (1974) also supports this contention, as is revealed by their conclusions to the research conducted in 1968 into 'relative deprivation in work':

> This review of the current position in Britain suggests that manual workers' 'market situation', despite some changes, remains inferior in most respects to that of most non-manual workers. The non-manual group, however, is extremely heterogeneous and there are some occupations where security of employment, and opportunities for promotion seem more akin to those of manual workers. Similarly, in respect of the 'work situation' – that is the nature of the work task, the experience of work constraints and the experience of power – it is possible to generalise and say that non-manual workers are better off than manual workers, but there are many differences within the non-manual group. To summarise, it might be said that the overall picture is one of considerable inequality in all aspects of the employment relationship; where the traditional dividing line between manual and non-manual occupations still represents a fairly sharp break in conditions... (pp. 153–4).

There is, of course, a degree of overlap between manual and non-manual workers, particularly with regard to weekly earnings. However, this is not necessarily an adequate indicator of market situation since the latter includes prospects for future earnings as well as present earnings. Many lower-level non-manual workers are, in fact, at the point of departure in a career which, even if loosely structured, promises considerable pecuniary improvement.[9] Many skilled manual workers, on the other hand, experience considerable economic insecurity, particularly in the form of unemployment, which has been revealed by (amongst other sources) a series of pieces of research into the skill shortages in the British engineering industry.[10] If these differences in typical market situation are coupled with the considerable differences in work situation experienced by manual and non-manual employees, it becomes apparent that there are few grounds to justify any abandonment of this line of cleavage.

Consequently, this research follows Lockwood and Parkin in particular, and the broad neo-Weberian tradition in general, by advocating the following three contentions initially. Firstly, it accepts the centrality of the capital/labour divide in the structuration of class in industrial capitalist societies. Secondly, it regards this distinction as insufficient for class analyses since the broad category of labour (the 'propertyless') has a definite line of class division within it. Finally, it holds that this secondary 'fault' within the class hierarchy in industrial capitalist societies is encapsulated by the non-manual/manual 'divide'.

Furthermore, each of these three classes is seen as comprising distinct elements or 'strata'. The capitalist class is seen to be constituted by a bourgeois and a petty bourgeois element. The bourgeois stratum refers to the owners of large-scale capital, like factory proprietors and company directors, whereas the petty bourgeoisie comprises owners of small-scale capital, like shopkeepers and small businessmen. The capitalist class was identified in order to locate the dominant class in a capitalist society and it was divided in order to take into account variations in the size of property owned – a variable which Bechhofer *et al.,*[11] amongst others, have shown to be of considerable sociological importance. The manual working class is seen as containing three elements differentiated in terms of their level of skill which, as was seen in chapters 6 and 7, are of central relevance in the internal structuration of the British manual working class. Two main strata were identified within the middle class: a routine white-collar stratum or 'lower middle class' and a stratum labelled 'co-ordinators'. This latter stratum included professional, bureaucratic and supervisory employees. They could have been labelled the 'service class', a term derived from Renner[12] and Dahrendorf (1964) and popularized recently by Goldthorpe in a different context, but the term 'co-ordinator'[13] was preferred as this indicates the precise function of these strata in the class structure of industrial capitalist societies, which is to perform a wide array of organizational tasks. If these three classes and their constitutive seven strata are accepted then the central problem for this research becomes how to locate occupations within these categories.

This leads to the vexed question of the relationship between 'occupation' and 'class'. The problem is that 'occupation' and 'class' are not fixed conceptual entities. Blackburn,[14] in his discussion of these issues, associates occupation with economic role differentiation within the 'propertyless' and, consequently, regards occupational analysis as central to the examination of stratification amongst the non-propertied elements of society. Such an approach is integral to such diverse activities as the Registrar-General's classification of occupations (1970) and Blau and Duncan's (1967) work on stratification in the United States of America. However, as the Oxford mobility team have shown, such conceptual assumptions are not logically required by the data themselves. It *is* possible to discover classes from data which are often regarded as occupational. Goldthorpe (1980) achieved this to a degree with his discussion of the petty bourgeoisie, but unfortunately he failed to take the analysis sufficiently far and discover the capitalist class *tout court*. It is not always possible to gain precise information about possession of property from such documents as marriage returns, but it is possible to produce powerful presumptions. Indeed, the information required on such documents as marriage and birth certificates, and even passports, is not 'occupation' but 'rank' and/or 'profession'. What is being asked, in essence, is 'what is your or your father's economic function?' If this is taken to be synonymous with

Diagram 9.1. *Occupational categories used in the Rochdale research*[15]

Stage A: The initial categorization	Stage B	Stage C: The categorization used to classify the data in this research
1. Unclassified	—	—
2. Agricultural	—	—
3. Manufacturers and proprietors	Bourgeoisie	Bourgeoisie
4. Directors		
5. Shopkeepers and merchants	Petty bourgeoisie	Petty bourgeoisie
6. Small businessmen		
7. Professionals	Professionals	
8. Technicians	—	
9. Managers	Bureaucrats	Co-ordinators
10. Administrators		
11. Supervisors	Supervisory	
12. Salesworkers	Routine white-collar	Routine white-collar
13. Clerical		
14. Shop assistants		
15. Skilled manual	Skilled manual	Skilled manual
16. Semi-skilled manual	Semi-skilled manual	Semi-skilled manual
17. Unskilled manual	Unskilled manual	Unskilled manual

occupation, then 'occupation' includes different classes in the sense of distinct property relationships (i.e. relations to the means of production, distribution and exchange). If occupation is limited to the propertyless then the data analysed in this research involve more than occupational information and include evidence on class situation. There appear to be no methodological or substantive reasons to adopt Blackburn's narrow definition of occupation, and this research uses the term 'occupation' to include economic roles that are *both* propertied and propertyless.

In fact, seventeen occupational categories were used in the initial classification. These seventeen categories were collapsed into the seven strata and *pari passu* the three classes used for the data analyses in chapters 11 and 12 as shown in diagram 9.1.

Three of the initial occupational categories, skilled manual, semi-skilled manual and unskilled manual workers were retained as strata in the seven strata model. The unclassified were dropped from the analysis for obvious reasons, and all the agricultural occupations were excluded since it had been decided not to focus on the rural class structure around Rochdale. The petty bourgeois stratum contained two occupational categories – 'shop-keepers and merchants' and 'small businessmen' and the bourgeois stratum comprised 'manufacturers and proprietors' and 'directors'. Of the eight remaining middle class occupational categories, three were placed in a routine white-collar or 'lower middle class' stratum. Four categories made up the stratum of 'co-ordinators' – which may be regarded as either the 'middle class proper' or the 'service' class. One occupational grouping, technicians, was so small that it was excluded from the seven strata model.

This three class model and its seven strata foundation are hopefully an improvement sociologically over other class categorizations in use by contemporary social scientists. Unlike the Registrar General's (1970), this categorization does not disguise the *capitalist* nature of the British class structure between the 1850's and the present. Nor does it use notions of 'intermediate' classes, which simply serve to obscure class analyses. Unlike Goldthorpe's (1980), the categorization does not place the bourgeoisie in with the middle class nor does it place the petty bourgeoisie in with routine white-collar workers.[16]

This model also has the advantage of being relatively easy to grasp and being usable at different levels of generality, either as three classes, seven strata or seventeen categories, depending upon the problems that have been posed. Finally, this model approximates to the class distinctions often made in everyday discourse. It is not synonymous with that discourse, but it is not difficult to translate many popular conceptions about class and stratification within its framework at one of the three levels of generality. Nevertheless, in the end, the proof is in the eating, and it is to the analysis of intermarriage data *by means of* this categorization that the research now turns.

10

Class analysis and marital endogamy

This third section of the book investigates the degree to which the economic structuration of class has been translated into parallel patterns of social boundedness during the period between 1856 and 1964 in Rochdale. It was suggested in the preceding chapter that such an analysis would permit a systematic, empirical assessment of the assumption amongst authors like Foster, Gray, Hobsbawm and Mackenzie, that the economic and social structuration of class co-vary chronologically. This chapter will explain why the question of social boundedness has been operationalized in terms of marital endogamy and also provide a review of the social scientific literature on intermarriage as a prelude to the empirical examination of the material from Rochdale in chapters 11 and 12.

The study of social endogamy has been a relatively neglected area of sociological investigation, especially in Britain. Most studies of marital endogamy have been conducted within the parameters of the sociology of the family. Major topics of research in this area have concentrated on social factors determining mate-selection, varying from general cultural factors,[1] such as notions of 'romantic love'[2] to specific social characteristics like race,[3] residential propinquity[4] and occupation.[5] In addition, there has been interest shown in Winch's[6] theory of complementary psychological needs in the determination of mate-selection. Whilst of considerable value, all this research (which is predominantly American in origin) suffers from its location within a general structural-functionalist theoretical framework and, in particular, from its failure to consider dynamic forces within its range of focus. Consequently, we are informed that for example, in post-1945 American society, there is a marked marital homogamy or, in other words, most Americans marry people with social and psychological characteristics similar to their own. What we do not know is the extent to which such patterns differ significantly from those of the recent (and less recent) past, or the typicality of American patterns for other advanced societies.

Notions of endogamy as a feature of the structuration of class relationships were stressed earlier in the century by Weber (1968) and Sorokin (1959), but little has been made of their remarks. The main reason for the absence of questions about endogamy from the traditional corpus of stratification research derives from the overwhelming emphasis in most studies on samples of adult males. Such approaches have had two unfortunate effects: they have ignored the role of women in the class structure, but also they have displaced the family from the focus of investigation. Nevertheless, for many questions about class structuration, the family is the most appropriate unit of analysis – particularly questions about the ownership and transmission of property and about social mobility. As will be seen, the family is taken as the basic unit of stratification for this research and, consequently, an entire chapter will be devoted to the investigation of class marital endogamy from the perspective of brides and grooms.

Recently, both Giddens (1973) and Parkin (1974 and 1979) have stressed the importance of social closure for the determination of the degree of structuration of class relationships, and Goldthorpe (1980) has attempted to develop similar conceptual points in his Nuffield social mobility research. Nevertheless, there is a serious gap in historical knowledge between recently published historical demography like the work of Stone (1977) and the analyses of Laslett *et al.*[7] at the Cambridge Group for the History of Population and Social Structure, which focus on pre-industrial structures, and the evidence produced by Goldthorpe and his Oxford colleagues on twentieth century patterns. The only other major systematic source for historical trends in social endogamy in British society is Glass's *Social Mobility in Britain* (1954). As will be shown later in this chapter, the Glass study's conclusions are open to question from a methodological angle. However, even with its limitations, Glass's research can only take us back to the last decades of the nineteenth century. For any earlier periods, his research is silent and all that can be done, at present, is to fill the gap with studies like Foster's (1974) research on Oldham, Northampton and South Shields, Gray's (1976) study of Edinburgh and various monographs on the ruling elite (particularly its landed component).[8] Unfortunately, for the most part the terrain is left by default to the various versions of the 'traditional' working class – which it was attempted to show earlier are, to say the least, suspect. One of the main contributions that this part of the research attempts to make is to offer empirical material for the whole period between the 1850's and the 1960's; for what can be termed the 'longue durée' of British industrial capitalism. Of course, it only refers to one specific geographical location – Rochdale – but it is, nevertheless, better to have some systematic empirical guide than none.

If the study of intermarriage has not formed an important element in traditional studies of class structure in Britain, there are strong grounds *prima facie* to suggest that it could provide a useful extension to class analysis. At any given moment, there is a set of families which provides the sum of potential marriage partners in a social system. These families are likely to reflect the overall distribution of economic class positions very strongly and, therefore, we can envisage a model in which a society is divided into two sub-sets of families: one containing sons and the other daughters. From what we know of British society and the evidence of homogamy from America and elsewhere, it would appear reasonable to expect that the combination of sons and daughters by marriage to form new families would reflect the class structure. In other words, we would expect a degree of class endogamy or, more plainly, there would be a strong presumption that sons of a certain class would tend to marry daughters from the same class more often than those of a different class. Indeed, this is often what is meant by the term 'class structure' in everyday discourse and in particular notions of 'rigid' versus 'open' class structures frequently involve notions of relative endogamy[9] chances. However, before proceeding with the substantive material gathered in Rochdale on patterns of intermarriage, it is necessary to investigate previous work in this area, in order to clarify the nature of the hypotheses to be examined.

One of the most notable studies of marital endogamy is that of the French bio-demographers, Sutter and Tabah (1951), which has been brought to the wider attention of contemporary sociologists by Lévi-Strauss's *Structural Anthropology* (1973). Sutter and Tabah's research involves an investigation of the inter-relationship between the genetic concept of an 'isolate' and the demographic notion of a 'minimum population'. The notion of endogamy enters the analysis in terms of the orthodox anthropological notion of marriage relations established between and within kinship structures. Clearly, this has a great appeal for Lévi-Strauss in his project for establishing a structural anthropology which can provide 'more directly... a mathematical expression of social phenomena', and in particular a quantitative measure of kinship boundaries. Although such anthropological notions about kinship structures are tangential to the aims of this research, they do contribute a useful metaphor. Lévi-Strauss suggests that intermarriage has constituted a vital 'deep structural' element in the reproduction of the social structures of non-advanced societies.[10] One heuristic assumption of the empirical investigations that follow is that intermarriage may perform a similar structural role in the reproduction of the economic class structure of advanced societies. If there is empirical evidence suggesting that there are 'deep structural' social class boundaries sustained and recreated through mechanisms of marital endogamy, it would be reasonable to argue that the underlying economic class matrix formed a major 'principle of boundedness'.

The analogy with anthropology may be pushed even further. The main reasons that lie behind the 'deep structures' of marital endogamy in non-advanced societies would appear to be the problems associated with the transfer of property and relative social status. Similar notions lie behind a succession of pieces of research into intermarriage and class, and which further suggest that an assumption of marital class endogamy is a sensible *a priori*. A clear example of this type of approach can be seen in Hollingsworth's (1964) study of the British peerage, which demonstrated a high degree of marital endogamy. Thomas (1972) has elaborated Hollingsworth's work to involve an examination of the sources of brides from non-peerage backgrounds. He found that the peerage had a high level of internal recruitment across the generations and that the sources of external recruitment were heavily concentrated within those classes or strata most proximate to the peerage (what Thomas refers to as the 'gentlemenly' class). Thomas's work is vitiated by his *ad hoc* class categories, especially his miscellaneous 'lowest social class' which includes more or less everyone not associated with either land ownership or the old petty bourgeoisie (traditional professionals and higher officers of the state). Nevertheless, two clear conclusions can be derived from such studies of aristocratic endogamy. Firstly, the peerage has had a high level of internal recruitment across generations and secondly, the sources of external recruitment to the landed aristocracy are heavily concentrated within those classes or strata most proximate to the peerage.

The first major study of internal recruitment across the entire class structure in Britain was made by the Glass mobility team (1954). Glass's research constitutes an extension of the Hollingsworth–Thomas mode of analysis to a series of occupational groupings and, consequently, suggests answers as to the likely typicality of the high levels of class endogamy revealed within the British landed aristocracy. The study of intermarriage provides the logical converse to the study of relative mobility, since mobility and immobility (exogamy and endogamy) are but opposite sides of the same coin. As Berent (1954) points out in a chapter on 'Social Mobility and Marriage' in the Glass study, following Sorokin's (1959) original thoughts on the subject, 'one of the tests of the "openness" of social structure is the extent of marriage between persons of different social origins' (p. 321). The results of the analysis were presented as clear and definite:

First, whether measured in terms of social origin or educational level, there is a significant amount of assortative mating in England and Wales, the degree of association between husband and wife being greatest in the top and bottom status categories. As in the case of mobility obtained by occupational achievement, the category of skilled manual worker shows the least rigidity. So far as education is concerned, the least marital mobility is found among individuals who have had university or other 'higher' education. Secondly, in those marriages in which the partners differ with respect to one or other of the variables selected, there is a slight tendency for men to marry 'downwards'. Thirdly, over the past fifty years the degree of social endogamy appears to have declined (Berent, 1954, pp. 337–8)

The evidence appears unambiguous, the British peerage is not untypical in its endogamous structure; indeed, its high rate of internal recruitment is mirrored to a lesser degree by other high status (and some low status) groupings in British society. In addition, the overall trend in Britain between 1900 and 1950 has been towards increasing permeability of the class structure and, consequently, less endogamy – although most of this increase is accounted for by short-distance mobility between adjacent status categories.[11] However, when Berent's classification of occupations is examined, it becomes apparent that the 'skilled' category comprises *both* skilled manual workers *and* routine grades of non-manual labour (i.e. clerical work). In addition, Berent fails to distinguish the difference between endogamy as a *logically necessary* feature of an intermarriage matrix and endogamy that is greater (or lesser) than the structure of potential marriage partners. This methodological point can be illuminated by using the example of Berent's own Table 1 (p.325), where the proportion of category III (the 'skilled') men who marry category III women is 53.8%. Given that 45.7% of women are located in category III, it would be expected at random that 45.7% of category III men's wives would be category III women. Clearly, absolute amounts of endogamy or exogamy are affected by the relative size of the groups under investigation – a point made by a series of researchers into social mobility (cf. Yasuda, 1964 and Boudon, 1973). These methodological objections suggest that we cannot place too much reliance on the *precise* findings reported by Berent, but his overall results do suggest the strong plausibility of any hypothesis that holds that marital endogamy is a reflection of the underlying class matrix and suggests that it would vary concomitantly with changes in that structure.

Such assumptions, as was shown in chapter 3, also underlie much of the literature on the labour aristocracy. Hobsbawm (1964) has asserted, and both Foster (1974) and Gray (1976) have sought to demonstrate, that marital endogamy is strongly affected by the nature of the economic class structure. Changes in the latter are seen as causally related to changes in the former by all these writers in the 'labour aristocracy' tradition. Mackenzie (1973) also sees patterns of social interaction as a reflection of an underlying economic class structure.

All this evidence, despite its patchiness and methodological limitations, does suggest that intermarriage is a significant aspect of social class structuration. The central image is of an economic class structure which underlies intermarriage and strongly delimits openness or 'pure choice'. This may be because different classes and strata have distinct value systems with cultural norms involving precepts about moral 'worthiness' and associated principles of derogation and superordination, or it may be because the class system prevents interaction between potential marriage partners from different class backgrounds, but the imagery is clear enough. The economic structuration of class, which is formed initially in the economic structures associated with property, market and the division of labour, strongly influences patterns of non-economic interaction and sociability and is revealed most starkly in the structuration of inter-marriage. The next two chapters will probe this imagery by means of a systematic analysis of material gathered in Rochdale on marital class endogamy.

11

Intermarriage in Rochdale: class endogamy of brides and grooms

It was stated in the preceding chapter that the purpose of collecting data on intermarriage in Rochdale was to permit an analysis of the extent to which economic divisions within the class structure based upon the spheres of work and market relations were translated into non-economic, 'social' divisions. Clearly, such a problem requires an adequate instrument with which to classify occupations into classes and strata and this was outlined in chapter 9. However, there is also the need to operationalize the overall research problem into a set of specific questions amenable to empirical scrutiny. In particular, given that marriage records provide information on the occupation and, by implication, class position of four people,[1] there is a problem of deciding which set of marital relationships should be taken as exemplifying the basic class relation. Should the investigator analyse the relationship between bride and groom or between the father of the bride and the father of the groom, for instance?

There are at least two conceptual problems involved here. Firstly, there is the question of the class position of women and of brides in particular. Recent sociological research has asserted that the family is the correct unit for class or stratification research and that the class position of a family is determined by the occupation of the male head of household.[2] Such views have, justifiably, been questioned by some contemporary sociologists and have been criticized by Garnsey (1978) as highly misleading. Without wishing to enter into the specific merits of the debate, it is important to recognize that there are *no universally correct units for class analysis or stratification research,* because there are no *a priori* criteria upon which they can, or must, be based. The appropriate unit for research depends upon the purpose of the investigator and, more mundanely, upon the availability of data. Consequently, the multiple sources of information about the class situations embodied in a marriage return, permit and require multiple modes of analysis. Given that one primary aim of this research is to demonstrate the complexity of class relations and the dangers of 'essentialism'[3] in class analyses, the sample of Rochdale marriage returns will be examined from a series of angles.[4] Initially, the relationship between bride and groom will be examined and this will be followed by an investigation of the marriage returns from the perspective of the class relationship exemplified by the fathers of the bride and the fathers of the groom. The reason for adopting the multiple perspective is not to produce a situation where the wood cannot be seen for the trees but to demonstrate the complex issues involved in the seemingly simple question, 'have skilled manual workers in Rochdale become more or less endogamous between 1856 and 1964?' In addition, such a multiple approach permits an *empirical* discussion of the issues raised when one operationalization from amongst many is actually chosen for research purposes.

The same points apply to the other conceptual difficulty that surrounds the investigation of the structuration or 'boundedness' of the class structure by means of intermarriage data. This concerns the changing nature of the occupational structure. This affects the question of class endogamy in one major way. If the manual working class is a high proportion of the total population, then the investigator would expect high degrees of absolute endogamy at random. It is clearly of major importance to separate propositions about *absolute* social closure from those about *relative* social closure.[5] However, this is rarely done but it seems likely that most of the propositions from the literature on the traditional working class and the aristocracy of labour are, in fact, statements about relative social closure. Consequently, it will be necessary to assess the propositions in this literature from the perspectives of both absolute and relative endogamy.

It is worth restating these propositions again. Three main hypotheses were discovered from the literature on the homogeneity of the traditional working class. If class 'homogeneity' is operationalized in terms of marital endogamy, the following propositions can be deduced:

a) the manual working class has been endogamous throughout the period between 1856 and 1964.
b) the manual working class was at its most endogamous between 1875 and 1914.
c) the manual working class was at its most endogamous between the First and Second World Wars.

The model of rhythms in working class sectionalism produces the following set of propositions:

i) the industrial revolution created an undifferentiated working class by 1850.
ii) this disintegrated in the period between 1850 and 1880 amid increasing sectionalism between the skilled and non-skilled.

iii) This sectionalism collapsed in the period 1880–1900.
iv) The working class remained undifferentiated until after 1945.
v) The post-war period witnessed the progressive redifferentiation of the manual working class around the axis of skill.

Clearly, there are two sets of questions that need to be asked. Firstly, has the manual working class *as a whole* become more or less fluid (i.e. more or less exogamous – the terms are used synonymously)? Secondly, have the relationships between the skilled and non-skilled strata within the manual working class become more or less sectional (i.e. more or less endogamous again)? The first set of questions concerns the *external* endogamy of the manual working class as a whole, and refers to those propositions raised primarily by the advocates of a 'traditional working class'. The second concerns the *internal* endogamy or 'structuration' of the manual working class around the axis of skill and focuses on the rhythms of working class sectionalism. Those propositions derived from the literature on the labour aristocracy in the nineteenth century and skilled manual workers in the twentieth century are of most relevance here. Both sets of questions will be assessed in this and the next chapter.

A brief characterization of the matrices as a whole[6]

The matrices analysed in this section were derived from the data collected in Rochdale for the period between 1856 and 1964. Information on the occupational characteristics of grooms, brides, fathers of grooms and fathers of brides was collected for a series of decennial time-periods by means of a stratified systematic random sample (see Appendix A and chapter 5 for the full details of the sample). The decennial periods selected were 1856–1865, 1875–1884, 1900–1909, 1920–1929 and 1955–1964. They were selected in order to furnish evidence that could be compared over a lengthy time-span, and the cases within each decennial matrix were assumed to be 'homogeneous'. In other words, no importance was placed upon whether a marriage in the first decennial period, for example, had occurred in either 1856 or 1865. The major problem for this research was taken to be secular trends in class endogamy over relatively long periods of time and, consequently, such an assumption produced a method of analysis that made it unnecessary to capture trends in intermarriage within any decennial matrix. However, this loss is more than compensated for by the size of the ensuing decennial sub-samples and the ability of such matrices to furnish evidence that helps to illuminate the central focus of this work – namely, the structural position of skilled manual workers within

Table 11.1. *Social endogamy in Rochdale, 1856–1865: brides and grooms*

Groom's occupational grouping	Bride's occupational grouping		
	Semi-skilled manual	Unskilled manual	N_r
Routine white-collar	0	1	1
Skilled manual	12	0	12
Semi-skilled manual	12	0	12
Unskilled manual	3	0	3
N_c	27	1	28

the British class structure between the mid-nineteenth and mid-twentieth centuries.

Decennial Period 1 (1856–1865). In the period 1856–1865, few brides gave their occupations. This was partly because of a normative expectation that marriage for women meant the ending of paid labour; an expectation more faithfully fulfilled amongst non-working class women than within the working class. It also reflected real differences in labour market participation by women, many of whom were domestic servants for whom marriage provided the mechanism for setting up an independent household. However, beyond such general points, it is clear that all women giving their occupations on the marriage certificate during this period were manual workers. All but one were semi-skilled, reflecting the preponderance of women as textile operatives, and all but one married a working class husband. The picture is of an endogamous working class, with little difference between skilled and non-skilled in terms of the social origins of husbands, but obviously not too much reliance should be placed upon such a small sub-sample. Indeed, when the evidence on marital endogamy is investigated from the perspective of the fathers of the brides and of the grooms in the next chapter the picture presented here will need to be revised.

Decennial Period 2 (1875–1884): Table 11.2. In the period between 1875 and 1884 more brides gave their occupations. The picture is similar to the previous period (1856–1865); three-quarters of the brides giving an occupation were semi-skilled manual workers and three-quarters of the grooms were manual workers.

Decennial Period 3 (1900–1909): Table 11.3. The evidence for this period, 1900–1909, gives far more detail than the previous two tables. Nevertheless, 68% of brides were semi-skilled manual workers and, as

Table 11.2. *Social endogamy in Rochdale, 1875–1884: brides and grooms*

Groom's occupational grouping	Bride's occupational grouping															N_r	%
	Petty bourgeois			Co-ordinators			Skilled manual			Semi-skilled manual			Unskilled manual				
	%r	N	%c	%r	N	%c	%r	N	%c	%r	N	%c	%r	N	%c		
Bourgeoisie	0	0	0	0	0	0	0	0	0	100	2	3.6	0	0	0	2	2.7
Petty bourgeois	25.0	1	50.0	0	0	0	0	0	0	50.0	2	3.6	25.0	1	11.1	4	5.5
Co-ordinators	0	0	0	33.3	1	50.0	33.3	1	20.0	33.3	1	1.8	0	0	0	3	4.1
Routine white-collar	0	0	0	11.1	1	50.0	11.1	1	20.0	44.4	4	7.3	33.3	3	33.3	9	12.3
Skilled manual	3.6	1	50.0	0	0	0	10.7	3	60.0	78.6	22	40.0	7.1	2	22.2	28	38.4
Semi-skilled manual	0	0	0	0	0	0	0	0	0	100	19	34.5	0	0	0	19	26.0
Unskilled manual	0	0	0	0	0	0	0	0	0	62.5	5	9.1	37.5	3	33.3	8	11.0
N_c		2			2			5			55			9		73	
%		2.7			2.7			6.8			75.3			12.3			

Key: %r gives row percentages (the row sum equals 100)
%c gives column percentages (the column sum equals 100)

Table 11.3. *Social endogamy in Rochdale, 1900–1909: brides and grooms*

Groom's occupational grouping	Bride's occupational grouping																			
	Petty bourgeois			Co-ordinators			Routine white-collar			Skilled manual			Semi-skilled manual			Unskilled manual			N_r	%
	%r	N	%c	%r	N	%c	%r	N	%c	%r	N	%c	%r	N	%c	%r	N	%c		
Petty bourgeois	0	0	0	0	0	0	8.3	1	20.0	8.3	1	4.8	58.3	7	6.1	25.0	3	16.7	12	7.1
Co-ordinators	14.3	1	33.3	42.9	3	42.9	0	0	0	0	0	0	42.9	3	2.6	0	0	0	7	4.1
Routine white-collar	4.2	1	33.3	12.5	3	42.9	8.3	2	40.0	29.2	7	33.3	33.3	8	7.0	12.5	3	16.7	24	14.2
Skilled manual	1.6	1	33.3	0	0	0	1.6	1	20.0	13.1	8	38.1	73.8	45	39.1	9.8	6	33.3	61	36.1
Semi-skilled manual	0	0	0	2.6	1	14.3	2.6	1	20.0	2.6	1	4.8	82.1	32	27.8	10.3	4	22.2	39	23.1
Unskilled manual	0	0	0	0	0	0	0	0	0	15.4	4	19.0	76.9	20	17.4	7.7	2	11.1	26	15.4
N_c		3			7			5			21			115			18		169	
%		1.8			4.1			3.0			12.4			68.0			10.7			

Key: %r gives row percentages (the row sum equals 100)
   %c gives column percentages (the column sum equals 100)

163

Table 11.4. *Social endogamy in Rochdale, 1920–1929: brides and grooms*

Groom's occupational grouping	Bride's occupational grouping																			
	Petty bourgeois			Co-ordinators			Routine white-collar			Skilled manual			Semi-skilled manual			Unskilled manual				
	%r	N	%c	%r	N	%c	%r	N	%c	%r	N	%c	%r	N	%c	%r	N	%c	N_r	%
Bourgeoisie	0	0	0	0	0	0	100	1	2.3	0	0	0	0	00	0	0	0	0	1	0.3
Petty bourgeois	0	0	0	5.3	1	5.3	26.3	5	11.4	10.5	2	4.4	57.9	11	6.4	0	0	0	19	6.5
Co-ordinators	0	0	0	31.3	10	52.6	21.9	7	15.9	12.5	4	8.9	31.3	10	5.8	3.1	1	7.7	32	10.9
Routine white-collar	1.4	1	50.0	9.7	7	36.8	34.7	25	56.8	6.9	5	11.1	44.4	32	18.7	2.8	2	15.4	72	24.5
Skilled manual	0	0	0	1.2	1	5.3	6.2	5	11.4	16.0	13	28.9	70.4	57	33.3	6.2	5	38.5	81	27.6
Semi-skilled manual	1.6	1	50.0	0	0	0	1.6	1	2.3	20.3	13	28.9	75.0	48	28.1	1.6	1	7.7	64	21.8
Unskilled manual	0	0	0	0	0	0	0	0	0	32.0	8	17.8	52.0	13	7.6	16.0	4	30.8	25	8.5
N_c		2			19			44			45			171			13		294	
%		0.7			6.5			15.0			15.3			58.2			4.4			

Key: %r gives row percentages (the row sum equals 100)
%c gives column percentages (the column sum equals 100)

Table 11.5. *Social endogamy in Rochdale, 1955–1964: brides and grooms*

Groom's occupational grouping	Bride's occupational grouping																			
	Petty bourgeois			Co-ordinators			Routine white-collar			Skilled manual			Semi-skilled manual			Unskilled manual			N_r	%
	%r	N	%c	%r	N	%c	%r	N	%c	%r	N	%c	%r	N	%c	%r	N	%c		
Petty bourgeois	0	0	0	16.7	1	1.4	66.7	4	2.9	16.7	1	3.8	0	0	0	0	0	0	6	1.8
Co-ordinators	1.3	1	100	46.2	36	51.4	39.7	31	22.1	2.6	2	7.7	9.0	7	7.7	1.3	1	7.7	78	22.9
Routine white-collar	0	0	0	20.8	21	30.0	55.4	56	40.0	3.0	3	11.5	17.8	18	19.8	3.0	3	23.1	101	29.6
Skilled manual	0	0	0	9.3	10	14.3	36.4	39	27.9	12.1	13	50.0	38.3	41	45.1	3.7	4	30.8	107	31.4
Semi-skilled manual	0	0	0	3.4	1	1.4	34.5	10	7.1	13.8	4	15.4	41.4	12	13.2	6.9	2	15.4	29	8.5
Unskilled manual	0	0	0	5.0	1	1.4	0	0	0	15.0	3	15.0	65.0	13	14.3	15.0	3	23.1	20	5.9
N_c		1			70			140			26			91			13		341	
%		0.3			20.5			41.1			7.6			26.7			3.8			

Key: %r gives row percentages (the row sum equals 100)

%c gives column percentages (the column sum equals 100)

would be anticipated from the previous periods, most married working class husbands. Nevertheless, when the row of figures for petty bourgeois husbands and for routine white-collar husbands are examined, it can be seen that there are high absolute levels of class permeability, with 7 of the 12 wives of the petty bourgeoisie being semi-skilled manual workers, and 8 of the wives of the 24 routine white-collar husbands coming from the semi-skilled stratum.

Decennial Period 4 (1920–1929): Table 11.4. The detail for this period is almost complete since most brides gave an occupation. 58% of brides were semi-skilled manual workers and 69% of these semi-skilled brides married working class husbands. Nevertheless, 58% of the wives of the petty bourgeoisie were semi-skilled manual workers, as were 44% of routine white-collar workers' wives. However, there is considerable evidence for a certain degree of endogamy amongst the middle class, for when the figures for co-ordinators are examined it can be seen that 53% of the wives of co-ordinators came from the categories of either co-ordinator or routine white-collar.

Decennial Period 5 (1955–1964): Table 11.5. The decennial period 1955–1964 witnessed the first dramatic transformation in the occupational structure of wives: 62% came from either capitalist or middle class backgrounds. Of considerable interest is the disappearance of the petty bourgeoisie from the local class structure. The processes of concentration and agglomeration in manufacturing industry and in retailing can be clearly discerned in terms of their class effects. The Rochdale class structure can be seen to be increasingly approximating a simple working class:middle class dichotomy.

The endogamy of the manual working class

The dominant impression from these tables is one of high levels of absolute manual working class endogamy throughout the period, which are the consequence of the massive preponderance of manual workers in the sub-samples, at least until the period 1955–1964. In this sense, there is strong support for the idea put forward by Anderson (1965) that there has been a traditional working class, separate from the remainder of the class structure, throughout the period between 1856 and 1964. However, as was argued above, most of the propositions about the development of the British class structure are not about absolute mobility – indeed, it would be rather strange to argue that the working class represented an 'enclave', 'a caste apart' or was 'hermetically sealed' simply in terms of its numerical preponderance – but rather about relative mobility (or closure).

However, if one wants to ask the extent to which the working class as a

Table 11.6. *Working class marital endogamy: original data, brides and grooms*

1875–1884	1900–1909	1920–1929	1955–1964

	a	b		a	b		a	b		a	b
a	3	15		11	32		57	67		150	35
b	1	54		4	122		8	162		61	95
		73			169			294			341

Key: a = classes other than manual working class
b = manual working class
columns = brides
rows = grooms

whole has become *relatively* more fluid or closed, we need to do more than inspect the tables visually. It is necessary to provide a statistical measure with which to assess *relative* marital endogamy. The measure used in this research, Yule's Q, was first suggested in 1912 (Yule) but was not really considered by social scientists until after Goodman and Kruskal's (1954) seminal article on 'Measures of Associations for Cross Classifications'. It has been recommended for general use by Davis (1971) and the summary of the properties of Yule's Q is taken from his text.

Yule's Q is a coefficient of association for two variables that can vary between -1 and $+1$. It is, therefore, far easier to interpret sets of coefficients of association using this measure than others in the field like the coefficients suggested by Glass (1954), Yasuda (1964) or Boudon (1973) which do not have this simple property.[7] Davis sets the arbitrary designations for verbal representation of strengths of relationships of Q in Table 11.7. This research will follow these conventions in its analysis of marital class endogamy.

Yule's Q is defined mathematically as the difference in cross products of a dichotomous matrix divided by the sum of those same cross products.[8] Q takes a value of zero when the two variables are independent and a value of unity when one of the cells contains zero counts (Blalock, 1972, p. 298). One particularly important (and desirable) feature of Q is that it is unaffected by changes in the total size of the data matrix and consequently it is insensitive to multiplication or division of the row or column frequencies by a constant value. Goodman and Kruskal suggest that a positive Q value of QI, for example, would indicate that we would do

Table 11.7. *Conventions for describing Q values*

Value of Q	Appropriate phrase
+ 0.70 or higher	A very strong positive association
+ 0.50 to + 0.69	A substantial positive association
+ 0.30 to + 0.49	A moderate positive association
+ 0.10 to + 0.29	A low positive association
+ 0.01 to + 0.09	A negligible positive association
0.00	No association
− 0.01 to − 0.09	A negligible negative association
− 0.10 to − 0.29	A low negative association
− 0.30 to − 0.49	A moderate negative association
− 0.50 to − 0.69	A substantial negative association
− 0.70 or lower	A very strong negative association

Source: J. Davis, *Elementary Survey Analysis* (1971, p. 49).

$(100 \times QI)\%$ better than chance if we predict some non-random pattern of association between the two variables (cf. Davis, 1971, pp. 48–9).

Yule's Q gives a single coefficient and it is, of course, necessary to provide confidence intervals. This is because the observed value of Q in any particular example represents only one of a number of possible values that could occur with repeated sampling. We shall follow Fisher (1926), Davis (1971) and general social scientific convention in arbitrarily deciding that a result of less than 5/100 is 'rare' and one more than 5/100 is 'frequent'. Given the fact that Q varies between + 1.00 and − 1.00, we shall follow Davis and use a two-tailed test. This will mean that statistical significance will be reported in terms of the 0.025 level. Essentially, we will regard a Q coefficient as statistically significant if its confidence interval is positive or negative but as insignificant if the confidence interval ranges over the value of zero. The reason for the non-significance of confidence intervals containing zero values is that they indicate that we cannot be confident that the data diverge significantly from a situation where there is no interaction between variables other than randomness.

It is worth pointing out that Q assumes simple random sampling and that the data diverge significantly from a situation where there is no interaction stratified random sample. However, this does not matter in the case of relationships shown to be not significant since the confidence intervals calculated in this research may be interpreted as *narrower* than their true values (see Davis, 1971, pp. 59–60). Conversely, any relations shown to be significant but with a confidence interval close to a zero value may, in fact,

Table 11.8. *Value of Q for working class marital endogamy: brides and grooms*

	Q	Magnitude	Confidence interval	Statistical significance
1875–1884	+ 0.83	very strong	± 0.36	Significant at 0.025 level
1900–1909	+ 0.83	very strong	± 0.19	Significant at 0.025 level
1920–1929	+ 0.89	very strong	± 0.08	Significant at 0.025 level
1955–1964	+ 0.74	very strong	± 0.11	Significant at 0.025 level

be non-significant. As will become apparent from an examination of the specific results in this and the subsequent chapter, this is not, in fact, a problem with the interpretation of the data collected in Rochdale.

What then are the values of Q for the data on working class external marital endogamy reported in Table 11.6? They are shown in Table 11.8. These results suggest two conclusions of interest. Firstly, there has been a very strong positive class interaction throughout the entire period of the research. Despite the absolute decline of the manual working class and the absolute rise in numbers of bourgeois and particularly middle class occupations in Rochdale, the relative endogamy of the working class, on the one hand, and of the remainder of the class structure, on the other, has been most marked. A small rise can be seen from the 1900's to the 1920's and a slightly larger decline between the 1920's and the figures for the period between 1955 and 1964. The results therefore suggest one major conclusion: there has been *no major shift in the relative external boundedness of the manual working class throughout the period of this research.* However, there has been one interesting change. In the periods before 1955–1964, manual working class boundedness was accounted for more in terms of the low chances of manual grooms marrying a bride with either a middle class or a capitalist occupation, whereas in the period 1955–1964 the situation was reversed. This suggests that as the class structure became less manual in content, there has been a changing relationship of gender to class in favour of a greater chance for manual men to marry outside their class than for manual women. Such a conclusion clearly warrants further research.

What light do these results shed upon the hypotheses about class structuration associated with the images of the traditional working class? There is no evidence to support either Hoggart, Williams, Lockwood or Young in their conjunctural theories of changes in relative endogamy. The overwhelming picture is one of marked structural stability in relative class endogamy throughout the period between 1856 and 1964. Indeed, whether one looks at working class marital boundedness from the perspective of absolute or relative endogamy, there is no support for theories of conjunctural change but overwhelming support for the view that there have been no significant changes in marital working class endogamy in Rochdale since the mid-nineteenth century. Anderson's vision of a 'hermetically sealed' manual working class 'enclave' throughout the epoch of British industrial capitalism is, therefore, closest to the mark.

The social endogamy of skilled manual husbands and wives

Skilled manual wives. In the period 1875–1884 there were only 5 skilled manual wives (6.8%). Three married skilled men and the remaining two married husbands who were not working class. During the period 1900–1909, 21 wives (12.4%) were skilled manual workers; and of these, eight married skilled men, seven married routine white-collar workers and only five non-skilled manual husbands. In the 1920's, 45 wives are classified as skilled (15.3%); 13 married skilled manual men and 75.6% married working class husbands overall; whilst in the 1950's only 26 women were skilled (7.6%) though 76.9% married working class men. The general picture therefore is one of small numbers of skilled women in Rochdale throughout the period of the research. This confirms strongly the recent work on skill and gender in Britain by Cockburn (1981 and 1983) and Coyle (1982).

Skilled manual husbands. During the period 1875–1884, 28 men were skilled (38.4%) and all but one married working class wives (96.4%). A similar picture is forthcoming for 1900–1909; 61 men were skilled and 96.8% of them married working class wives. In the 1920's, 81 men were skilled and 92.6% married working class wives. The only deviation from this overwhelming picture of working class endogamy comes from the period between 1955 and 1964. Of the 107 skilled husbands, only 54.1% had working class wives whilst 36.4% had routine white-collar wives. So far, the evidence suggests a picture of an homogeneous manual working class, socially endogamous until at least the end of the 1920's but becoming somewhat more permeable with the occupational shifts in women's paid labour during the post-1945 era. However, so far all that have been presented are general impressions backed up with certain evidence. A further question, more precise and more illuminating, presents itself – did the patterns of intermarriage of skilled manual husbands diverge significantly from what would have been expected at random?

In Table 11.9 the discussion of the skilled 'divide' within the manual working class has been restricted to the three twentieth century matrices.[9] It is apparent that there is no support for the view that there has been a

Table 11.9 *Marital endogamy of skilled workers: original data and Q values, brides and grooms.*

1900–1909	1920–1929	1955–1964

	x	y
x	8	51
y	5	58

122
$Q = +0.29 \ (\pm 0.54)$,
not statistically
significant
$(p = \geq 0.025)$

	13	62
	21	66

162
$Q = -0.21 \ (\pm 0.37)$
not statistically
significant
$(p = \geq 0.025)$

	13	45
	7	30

95
$Q = +0.11(\pm 0.51)$
not statistically
significant
$(p = \geq 0.025)$

Key: x = skilled manual workers
y = non-skilled manual workers
columns = brides
rows = grooms

skilled 'divide' in Rochdale in the twentieth century. The general model of working class sectionalism suggested homogeneity between the later nineteenth century and the end of the Second World War. The evidence from Rochdale supports this view that there was no sectional social division within the manual working class in Rochdale around the axis of skill during that period. However, no support is forthcoming for the views of an increasingly differentiated working class after 1945 that are associated with Dahrendorf (1959) and Mackenzie (1973).

Indeed, the results from the examination of the *external* and *internal* boundedness of the manual working class in Rochdale in this chapter produce a remarkably consistent picture of structural stability. No evidence of secular or conjunctural changes in the social structuration of class, as measured by marital endogamy, can be seen in these data. Consequently, the dominant picture is of a stable social structuration of class in Rochdale, with a strongly homogeneous manual working class where the economic divisions between skilled and non-skilled manual workers outlined in chapters 6 and 7 are not translated into equivalent patterns of social boundedness. The next chapter will examine the generality of these conclusions by means of examining patterns of class interaction with evidence pertaining to the fathers of the brides and the fathers of the grooms.

12

Intermarriage in Rochdale: class endogamy of fathers of brides and fathers of grooms

The evidence from the Rochdale sub-samples on marital endogamy when viewed from the perspective of fathers of brides and fathers of grooms is much fuller than the data investigated on brides and grooms. As can be seen from Tables 12.1, 12.2, 12.3, 12.4 and 12.5 the number of cases in each matrix is always greater than 200 and for the last two sub-samples, the 1920's and the period between 1955 and 1964, it is almost 400. The reason for this is simple; quite a number of the marriage certificates had only three pieces of occupational data rather than the full four, as a consequence of the bride not giving her occupation. This was a result of a series of factors. Some brides had no occupation prior to marriage. Such women would tend to be from bourgeois or petty bourgeois backgrounds and evidence to support this view can be seen in each of the matrices in this chapter, where the proportion of fathers of brides from such backgrounds oscillates between about 7% to around 15%, whereas the proportion of brides with such class positions was much lower. It is also worth remembering that, in the early periods at least, there were strong taboos about women remaining in employment once married, particularly in textiles and, consequently, many women would give up paid work. This retreat from the labour market, coupled with communal values emphasizing the domestic role of married women, tended to produce a situation whereby brides did not record an occupation on the marriage certificate. These points support the need for multiple perspectives on marital endogamy as argued in the last chapter. Given the biases involved in the recording or non-recording of bridal occupation, it is vital to check the conclusions on class endogamy derived from data on brides and grooms from the perspective of the fathers who were involved in the marriage.

A brief characterization of the matrices as a whole

Decennial Period 1 (1856–1865): Table 12.1. The class structure in Rochdale during the mid-Victorian era is a 'mature' capitalist one. The

Table 12.1. *Social endogamy in Rochdale, 1856–1865: fathers of brides and fathers of grooms*

Fathers of groom's occupational grouping	Father of bride's occupational grouping																					N_r	%
	Bourgeoisie			Petty bourgeois			Co-ordinators			Routine white-collar			Skilled manual			Semi-skilled manual			Unskilled manual				
	%r	N	%c	%r	N	%c	%r	N	%c	%r	N	%c	%r	N	%c	%c	N	%r	%c	N	%r		
Bourgeoisie	20.0	3	50.0	26.7	4	13.8	6.7	1	5.9	13.3	2	40.0	20.0	3	2.9	2.6	2	13.3	0	0	0	15	5.4
Petty bourgeois	3.8	1	16.7	30.8	8	27.6	19.2	5	29.4	3.8	1	20.0	30.8	8	7.7	1.3	1	3.8	4.8	2	7.7	26	9.3
Co-ordinators	0	0	0	14.3	2	6.9	7.1	1	5.9	0	0	0	50.0	7	6.7	3.9	3	21.4	2.4	1	7.1	14	5.0
Routine white-collar	0	0	0	33.3	1	3.4	0	0	0	0	0	0	33.3	1	1.0	0	0	0	2.4	1	33.3	3	1.1
Skilled manual	1.0	1	16.7	7.2	7	24.1	5.2	5	29.4	1.0	1	20.0	40.2	39	37.5	35.5	27	27.8	40.5	17	17.5	97	34.6
Semi-skilled manual	0	0	0	6.4	5	17.2	6.4	5	29.4	0	0	0	39.7	31	29.8	35.5	27	34.6	23.8	10	12.8	78	27.9
Unskilled manual	2.2	1	16.7	4.3	2	6.9	0	0	0	2.2	1	20.0	32.6	15	14.4	21.1	16	34.8	26.2	11	23.9	46	16.4
N_c		6			29			17			5			104			76			42		279	
%		2.2			10.4			6.1			1.8			37.3			27.2			15.1			

Key: %r gives row percentages (the row sum equals 100)
%c gives column percentages (the column sum equals 100)

Table 12.2. *Social endogamy in Rochdale, 1875–1884: fathers of brides and fathers of grooms*

Father of groom's occupational grouping	Father of bride's occupational grouping																						
	Bourgeoisie			Petty bourgeois			Co-ordin-ators			Routine white-collar			Skilled manual			Semi-skilled manual			Unskilled manual			N_r	%
	%r	N	%c	%r	N	%c	%r	N	%c	%r	N	%c	%r	N	%c	%r	N	%c	%r	N	%c		
Bourgeoisie	42.9	3	37.5	14.3	1	4.0	0	0	0	0	0	0	42.9	3	3.1	0	0	0	0	0	0	7	3.2
Petty bourgeois	0	0	0	0	0	0	14.3	2	16.7	0	0	0	35.7	5	5.1	28.6	4	7.8	21.4	3	14.3	14	6.4
Co-ordinators	6.7	1	12.5	40.0	6	24.0	6.7	1	8.3	0	0	0	33.3	5	5.1	13.3	2	3.9	0	0	0	15	6.9
Routine white-collar	16.7	1	12.5	16.7	1	4.0	16.7	1	8.3	0	0	0	50.3	3	3.1	0	0	0	0	0	0	6	2.8
Skilled manual	3.0	3	37.5	15.0	15	60.0	5.0	5	41.7	2.0	2	100	44.0	44	44.9	24.0	24	47.1	7.0	7	33.3	100	46.1
Semi-skilled manual	0	0	0	2.3	1	4.0	7.0	3	25.0	0	0	0	51.2	22	22.4	30.2	13	25.5	9.3	4	19.0	43	19.7
Unskilled manual	0	0	0	3.1	1	4.0	0	0	0	0	0	0	50.0	16	16.3	25.0	8	15.7	21.9	7	33.3	32	14.7
N_c		8			25			12			2			98			51			21		217	
%		3.7			11.5			5.5			0.9			45.2			23.5			9.7			

Key: %r gives row percentages (the row sum equals 100)
    %c gives column percentages (the column sum equals 100)

174

Table 12.3. *Social endogamy in Rochdale, 1900–1909: fathers of brides and fathers of grooms*

Father of groom's occupational grouping	Father of bride's occupational grouping																			
	Petty bourgeois			Co-ordinators			Routine white-collar			Skilled manual			Semi-skilled manual			Unskilled manual			N_r	%
	%r	N	%c	%r	N	%c	%r	N	%c	%r	N	%c	%r	N	%c	%r	N	%c		
Petty bourgeois	16.0	4	22.2	12.0	3	14.3	12.0	3	16.7	44.0	11	9.4	12.0	3	4.9	4.0	1	3.4	25	9.5
Co-ordinators	12.1	4	22.2	15.2	5	28.8	15.2	5	27.8	45.5	15	12.8	6.1	2	3.3	6.1	2	6.9	33	12.5
Routine white-collar	8.3	1	5.6	16.7	2	9.5	8.3	1	5.5	33.3	4	3.4	33.3	4	6.6	0	0	0	12	4.5
Skilled manual	5.2	6	33.3	7.8	9	42.9	6.1	7	38.9	46.1	53	45.3	25.2	29	47.5	9.6	11	37.9	115	43.6
Semi-skilled manual	4.2	2	11.1	2.1	1	4.8	2.1	1	5.5	45.8	22	18.8	35.4	17	27.9	10.4	5	17.2	48	18.2
Unskilled manual	3.2	1	5.6	3.2	1	4.8	3.2	1	5.5	38.7	12	10.3	19.4	6	9.8	32.3	10	34.5	31	11.7
N_c		18			21			18			117			61			29		264	
%		6.8			8.0			6.8			44.3			23.1			11.0			

Key: %r gives row percentages (the row sum equals 100)
%c gives column percentages (the column sum equals 100)

bourgeois and petty bourgeois class comprise about 14% of the sub-sample and the manual working class a massive 80%. Between these classes lies a small non-manual section of about 7%.

Decennial Period 2 (1875–1884): Table 12.2. The class structure in the period 1875–1884 is similar in profile to the mid-nineteenth century picture. The manual working class comprises almost 80% of the whole, whilst the bourgeois and petty bourgeois classes are about 12%. Occupational differentiation associated with the growth of the middle class has had little impact on Rochdale by this period.

Decennial Period 3 (1900–1909): Table 12.3. This is the only period for which there are no reports of marriages concerning the offspring of 'bourgeois' parents. However, there is unlikely to be any great mystery involved in such findings. The number of 'bourgeois' children throughout the periods under review has been very small, and only a handful are found in the next two, twentieth century sub-samples (see Tables 12.4 and 12.5). The most likely explanation for this lack of any 'bourgeois' offspring involves the statistical variations associated with sampling. Of greater interest is the increasing proportion of fathers from middle class backgrounds – now around 16%. The proportional growth of professional, managerial and clerical occupations is partly explained by a small decline in the proportion of manual workers and partly by a somewhat larger decrease in the proportion of bourgeois and petty bourgeois cases. Nevertheless, about three-quarters of the entire set of fathers remain manual workers in this period.

Decennial Period 4 (1920–1929): Table 12.4. The trend during the 1920's follows the secular path discernible over the previous three periods. There is a tendency for the middle class, non-manual sector to expand proportionately, particularly the managerial and professional stratum. At the same time, the proportion of skilled manual workers has declined from about 44% in the 1900's to about 40% in the 1920's. The proportion of semi-skilled manual workers has declined in the first decades of the twentieth century from about 21% to about 16%, whilst the unskilled have witnessed an expansion from about 11% to about 17%. The main reasons for these trends within the manual working class centre around the blighted industrial history of Rochdale in the inter-war years. Engineering stagnated after the early 1920's and the proportion of skilled men diminished. The cotton industry declined disastrously, particularly towards the second half of the decade and, consequently, many semi-skilled textile workers were displaced from the labour market and forced into unskilled jobs. These two trends help to explain such relative shifts within the manual working class. The small increase in the proportion of managerial and professional workers is simply the manifestation in Rochdale of a general

Table 12.4. *Social endogamy in Rochdale, 1920–1929: fathers of brides and fathers of grooms*

Father of groom's occupational grouping	Father of bride's occupational grouping																						
	Bourgeoisie			Petty bourgeois			Co-ordin- ators			Routine white- collar			Skilled manual			Semi- skilled manual			Unskilled manual			N_r	%
	%r	N	%c	%r	N	%c	%r	N	%c	%r	N	%c	%r	N	%c	%r	N	%c	%r	N	%c		
Bourgeoisie	20.0	1	16.7	0	0	0	20.0	1	2.5	20.0	1	5.9	40.0	2	1.3	0	0	0	0	0	0	5	1.3
Petty bourgeois	5.6	2	33.3	8.3	3	10.7	13.9	5	12.5	2.8	1	5.9	38.9	14	8.9	22.2	8	11.4	8.3	3	4.8	36	9.4
Co-ordinators	1.9	1	16.7	9.6	5	17.9	21.2	11	27.5	5.8	3	17.6	32.7	17	10.8	13.5	7	10.0	15.4	8	12.7	52	13.6
Routine white-collar	3.7	1	16.7	37.	1	3.6	14.8	4	10.0	11.1	3	17.6	29.6	8	5.1	22.2	6	8.6	14.8	4	6.3	27	7.1
Skilled manual	0.7	1	16.7	6.3	9	32.1	9.0	13	32.5	4.2	6	35.3	50.0	72	45.9	16.0	23	32.9	13.9	20	31.7	144	37.8
Semi-skilled manual	0	0	0	13.5	7	25.0	7.7	4	10.0	1.9	1	5.9	34.6	18	11.5	25.0	13	18.6	17.3	9	14.3	52	13.6
Unskilled manual	0	0	0	4.6	3	10.7	3.1	2	5.0	3.1	2	11.8	40.0	26	16.6	20.0	13	18.6	29.2	19	30.2	65	17.1
N_c		6			28			40			17			157			70			63		381	
%		1.6			7.3			10.5			4.5			41.2			18.4			16.5			

Key: %r gives row percentages (the row sum equals 100)
%c gives column percentages (the column sum equals 100)

Table 12.5. *Social endogamy in Rochdale, 1955–1964: fathers of brides and fathers of grooms*

Father of groom's occupational grouping	Father of bride's occupational grouping																					N_r	%
	Bourgeoisie			Petty bourgeois			Co-ordinators			Routine white-collar			Skilled manual			Semi-skilled manual			Unskilled manual				
	%r	N	%c	%r	N	%c	%r	N	%c	%r	N	%c	%r	N	%c	%r	N	%c	%r	N	%c		
Bourgeoisie	0	0	0	28.6	2	9.1	0	0	0	14.3	1	2.6	42.9	3	1.9	14.3	1	1.5	0	0	0	7	1.8
Petty bourgeois	4.5	1	20.0	0	0	0	18.2	4	8.5	0	0	0	45.5	10	6.3	22.7	5	7.4	9.1	2	5.0	22	5.8
Co-ordinators	3.1	2	40.0	9.2	6	27.3	24.6	16	34.0	13.8	9	23.1	33.8	22	13.8	7.7	5	7.4	7.7	5	12.5	65	17.1
Routine white-collar	0	0	0	7.4	2	9.1	11.1	3	6.4	18.5	5	12.8	63.0	17	10.6	0	0	0	0	0	0	27	7.1
Skilled manual	1.4	2	40.0	5.6	8	36.4	9.9	14	29.8	10.6	15	38.5	42.3	60	37.5	19.0	27	39.7	11.3	16	40.0	142	37.3
Semi-skilled manual	0	0	0	4.1	3	13.6	9.6	7	14.9	11.0	8	20.5	39.7	29	18.1	27.4	20	29.4	8.2	6	15.0	73	19.2
Unskilled manual	0	0	0	2.2	1	4.5	6.7	3	6.4	2.2	1	2.6	42.2	19	2.6	22.2	10	14.7	24.4	11	27.5	45	11.8
N_c		5			22			47			39			160			68			40		381	
%		1.3			5.8			12.3			10.2			42.0			17.8			10.5			

Key: %r gives row percentages (the row sum equals 100)

%c gives column percentages (the column sum equals 100)

tendency in all advanced capitalist societies in the twentieth century towards an increasing proportion of occupations in what Renner (1978) and Goldthorpe (1980) refer to as 'the service class'.

Decennial Period 5 (1955–1964): Table 12.5. Table 12.5 reveals the full force of the processes that have been at work in the twentieth century on the occupational structure. The bourgeois and petty bourgeois classes have shrunk considerably from about 14% in the 1850's to about $7\frac{1}{2}$% in the period 1955–1964. The manual working class has shrunk from 80% to 69%, whilst the middle class of managerial, professional and routine white-collar workers has increased from 7% in the period 1856–1865 to 23% in the post-1945 period.

The endogamy of the manual working class

The overwhelming impression from these tables is of massive absolute working class endogamy. It is also clear that the absolute amounts of endogamy amongst the capitalist and middle classes are rather less, since there is clear evidence of considerable marriages between brides and between grooms from these backgrounds and working class spouses. Such evidence is consistent with the initial picture of marital class endogamy painted in the previous chapter and provides no support for the conjunctural versions of the traditional working class associated with Hoggart, Williams, Lockwood or Young. As with the preceding chapter, the initial impression in terms of absolute rates of marital class endogamy is one of a massive, unchanging pattern, mainly explicable in terms of the overwhelming numerical preponderance of the manual working class in the population of Rochdale. Such results therefore offer support once more to Anderson's notion of an homogeneous working class 'enclave' throughout the period between 1856 and 1964. Nevertheless, as was argued in the preceding chapter, this is not perhaps a very surprising result. What is of more interest is the pattern of *relative* marital class endogamy between fathers of brides and fathers of grooms and this is revealed in Table 12.7.

These results suggest two main conclusions. Firstly, there has been a positive class marital association throughout the period under review.[1] It also appears that the degree of positive class marital relative endogamy between the manual working class and the rest of the population has undergone a secular decline between the mid-nineteenth and mid-twentieth centuries. Such results disconfirm Hoggart, Williams and Lockwood, whose theories would have led one to expect a rise in relative marital class endogamy between the 1900's and 1920's but a subsequent fall after the end of World War II in the period between 1955 and 1964. Nor is there evidence to suggest any rise in relative marital endogamy in the last quarter of the

Table 12.6. *Working class marital endogamy: original data, fathers of brides and fathers of grooms*

1856–1865		1875–1884		1900–1909		1920–1929		1955–1964	
a	*b*								
a 29	29	17	25	28	42	43	77	51	70
b 28	193	30	145	29	165	48	213	62	198
	279		217		264		381		381

Key: *a* = classes other than manual working class
        b = manual working class

Table 12.7. *Values of Q for working class marital endogamy, fathers of brides and fathers of grooms*

	Q	Magnitude	Confidence interval	Statistical significance
1856–1865	0.75	Very Strong	± 0.14	Significant at 0.025 level
1875–1884	0.53	Substantial	± 0.26	”
1900–1909	0.58	Substantial	± 0.20	”
1920–1929	0.42	Moderate	± 0.20	”
1955–1964	0.40	Moderate	± 0.19	”

nineteenth century as predicted by Young. Finally, this evidence suggests that there has been a general, structural trend towards *decreasing relative marital class endogamy between fathers of brides and fathers of grooms.* Such results therefore fail to confirm Anderson's picture of the traditional working class but indicate a definite trend towards a greater 'openness' or fluidity between the manual working class and the remainder of the population. However, a note of caution should be inserted, the spread of the confidence intervals also suggests that a theory of no structural change throughout the entire period between 1856 and 1964 would not be inconsistent with the data.[2]

When the results in this chapter are compared with those for the preceding one, the following overall conclusions emerge concerning the external boundedness of the manual working class between 1856 and 1964

Table 12.8. *Marital endogamy of skilled workers: original data and Q values, fathers of brides and fathers of grooms*

	1856–1865		1875–1884		1900–1909		1920–1929		1955–1964	
	x	y								
x	39	44	44	31	53	40	72	43	60	43
y	46	64	38	32	34	38	44	54	48	47
		193		145		165		213		198

1856–1865	1875–1884	1900–1909	1920–1929	1955–1964
$Q = 0.10$	$Q = 0.09$	$Q = 0.19$	$Q = 0.35$	$Q = 0.15$
(± 0.28)	(± 0.33)	(± 0.30)	(± 0.24)	(± 0.27)
not statistically significant	not statistically significant	not statistically significant	Statistically significant at the	not statistically significant
$(p = \geq 0.025)$	$(p = \geq 0.025)$	$(p = \geq 0.025)$	0.025 level	$(p = \geq 0.025)$

Key: x = skilled manual workers
     y = non-skilled manual workers

in Rochdale. In terms of absolute rates both chapters suggest massive amounts of working class endogamy. Such results indicate a distinct separateness of the working class from the remainder of the population in Rochdale. When the focus is directed towards relative marital class endogamy, the picture becomes more complex. Both chapters suggest high levels of relative endogamy throughout the period, but the preceding chapter indicated little trend within these high rates whereas the present chapter suggested a secular decline – although this was by no means the only interpretation possible. Nevertheless, despite these differences in perspective, neither chapter provided support for the conjunctural theories of the traditional working class outlined in chapter 2 based upon the works of Hoggart, Williams, Lockwood and Young. Only Anderson's structural theory of a 'steady-state' to the class structures of industrial capitalist societies receives any empirical confirmation from this material. The major conclusions, therefore, to be drawn from this material on the external boundedness of the manual working class is that such boundedness has been a marked and persistent feature of the social structuration of class in Rochdale between 1856 and 1964, although there is some evidence (by no means unequivocal) to suggest a slight diminution in the strength of manual working class external marital endogamy.

The social structuration of the manual working class around the axis of skill from the perspective of fathers of grooms and fathers of brides

It is evident that, apart from the 1920's, all the results reported in Table 12.8 are statistically non-significant at the 0.025 level. This suggests that there was no significant social structuration of the manual working class around the axis of skill except between 1920 and 1929. Such results bear no relationship to the rhythms hypothesized in the general model of working class sectionalism outlined at the end of chapter 3. Far from the periods 1856–1865 or 1955–1964 being the time of maximum sectionalism around the axis of skill, it would appear that the 1920's witnessed its major impact. Indeed, it is during the inter-war years, which Lockwood, Hoggart and Williams imagine to have been the golden age of working class solidarity, that there is the only evidence in this research for a sectional divide within the manual working class in terms of intermarriage.

If we compare the results in this chapter on the social structuration of class from the perspective of marital endogamy with those from the preceding chapter, it becomes apparent that, overall, *no support is forthcoming for the general model of sectionalism outlined in chapter 3.* Indeed, apart from the one instance reported above (the 1920's from the perspective of fathers of brides and fathers of grooms) there is *no support for the assumption that skill has been a salient factor in the structuration of marital class endogamy in Rochdale between 1856 and 1964.*

13

Skilled manual workers in the British class structure

The internal division within the manual working class around the axis of skill has been a central feature of work and market relations in Rochdale during the period between 1856 and 1964. Evidence from trade union organization in the cotton and engineering industries suggested that the battle for skill has been a persistent feature of class relations over the last hundred years or so. The material presented in chapter 7 on wage differentials between skilled and non-skilled showed that the belief, popularized by Knowles and Robertson and by Turner, that skill differentials within the working class have narrowed in the twentieth century is mistaken, certainly as far as earnings since the mid-1930's are concerned. Furthermore, the trajectory of skilled differentials in these two industries revealed distinct paths over the span covered by this research and, it was argued, only an intimate knowledge of the localized bargaining practices in the two industries themselves could provide an adequate explanation of the causal processes at work. Such results vindicate the strategy of conducting research into such issues in a specific industrial location. Although the research only dealt with two industries in one place, the explanations provided were of a general rather than specific kind. Consequently, it was hypothesized that, in the absence of empirical material to the contrary, the evidence analysed for Rochdale provided a useful first approximation for the wider societal pattern in Britain during the period under discussion.

The manual working class has been sectionally organized in skilled unions throughout the period. These sectional unions have concentrated upon the maintenance of mechanisms of social closure in the sphere of work, particularly upon exclusive rules governing the manning of machinery. These monopolistic strategies cannot be separated empirically from the structure of market relations within the manual working class since they not only serve to reproduce 'skill' but also to maintain economic differentials as well. Differentials, status and skill are all aspects of an overall strategy to maintain the privileged position of craftsmen within the manual workforce. The strong organization of skilled engineering and cotton workers, often pre-dating the widespread automation of factory production in the mid-nineteenth century, has enhanced their position *vis à vis* capitalist employers in Rochdale, who themselves have been in a competitive market for skilled labour. One of the most significant features of this overall strategy of exclusion is that it *actively* divided the manual working class at the point of production. Occupation and skill have been far more central to the everyday activities of manual workers in the industries investigated than class *per se*. The fact that the skilled are generally the best organised, the most combative and the most militant in their relations with capitalist employers should not blind sociologists to the complex, and often contradictory, position of skilled manual workers within the working class as a whole. Clearly the working class is unified in the sense that it shares a propertyless condition and the performance of 'manual' labour, but in another, vitally significant sense the manual working class is divided in the workplace. In terms of the wider class matrix, this means that the manual working class is stratified into skilled and non-skilled components. Despite superficial changes this skilled divide has persisted in Rochdale throughout the period between 1856 and 1964.

The proportion of skilled manual workers within the Rochdale working class has remained more or less constant throughout the period of this research, whereas the working class itself has declined significantly. The distinction between skilled and non-skilled manual workers at work is powerful and reproduced via the mechanisms of closure discussed in chapters 6 and 8. Workshop relations are strongly structured around the skilled divide. Consequently, there is little support provided in this research for Braverman's (1974) contention that the manual working class is becoming or has become de-skilled and consequently an increasingly homogeneous class entity. The content of jobs may have become less skilled, although this research offers no definitive comment on this suggestion, but the thrust of Braverman's argument is that social relations within the manual working class at the point of production have become progressively more homogeneous. This research offers no support for such a view. Nor, for that matter, does it corroborate the opposite theoretical position that suggests that the manual working class has become more fragmented. This viewpoint, exemplified by Roberts *et al.* (1977) and relying heavily on a developmental model underpinned by notions of a historical, homogeneous, 'traditional' working class, is no more plausible. *The skilled divide within the manual working class has been a permanent feature of workshop relations throughout the period of this research.*

This absence of any consideration of skill is the strongest weakness of the various models of the traditional working class outlined in chapter 2. Indeed, it was the attempt by Lockwood, Williams, Hoggart, Anderson and Young to provide a structural model of the working class from a starting-point that emphasized class imagery and class consciousness that represented their common weakness. Any sociological model of the structure of the British manual working class should be premised upon the historical centrality of the skilled:non-skilled divide. Questions about attitudes, imagery and consciousness should follow the erection of a structural model rather than pre-empt it. None of the authors mentioned above have anything to say about the relations between skilled and non-skilled manual workers. Such 'silences' should be seen as symptomatic of a set of class models that should be abandoned by contemporary sociologists.

How adequate is the general model of working class sectionalism outlined at the end of chapter 3 for an understanding of the rhythms of economic structuration of the manual working class around the axis of skill? The evidence presented in chapter 6 on trade union structures and in chapter 7 on wage differentials provided little empirical support for that model. Trade unions have always been structured around the axis of skill and there is no evidence to support the cadences of sectionalization and homogenization embodied in the model. Nor did the data on wage differentials. There was no isomorphic trend in relativities between skilled and semi-skilled or unskilled workers in both industries. Consequently, it makes little sense to talk about *the* trend in skill differentials. Nevertheless, long periods of relative stability in differentials have been apparent *within specific industries*. In cotton, the period between 1886 and 1920 revealed a constant set of ratios between the earnings of minders and piecers. The two shifts in secular trend occurred in the late 1870's and in the 1920's. The main cause of the first, a narrowing of differentials in the late 1870's, was the progressive implementation of the 1876 Oldham piece list. The 1920's saw a widening set of differentials as a direct result of the spinners' attempt to offset the effects of the inter-war depression onto their assistants by reducing their relative earnings. The main factor in the success of this strategy lay in the sub-contracting system operating in the mule-spinning sector. In engineering, similar long periods of stable relativities were evident, with two shifts in the trend. The first occurred during the 1860's and the second in the period of oscillation between 1914 and 1925. A reduction in the skilled differential was evident during this latter period, but little evidence was found to support any theory of a continuing erosion of differentials in engineering, at least as far as earnings were concerned. None of this data on trends in earnings relativities between skilled and non-skilled manual workers corresponds to the general model of sectionalization outlined at the end of chapter 3. Industrialization created a factory-based working class endowed with clear economic differentials which persisted right up to 1914. The differential between skilled and unskilled engineering workers narrowed between 1859 and 1877 when, according to the model, they ought to have widened. In the period between 1877 and 1914, the skilled differential in engineering remained more or less constant when the model suggests that it should have decreased. In cotton spinning, differentials were wider than in engineering as a result of sub-contracted forms of payment. They narrowed somewhat around 1877 but remained approximately constant from the early 1880's until the 1920's. Nor is there any support for the idea that internal economic structuration associated with skill declined in the inter-war years or expanded after 1945. Evidence from the engineering industry showed that, despite a declining differential *rate* between 1914 and 1964, *earnings* differentials between skilled and non-skilled remained approximately proportional between the mid-1920's and the mid-1960's. Data from spinning suggested that differentials expanded in the 1920's and declined in the 1950's. The most important conclusions are that the model of the labour aristocracy in the nineteenth century and of skilled workers in the twentieth century is highly simplistic *and* when tested against empirical data it can be seen to be clearly erroneous.

The data on intermarriage presented in this research permit answers to the following three questions. Firstly, have skilled manual workers become more or less endogamous during the period under review? Secondly, do the patterns of skilled manual marital endogamy correspond to the rhythms of economic structuration revealed in this research? Finally, does the evidence on skilled marital endogamy provide any support for the general model of rhythms in working class sectionalism outlined in chapter 3?

The overwhelming impression from the data on marital endogamy throughout the period under review is that there has been *no significant social bifurcation of the manual working class around the axis of the skill.* When the class relationship embodied in marriage was examined by means of data on brides and grooms, there was no evidence of any statistically significant skilled endogamy within the manual working class at the .025 level. The data on the fathers of the brides and the fathers of the grooms did present some evidence of statistically significant skilled endogamy at the .025 level. Evidence from the period between 1920 and 1929 was significant but the evidence for all the other decennial periods (1856–1865, 1875–1884, 1900–1909 and 1955–1964) was not.

The general impression from this research is that *the clear bifurcation of the manual working class in the economic sphere has not been translated into a parallel or isomorphic set of social boundaries* – at least, as measured by data on intermarriage. The change in the trend of earnings differentials during the period around World War I has not been translated into a similar 'changed point' in the pattern of social boundedness. Furthermore, the data on intermarriage, like the material on the economic structuration of class, offer no support for the general model of rhythms of sectionalism suggested in chapter 3. The most efficient conclusion from all the data reported on skilled marital endogamy in chapters 11 and 12 is that there has probably not been a significant skilled social division within the manual working class throughout the period between 1856 and 1964. Far from there being rhythms of increasing and decreasing skilled endogamy there would appear little evidence of any skilled social divide. Nonetheless, the only evidence of skilled marital endogamy concerned relations between the fathers of the brides and the fathers of the grooms in the period between 1920 and 1929. Such findings run counter to the general imagery of social change suggested by the model in chapter 3 since the 1920's ought to have revealed similar skilled endogamy to the 1900's but less than that in the period betwen 1955 and 1964.

It is clear that the general model of skilled manual workers failed to capture the rhythms of skill discovered in this research. The evidence on economic structuration in chapters 6 and 7 offered no support for it, and neither did the evidence on the social structuration of the manual working class revealed in the last chapters on marital endogamy. It became apparent that the rhythms of the workplace and of market relations were not paralleled by those of marital endogamy. This suggests that the efforts of Foster, Gray and Hobsbawm to connect such spheres *a priori* are theoretically unsound. Such Marxist social history grossly over-simplifies the complex empirical structuration of class relations. Its easy generalizations are empirically mistaken and its explanations should be rejected by contemporary sociologists.

What, then, is needed from future research into the issues discussed in this analysis? There is a clear need to examine the typicality of the evidence by means of further empirical research. Given the localized nature of industrial relations in Britain, studies like the one reported here in Rochdale will be central to such an inquiry. There is also a strong case in favour of reintroducing a more phenomenological element into class analysis. The structural approach advocated in chapter 1 has been pushed to its heuristic limits in this research. In particular, there is a need for more research on the battle for skill in the workshop, particularly the strategies of organized workers and managerial representatives of capital. However, if one way forward would embody an increasing emphasis on the 'meanings' involved, another equally important task would involve a more sophisticated examination of the external structure of economic constraints, particularly the labour market and the product market. Needless to say such research would presuppose access to relevant data.

There is also a need for more data about the significance of marriage within the class structure. Little is known by sociologists about such issues as how and where couples meet who get married, what factors govern acceptance or rejection of 'courtship' or the role of agencies of socialization like the family and the school in the conditioning of such responses. Nevertheless, a return to the conceptual frameworks of class consciousness and class imagery is not being advocated. Both approaches suffer from too many dubious assumptions for this to be warranted. The phenomenological element is suggested as an additional element to 'fill out' structural accounts.

One empirical gap in the analysis presented in this research lies in the absence of any account of the political effects of the patterns of economic and social structuration discussed. Lack of time and data enforced this procedure, although chapters 6 and 8 did present discussions on such issues. It would seem probable that the politics of skill would reveal yet further empirical complexities since if there is no isomorphic relationship between the rhythms of the economic and the social it would seem reasonable to suggest that the political sphere would also reveal a further lack of 'essentialism'. Indeed, the work of Moss (1977) and Stein (1978) in France has demonstrated the autonomous nature of political developments there and the evidence presented in this research supports a general model of class like theirs which encapsulates a series of discrete, empirically variable arenas of structuration.

What, then, of the revolutionary potential of the manual working class that has so preoccupied British sociologists for the last two decades? Three points can be made about this debate. Firstly, there is little evidence to suggest that political changes are either caused or closely paralleled by rhythms within non-political spheres in any simple sense. The determinations and interactions are multiple and complex. Secondly, it is perhaps worth pointing out that *the question of revolutionary potential probably concerns revolutionary politics more than putative changes in the class structure*. Nevertheless, this research has not been about politics *per se*, but about economic and social structuration. Thirdly, skilled manual workers have been separately organized, economically advantaged and permanently concerned with the battle for the continuation of the structural supports of skill which, as has been shown, *actively* divides the manual working class at the point of production. The failure to grasp this central feature of the British manual working class throughout the period since industrialization is a clear weakness both of notions of a 'traditional' working class and of a 'labour aristocracy'. In the former case it is obvious enough but how could the theories of the labour aristocracy have failed as well? The main reason lies in their inadequate grasp of empirical data and their general desire to short-circuit complex empirical relationships by the use of single indicators – either wage rates or putative political changes. Theorists of the labour aristocracy have failed to recognize the structural continuity of the skilled divide within the British manual working class because they have not examined it in sufficient empirical detail. It is a general feature of discussion about class structuration in Britain (with some notable exceptions) that a desire for neat formulae overrides careful empirical scrutiny.

Nevertheless, the separate economic identity of skilled manual workers has not been translated into equivalent social boundaries. The evidence on marital endogamy suggested that their 'manualness' has been of greater significance for the determination of their social class situation than skill. Skilled manual workers do not constitute a part either of the middle class or of the lower middle class: they represent a distinct stratum within the British manual working class. They are part of the working class but *the top part* nonetheless. This would appear to characterize their present structural location.[1] Evidence from the conflicts between management and the National Graphical Association in the printing industry over the introduction of new forms of technology, the Isle of Grain lagging dispute, hostility between sectional unions like the A.U.E.W. (Engineering section) and the E.E.T.P.U. and the general unions all reveal the continued salience of the skilled divide and also the ambivalent position of skilled manual workers within the British manual working class. To paraphrase the words of Terry Duffy, leader of the A.U.E.W., to the T.U.C. Conference of 1980, *skilled workers are the defensive vanguard of the British working class*. This militant defensiveness was most nearly captured by the militant craftsman tradition associated with writers like Hinton and Montgomery. However, this body of literature emphasized the period between 1890 and 1930 as the historical 'moment' of the militant craftsman, thereby ignoring the persistence of the skilled divide in Britain throughout the period since 1850.

The manual working class in Rochdale has been relatively homogeneous socially but actively divided economically, particularly in the sphere of production. Such a contradictory state of affairs does not appear to explain the persistent non-revolutionary politics of the working class in the town. The *a priori* belief in the different rhythms and causal sequences of the political sphere is revealed as more plausible empirically than any theory of strong causal linkages between the political and the non-political. If one wishes to explain the absence of revolutionary attitudes and behaviour in advanced capitalist societies (and of course their residual variations), it is to the political sphere that one should address the questions. The 'failure' of working class revolution is more a failure of revolutionary theories and politics than the result of any secular trend in the historical structuration of the working class.[2]

What is likely to be the future of the skilled divide in an era of depression and potential radical technological innovation? It is not the role of social science to offer predictions, but it is clear that organized skilled workers will continue to contest the implementation of new technologies on terms disadvantageous to themselves. Theirs might appear a hopeless task but the evidence presented in this research should caution against certainty on this issue. New technologies offer opportunities for renewed skilled controls over machinery just as they offer possibilities for de-skilling. Only future research can reveal whether the battle for skill in the 1970's and 1980's will succeed or fail.[3]

Appendix A Notes on the Rochdale churches sampled

a) *All Saints, Hamer*
   Anglican. First registered marriage 24 July 1867. Continuous record.
b) *St Peter's, Newbold*
   Anglican. First registered marriage 1 June 1871. Continuous record.
c) *St Clement's, Spotland*
   Anglican. First registered marriage 9 August 1837. Continuous record.
d) *St Mary's, Balderstone*
   Anglican. First registered marriage 7 August 1872. Continuous record.
e) *St Chad's*
   Anglican. Register begins in 1582. All the other Anglican parishes were created out of this enormous parish, hence the present parish is much reduced in size, if not status. Continuous record. Vicar Hay read the Riot Act at Peterloo.
f) *St Edmund's, Falinge*
   Anglican. First registered marriage 28 May 1873. Continuous record.
g) *St Mary's, Wardleworth*
   Anglican. First registered marriage 19 May 1850. Continuous record.
h) *Jarvis Street*
   Originally Primitive Methodist but in 1932 became Methodist. First registered marriage 1919. Continuous record.
i) *Lowerfold, Thrum Hall*
   Methodist. First registered marriage 1959. Continuous record.
j) *William Street*
   United Methodist Church. First registered marriage 1909. Continuous record until 1964; subsequently transferred to Castlemere Methodist Church, Castlemere Street.
k) *Champness Hall*
   Methodist. Many records lost. Continuous record only for 1955–1964.
l) *Brimrod*
   United Methodist Church. First registered marriage 17 May 1913. Continuous record.
m) *Moorhouse, Milnrow*
   Free Methodist Chapel. An unofficial register from 31 July 1880 in which only a selection of marriages were recorded (according to ministerial notes in the

margin), the criteria for which remain unknown. The unofficial record ended on 25 October 1919. The official register began on 19 December 1931 and was continuous thereafter.

n) *Spotland*

Methodist Church. First registered marriage 8 October 1940. Continuous record.

o) *Trinity*

Wesleyan Chapel. First registered marriage 9 June 1908. Continuous record.

p) *Unitarian Church, Blackwater Street*

Unitarian. First registered marriage 14 November 1907. Continuous record. Also an unofficial nineteenth century record of marriages but this failed to record occupations and was most irregular in composition, only rare entries.

Appendix B Details of the sample from the Rochdale churches

Church	Denomination	Total number of marriages				
		1856–1865	1875–1884	1900–1909	1920–1934	1955–1964
All Saints, Hamer	Anglican	—	122	241	388	213
St Peter's, Newbold	Anglican	—	221	443	586	153
St Clement's	Anglican	409	205	349	399	265
St Mary's, Balderstone	Anglican	—	246	243	489	252
St Chad's	Anglican	2,560	711	383	690	215
St Edmund's	Anglican	—	236	222	297	110
St Mary's, Wardleworth	Anglican	327	239	359	522	114
Jarvis Street	Methodist	—	—	—	37	18
Lowerfold	Methodist	—	—	—	—	14
William Street	Methodist	—	—	—	223	25
Champness Hall	Methodist	—	—	—	—	28
Brimrod	Methodist	—	—	—	68	21
Moorhouse	Methodist	—	—	—	—	44
Spotland	Methodist	—	—	—	—	56
Trinity	Methodist	—	—	50	93	79
Unitarian	Unitarian	—	—	—	150	64
A. Total number of marriages in Rochdale churches used in sample		3,296	2,180	2,490	3,942	1,671
B. Total number of marriages in Rochdale		Incomplete evidence	9,323	10,211	Incomplete evidence	6,493
Proportion A/B		—	0.23	0.24	—	0.26
C. Number in actual Rochdale sample		366	267	324	665	419
Proportion C/A		0.11	0.12	0.13	0.17	0.25

Appendix C Details of the sampling frame of Rochdale churches

Church	Denomination	Type of sample				
		1856–1865	1875–1884	1900–1909	1920–1934	1955–1964
All Saints, Hamer	Anglican	—	C	C	C	C
St Peter's, Newbold	Anglican	—	C	C	C	C
St Clement's	Anglican	C	C	C	C	C
St Mary's, Balderstone	Anglican	—	C	C	C	C
St Chad's	Anglican	1856–1857 = B; 1858–1865 = C	A	C	C	C
St Edmund's	Anglican	C	C	C	C	C
St Mary's, Wardleworth	Anglican	—	C	C	C	C
Jarvis Street	Methodist	—	—	—	D	D
Lowerfold	Methodist	—	—	—	—	F
William Street	Methodist	—	—	—	D	D
Champness Hall	Methodist	—	—	—	—	F
Brimrod	Methodist	—	—	—	E	E
Moorhouse	Methodist	—	—	—	—	E
Spotland	Methodist	—	—	—	—	E
Trinity	Methodist	—	—	E	E	E
Unitarian	Unitarian	—	—	E	E	E

Key to Sample

A = 1/20 Manual + 1/3 Non-manual
B = 1/12 Manual + All Non-manual
C = 1/10 Manual + 1/3 Non-manual
D = 1/5 Manual + 1/3 Non-manual
E = 1/2
F = All

Appendix D Wages in the engineering industry

Table 1. *Average rates of wages for Manchester and neighbourhood in 1859 for the manufacture of machinery*

Occupation	Wage rate per week[1]
Pattern maker	32s
Smith	32s
Brass founder	34s
Joiner in engineering works	28s
Fitter in engineering works	32s
Turner in engineering works	30s
Erector in engineering works	33s
Boiler maker in engineering works	32s
Millwright in engineering works	32s
Moulder in engineering works	34s
	Unweighted average skilled: 31s 11d
Planer	22s
Borer	20s
Screwer	18s
Driller	18s
Slotter	18s
	Unweighted average semi-skilled: 19s 1d
Smiths' strikers	18s
Labourers in engineering works	15s 6d
	Unweighted average unskilled: 16s 9d

Source: *Labour Statistics – Returns of Wages 1830–1886* (H.M.S.O., 1887, c-5172), p. 181.

[1] Hours of labour given as 58 per week.

Table 2. *Average rates of wages paid in Manchester and neighbourhood in 1877 for the manufacture of machinery*

Occupation	Wage rate per week[1]
Pattern makers	31s
Moulders	34s
Blacksmiths	32s 6d
Boiler makers	34s
Turners	31s
Fitters	31s
Engineers and millwrights	32s 6d
Joiners	29s
	Unweighted average skilled: 31s 10½d
Planers, drillers, etc (unskilled men working machines)	24s[2]
	Unweighted average, semi-skilled: 24s
Blacksmiths' strikers	20s
Labourers	18s
	Unweighted average, unskilled: 19s

Source: *Labour Statistics – Returns of Wages 1830–1886*, p. 182.
[1] Hours of labour given as 54 per week.
[2] For piecework.

Table 3. *Average rates of wages of men employed in engineering and machinery works, including iron and brass foundries at 1 October 1886 in South Lancashire (except Manchester)*

Occupation	Number	Average weekly rate of wages[1]	
Pattern makers	128	30s 9d	
Moulders			
a. Time	523	32s 3d	
b. Piece	128	37s 7d	
Brass founders	19	32s 4d	
Turners	454	29s 0d	
Fitters and Erectors	579	29s 5d	
Millwrights	41	29s 5d	
Smiths	172	30s 1d	
Carpenters and joiners	123	28s 10d	
		Unweighted average	
		skilled: 31s 1d	*Weighted:* 30s 7$\frac{1}{2}$d
Planers and shapers	71	24s 10d	
Slotters	32	22s 11d	
Borers	35	26s 10d	
Drillers	205	19s 6d	
Screwers	19	19s 1d	
		Unweighted average	
		semi-skilled: 22s 0$\frac{1}{2}$d	*Weighted:* 21s 6d
Smiths' strikers	200	18s 9d	
Labourers	1,014	17s 6d	
		Unweighted average	
		unskilled: 18s 1$\frac{1}{2}$d	*Weighted:* 17s 8d

Source: 1886 Wage Census ('Accounts and Papers' LXX, H.M.S.O., 1889, c-5807).
[1]Hours of labour given as 54 per week; all rates are time rates unless otherwise indicated.

Table 4. *Average earnings of all male workpeople over 20 years of age employed in engineering, including those who were working full time and those who worked less or more than full time, in certain large Lancashire towns in 1906*

Occupation		Number	Average earnings		
Pattern makers	Time	350	38s 1d		
Joiners	Time	291	34s 7d		
	Piece	214	41s 11d		
Moulders					
a. Iron and steel	Time	1,491	38s 4d		
	Piece	1,242	36s 1d		
b. Brass	Time	60	36s 7d		
Smiths					
a. Textile machinery	Time	113	30s 9d		
	Piece	119	33s 6d		
b. Gen. eng.	Time	136	34s 9d		
Turners (other than brass)					
a. Textile machinery	Time	457	35s 1d		
	Piece	1,045	35s 9d		
b. Gen. eng.	Time	695	36s 7d		
Fitters, erectors, and millwrights					
a. Textile machinery	Time	1,388	35s 4d		
	Piece	1,105	36s 2d		
b. Gen. eng.	Time	1,011	39s 4d		
			Unweighted average for skilled: 36s 2d	*Weighted*: 36s 8d	
Machinemen (planers, borers, etc.)	Time	1,148	25s 8d		
	Piece	2,214	29s 2d		
			Unweighted average for semi-skilled: 27s 5d	*Weighted*: 27s 11½d	
Smiths' strikers	Time	332	22s 4d		
General labourers	Time	4,219	21s 0d		
	Piece	233	24s 4d		
			Unweighted average unskilled: 22s 6½d	*Weighted*: 21s 3d	

Source: *1906 Wage Census* ('Accounts and Papers', LXXXVIII, H.M.S.O., 1911, C-5814). Evidence for Rochdale District.

Table 5. *Average weekly earnings in engineering in Rochdale during July 1914 for men over the age of 21*

Occupation	Time workers		Payment-by-result workers		Combined	
	Number	Earnings	Number	Earnings	Number	Earnings
Fitter	286	36s 5d	49	42s $3\frac{1}{4}$d	335	37s $3\frac{1}{4}$d
Turner	120	34s $5\frac{1}{4}$d	74	40s $4\frac{3}{4}$d	194	36s $8\frac{1}{2}$d
Pattern maker	29	38s 10d	–	–	29	38s 10d
Moulder	141	36s $9\frac{1}{2}$d	46	47s 3d	187	39s $4\frac{1}{4}$d
Skilled weighted average	(*Time*): 36s $2\frac{1}{2}$d		(*Piece*): 42s $9\frac{1}{2}$d		(*Combined*): 37s $8\frac{1}{2}$d	
Labourer	311	22s $8\frac{1}{4}$d	14	26s $1\frac{3}{4}$d	325	22s 10d

Source: *Engineering Employers' Federation Wage Census, July 1914.* I am indebted for the data in this and subsequent tables on earnings in the Engineering industry to Mr Cartwright, Head of Statistics for the Engineering Employers' Federation.

Table 6. *Average weekly earnings in engineering in Rochdale during September 1918 for men over the age of 21*

Occupation	Time workers		Payment-by-result workers		Combined	
	Number	Earnings	Number	Earnings	Number	Earnings
Fitter	164	73s $10\frac{1}{2}$d	104	83s $6\frac{1}{4}$d	268	77s $7\frac{1}{4}$d
Turner	98	73s $5\frac{1}{2}$d	129	75s $7\frac{3}{4}$d	227	74s $8\frac{1}{2}$d
Pattern maker	20	74s $3\frac{1}{2}$d	6	67s 6d	26	72s $8\frac{3}{4}$d
Moulder	135	70s $0\frac{1}{2}$d	29	76s 0d	164	71s 1d
Skilled weighted average	(*Time*): 72s $6\frac{1}{2}$d		(*Piece*): 78s $6\frac{1}{2}$d		(*Combined*): 74s $10\frac{1}{2}$d	
Labourer	315	55s $6\frac{3}{4}$d	57	59s 10d	372	56s $2\frac{3}{4}$d

Source: *Engineering Employers' Federation Wage Census, September 1918.*

Table 7. *Average weekly earnings in engineering in Rochdale during October 1925 for men over the age of 21*

Occupation	Time workers		Payment-by-result workers		Combined	
	Number	Earnings	Number	Earnings	Number	Earnings
Fitter	367	58s 1¾d	135	68s 4½d	502	60s 10½d
Turner	202	55s 5¼d	57	62s 3¾d	259	56s 11¼d
Pattern maker	17	73s 3¾d	22	76s 2½d	39	74s 11¼d
Moulder	103	65s 8d	101	70s 8½d	204	68s 2d
Sheetmetal worker	77	55s 7d	4	81s 3d	81	56s 10¼d
Coppersmith	2	78s 4½d	3	62s 3d	5	68s 8½d
Skilled weighted average	(*Time*):	57s 11d	(*Piece*): 68s 8d		(*Combined*): 61s 6½d	
Labourer	391	42s 7½d	65	46s 0½d	456	43s 1½d

Source: *Engineering Employers' Federation Wage Census, October 1925.*

Table 8. *Average weekly earnings in engineering in Rochdale during October 1930 for men over the age of 21*

Occupation	Time workers		Payment-by-result workers		Combined	
	Number	Earnings	Number	Earnings	Number	Earnings
Fitter	190	57s 3d	149	57s 2d	339	57s 2½d
Turner	82	50s 6½d	63	63s 4¾d	145	56s 1½d
Pattern maker	5	55s 0d	35	70s 1¾d	40	68s 3d
Moulder	68	54s 4¼d	41	61s 5¾d	109	57s 0¼d
Sheetmetal worker	22	55s 0d	13	59s 7¼d	35	56s 8¼d
Skilled weighted average	(*Time*):	55s ½d	(*Piece*): 60s 8d		(*Combined*): 57s 7d	
Labourer	248	38s 1¼d	21	42s 2d	269	38s 5d

Source: *Engineering Employers' Federation Wage Census, October 1930.*

Table 9. *Average weekly earnings in engineering in Rochdale during October 1935 for men over the age of 21*

Occupation	Time workers		Payment-by-result workers		Combined	
	Number	Earnings	Number	Earnings	Number	Earnings
Fitter	215	66s 6d	153	66s $8\frac{3}{4}$d	368	66s $7\frac{1}{2}$d
Turner	100	66s $5\frac{1}{2}$d	57	71s $7\frac{3}{4}$d	157	68s 4d
Pattern maker	5	64s $4\frac{3}{4}$d	34	74s $10\frac{1}{4}$d	39	73s 6d
Moulder	120	63s 8d	59	67s 10d	179	65s 0d
Sheetmetal worker	39	61s 9d	17	69s $8\frac{1}{2}$d	56	64s 2d
Coppersmith	1	62s 0d	6	78s 4d	7	76s $10\frac{1}{4}$d
Skilled weighted average	(*Time*):	65s $4\frac{1}{2}$d	(*Piece*):	69s 0d	(*Combined*):	66s $9\frac{1}{2}$d
Machineman (below fitter's rate)	124	54s $11\frac{1}{2}$d	191	53s $6\frac{3}{4}$d	315	54s $1\frac{1}{4}$d
Labourer	275	45s 10d	19	52s $7\frac{1}{2}$d	294	46s 4d

Source: *Engineering Employers' Federation Wage Census, October 1935.*

Table 10. *Average weekly earnings of engineering workers in Rochdale in 1955*

Occupation	Time workers		Payment-by-result workers		Combined	
	Number	Earnings	Number	Earnings	Number	Earnings
Fitters (other than toolroom)	289	229s 5d	477	238s 10$\frac{1}{4}$d	766	235s 3$\frac{1}{2}$d
Turners and machinemen a. Rated at or above fitter's rate (skilled)	230	228s 7$\frac{1}{4}$d	266	237s 1d	496	233s 1$\frac{3}{4}$d
Toolroom fitters and turners	91	239s 9$\frac{1}{4}$d	18	214s 1$\frac{1}{4}$d	109	235s 6$\frac{1}{2}$d
Pattern makers	48	239s 1$\frac{1}{4}$d	30	259s 6$\frac{3}{4}$d	78	246s 11$\frac{3}{4}$d
Sheetmetal workers	46	238s 1$\frac{3}{4}$d	73	275s 11$\frac{1}{4}$d	119	261s 4d
Moulders (loose pattern)	48	266s 2$\frac{3}{4}$d	71	260s 0d	119	262s 6$\frac{1}{4}$d
Skilled weighted average	(*Time*): 233s 11$\frac{1}{2}$d		(*Piece*): 243s $\frac{1}{2}$d		(*Combined*): 239s 1d	
Turners and machinemen b. Rated below fitter's rate (semi-skilled)	140	193s 7$\frac{1}{2}$d	694	205s 8$\frac{1}{2}$d	834	203s 8d
Labourers	592	170s 11d	130	178s 5d	722	172s 3d

Source: *Engineering Employers' Federation Wage Census, 1955.*

Table 11. *Average weekly earnings of engineering workers in Rochdale in 1964*

Occupation	Time workers		Payment-by-result workers		Combined	
	Number	Earnings	Number	Earnings	Number	Earnings
Fitters	259	370s 1d	142	397s 8d	401	379s 10d
Turners and machinemen a. Who set their machines	173	358s 11d	139	338s 2d	312	349s 8d
Toolroom fitters and turners	42	333s 6d	—	—	—	—
Pattern makers	24	351s 5d	20	331s 6d	44	342s 5d
Sheetmetal workers	32	352s 2d	50	407s 10d	82	386s 1d
Moulders	35	335s 10d	62	381s 3d	97	364s 10d
Skilled maintenance a. Fitters	41	353s 7d	—	—	—	—
b. Electricians	30	364s 8d	1	531s 0d	31	370s 0d
c. Other	27	377s 1d	—	—	—	—
Skilled weighted average	(*Time*): 360s 6d		(*Piece*): 373s 7d		(*Combined*): 367s 1d	
Turners and machinemen b. Who do not set their machines	114	273s 7d	362	317s 1d	476	306s 8d
Labourers	425	258s 7d	123	298s 0d	548	267s 5d

Source: Engineering Employers' Federation Wage Census, 1964.

Appendix E Wages in the cotton industry

Table 1. *Average rates of wages for Manchester and district in 1859 for the production of cotton*

Occupation	Sex	Weekly wage rate
Spinners upon self-acting mules (average)	Men	21s 0d
Piecers upon self-acting mules	Women and young men	10s 0d
Throstle spinners	Women	9s 0d
	Girls	5s 0d
Grinders	Men	15s 0d
Cop reelers	Women	9s 0d
Bobbin winders	Women	9s 0d
Power loom weavers:		
2 looms	Principally women	10s 9d
3 looms	Principally women	15s 6d
4 looms	Principally women	18s 0d

Source: Labour Statistics – Returns of Wages, 1830 – 1886 (H.M.S.O. 1887, C-5172).

Table 2. *Average rates of wages for Manchester and district in 1877 for the production of cotton*

Occupation	Sex	Weekly wage rate
Spinners upon self-acting mules (average)	Men	32s 10d
Piecers upon self-acting mules (average)	Lads and boys	13s 8d
Throstle spinners	Women	17s 6d
Grinders	Men	23s 0d

Table 2 (*Contd.*)

Cop reelers	Women	12s	0d
Bobbin winders	Women	14s	2d
Power loom weavers:			
2 looms	Lads, Boys and Girls	12s	3d
3 looms	Men and Women	18s	6d
4 looms	Men and Women	22s	1d

Source: *Labour Statistics – Returns of Wages, 1830–1886* (H.M.S.O. 1887, C-5172).

Table 3. *Average weekly rate of pay for Rochdale, Heywood and neighbourhood in 1886 for the production of cotton textiles*

Occupation	Form of payment	Number	Sex	Weekly wage rate[1]
Minders of self-acting mules	Piece	194	Men	31s 3d
Big piecers	Time	183	Young men	14s 11d
Little piecers	Time	181	Young men[2]	9s 11d
Throstle spinners	Time	434	Women[3]	12s 2d
Strippers and grinders	Time	133	Men	18s 9d
Cop reelers	Piece	51	Women	11s 4d
Bobbin winder	Time	12	Women	12s 5d
	Piece	123	Women	12s 2d
Loom overlooker	Piece	43	Men	41s 6d
Weavers				
2 looms	Piece	52	Lads and boys	9s 7d
	Piece	14	Women	10s 10d
	Piece	74	Girls	9s 8d
3 looms	Piece	50	Men	14s 7d
	Piece	56	Young men	14s 10d
	Piece	779	Women	14s 9d
4 looms	Piece	257	Men	19s 7d
	Piece	183	Women	19s 0d
6 looms	Piece	31	Men	22s 10d

Source: *Return of Wages in the Principal Textile Trades of the U.K.* (H.M.S.O., 1889, C-5807).
[1] Weekly hours given as $56\frac{1}{2}$ per week.
[2] A few women and girls were returned as piecers at 14s 3d and 9s 0d per week, respectively.
[3] Also 9 girls who averaged 8s 5d per week.

Table 4. *Average weekly earnings in Rochdale district for all workpeople including those working full time and those working less or more than full time during the last pay-week of September 1906 for the production of cotton textiles*

Occupation	Form of payment	Number	Age and sex	Weekly earnings
Spinners (self-acting)				
a. Counts below 40	Piece	439 }	Men of or above 20 years of age	39s 8d
b. Counts above 40	Piece	248 }		42s 10d
			Spinners weighted average	= 40s 10d
Big piecers (1)	Time	519 }	Men of or above 20 years of age	19s 11d
	Piece	63 }		21s 4d
Big piecers (2)	Time	101 }	Lads and boys (under 20 years of age)	17s 3d
	Piece	26 }		18s 2d
			Big piecers weighted average	= 19s 7d
Little piecers	Time	596 }	Lads and boys (under 20 years of age)	13s 0d
	Piece	45 }		12s 4d
			Little piecers weighted average	= 12s 11½d
Ring spinners	Time	1,097 }	Women	15s 10d
	Piece	66 }		16s 4d
			Ring spinners weighted average	= 15s 10d

Grinder or card room jobber	Men	Time	288	28s 3d
Reeler (1)	Women (of and above 18 years of age)	Piece	288	15s 9d
Reeler (2)	Girls (under 18)	Piece	40	10s 8d
Winder (1)	Women (of and above 18)	Time	86 ⎫	14s 3d
		Piece	1,553 ⎭	15s 4d
Winder (2)	Girls (under 18)	Time	55 ⎫	10s 8d
		Piece	262 ⎭	13s 5d
Weavers 2 looms	Men	Piece	48	16s 3d
	Lads and boys (under 18)	Piece	135	10s 7d
	Women	Piece	326	16s 5d
	Girls (under 18)	Piece	486	10s 7d
Weavers 3 looms	Men	Piece	324	20s 8d
	Lads and boys	Piece	196	16s 5d
	Women	Piece	3,289	16s 10d
	Girls	Piece	804	15s 6d
4 looms	Men	Piece	1,578	23s 2d
	Lads and boys	Piece	54	20s 10d
	Women	Piece	3,264	22s 3d
	Girls	Piece	93	19s 0d
6 looms	Men	Piece	159	30s 9d

Source: 1906 Wage Census ('Accounts and Papers', Vol. LXX, H.M.S.O., 1909, C-4545).

Table 5. *Full time earnings by the minder and piecer in the spinning section between 1920 and 1932 for the Rochdale district*

Occupation	1920[1]		1932[1]	
Minder	112s	10d	87s	0d
Big piecer	52s	9d	36s	4d
Little piecer	38s	0d	26s	6d
Ring spinners	40s	2d	30s	10d

Source: J. Jewkes and E.M. Gray, *Wages and Labour in the Cotton Spinning Industry* (Manchester, 1935).

[1] The earnings data are taken by Jewkes and Gray from the Employers' Federation Inquiries into Wages taken in 1920 and 1932. These inquiries can no longer be traced, as a result of the destruction of the Federation's records by air raids during the war. I am indebted for this information to Mr J. Gill, the Industrial Director of the British Textile Employers' Association.

Table 6. *Earnings in the weaving and ancilliary sections of the cotton industry in Lancashire (and Rochdale) in 1937*

Occupation	Employment	Location	Average weekly earnings
Weavers	Including those not fully employed	Rochdale[1]	39s 3d
Automatic looms			
1. Men	Full-time	Lancashire	51s 11d
2. Women	Full-time	Lancashire	40s 1d
Winders[2]	Full-time	Rochdale	29s 5d
Warpers	Full-time	Lancashire	37s 3d
Reelers	Full-time	Lancashire	37s 0d
Sweepers and oilers			
1. Men	Full-time	Lancashire	38s 4d
2. Women	Full-time	Lancashire	29s 9d

Source: E.M. Gray, *The Weaver's Wage* (Manchester, 1937).
[1] 7.2% of the total were not in full-time employment, Gray, *op. cit.*, p. 29.
[2] Gray also gives figures on the earnings of winders for 1920. All the data for 1920, 1932 and 1937 are taken from the Employers' Federation Wage Inquiries which were destroyed in an air raid (cf. Table 5, note 1).

Table 7. *Average weekly earnings in the weaving and ancilliary sections of the cotton industry and the man-made fibre industry*

Occupation	Weekly earnings		
	1950	1958	1962–3
Weavers (average)	113s	169s	212s
Winders (pion; cotton and rayon)	95s	149s	179s
Overlookers			
a. Lancashire looms	190s	288s	342s
b. Automatic looms	204s	314s	370s
Tape sizers	161s	255s	304s
Weftmen and tape labourers	109s	166s	194s
Battery fillers (adult)	88s	139s	165s

Source: Wage Survey undertaken by the U.K. Textile Manufacturers Association in 1962–3. I am indebted to Mr Gill for furnishing me with the data.

Appendix F The terms of settlement of 1898

Final Agreement between the Federated Engineering and Shipbuilding Employers and the Amalgamated Society of Engineers, the United Society of Smiths and Hammermen, the London and Provincial Society of Coppersmiths, the London United Society of Drillers, the London United Society of Brass Finishers, the London and Provincial Society of Hammermen, the Amalgamated Society of Toolmakers, Scientific Instrument Makers, and the Marine and General Engineers' Society.

Dated 28 January 1898

General Principle of Freedom to Employers in the Management of Their Works

The Federated Employers, while disavowing any intention of interfering with the proper functions of Trade Unions, will admit no interference with the management of their business, and reserve to themselves the right to introduce into any federated workshop at the option of the employer concerned, any condition of labour, under which any members of the Trade Unions here represented were working at the commencement of the dispute in any of the workshops of the Federated Employers; but, in the event of any Trade Union desiring to raise any question arising therefrom, a meeting can be arranged by application to the Secretary of the Employers' Local Association to discuss the matter.

Nothing in the foregoing shall be construed as applying to the normal hours of work, or to general rises and falls of wages, or to rates of remuneration.

NOTE – No new condition of labour is introduced or covered by this clause. It simply provides for equality of treatment between the Unions and the Federation by reserving for all the members of all the Trade Unions, as well as for all the Federated Employers, the same liberty which many Trade Unionists and many employers have always had.

Special provision is made in the clause and in the subsequent 'Provisions for avoiding future Disputes' to secure workmen or their representatives, the right of bringing forward for discussion any grievance or supposed grievance.

1. Freedom of Employment
Every workman shall be free to belong to a Trade Union or not as he may think fit.

Every employer shall be free to employ any man, whether he belongs to a Trade Union or not.

Every workman who elects to work in a Federated Workshop shall work peaceably and harmoniously with all fellow employees, whether he or they belong to a Trade Union or not. He shall also be free to leave such employment, but no collective action shall be taken until the matter has been dealt with under the provisions for avoiding disputes.

The Federation do not advise their members to object to Union workmen or give preference to non-union workmen.

NOTE – The right of a man to join a Trade Union if he pleases involves the right of a man to abstain from joining a Trade Union if he pleases. This clause merely protects both rights. The Federation sincerely hope that a better understanding will prevent any question of preference arising in the future, and advise the members not to object to union workmen.

2. Piecework

The right to work piecework at present exercised by the Federated Employers shall be extended to all members of the Federation and to all their Union workmen.

The prices to be paid for piecework shall be fixed by mutual arrangement between the employer and the workman or workmen who perform the work.

The Federation will not countenance any piecework conditions which will not allow a workman of average efficiency to earn at least the wage at which he is rated.*

The Federation recommend that all wages and balances shall be paid through the office.

NOTE – These are just the conditions that have been for long in force in various shops. Individual workmen are much benefited by piecework.

A mutual arrangement as to piecework rates between employer and workman in no way interferes with the functions of the Unions in arranging with their own members the rates and conditions under which they shall work.

3. Overtime

When overtime is necessary the Federated Employers recommend the following as a basis and guide:

That no man shall be required to work more than 40 hours over time in any four weeks after full shop hours have been worked, allowance being made for time lost through sickness or absence without leave.

In the following cases overtime is not to be restricted: viz.

Breakdowns in plant.

General repairs, including ships.

---

* In reply to an inquiry as to the interpretation of this paragraph the employers' secretaries on 21 January 1898 wrote to the General Secretary of the A.S.E. stating that the general note (appended to the explanations) which disclaims any intention of reducing the wages of skilled men 'applies both to time wages, and to piecework earnings – in the latter case there is no intention of interfering with the usual practice of making extra payment for extra effort'.

Repairs or replace work, whether for the employers or their customers.
Trial Trips.

It is mutually agreed that in cases of urgency and emergency restriction shall not apply.

This basis to apply only to members of the Trade Unions who are represented at this Conference.

All other existing restrictions as regards overtime are to be removed.

It is understood that if mutually satisfactory to the Local Association of Employers and the workmen concerned, existing practices regarding overtime may be continued.

NOTE – The overtime conditions are precisely the conditions now in operation in various places, though in many Federated workshops no limitation whatever exists at the present time. In many cases this will be the first attempt to regulate or prevent excess of overtime.

4. Rating of Workmen

Employers shall be free to employ workmen at rates of wages mutually satisfactory. They do not object to the Unions or any other body of workmen in their collective capacity arranging among themselves rates of wages at which they will accept work, but while admitting this position they decline to enforce a rule of any Society or an agreement between any Society and its members.

The Unions will not interfere in any way with the wages of workmen outside their own Unions.

General alterations in the rates of wages in any district or districts will be negotiated between the Employers' Local Association and the local representatives of the Trade Unions or other bodies of workmen concerned.

NOTE – Collective bargaining between the Unions and the Employers' Associations is here made the subject of distinct agreement.

The other clauses simply mean that as regards the wages to be paid there shall be (1) Freedom to the Employer; (2) Freedom to the Union workmen both individually and in their collective capacity – that is to say collective bargaining in its true sense is fully preserved; and (3) Freedom to non-unionists.

These conditions are precisely those in operation at present on the North-East Coast, the Clyde, and elsewhere, where for years past alterations in wages have been amicably arranged at joint meetings of employers and representatives of the Trade Unions.

5. Apprentices

There shall be no limitation on the number of apprentices.

NOTE – This merely puts on record the existing practice and is to prevent a repetition of misunderstandings which have arisen in some cases.

6. Selection, Training and Employment of Operatives

Employers are responsible for the work turned out by their machine tools and shall have full discretion to appoint the men they consider suitable to work them, and determine the conditions under which such machine tools shall be worked. The employers consider it their duty to encourage ability wherever they find it, and shall have the right to select, train and employ those whom they consider best adapted to the various operations carried on in their workshops, and will pay them according to their ability as workmen.

NOTE – There is no desire on the part of the Federation to create a specially favoured class of workmen.

Provisions for Avoiding Disputes

With a view to avoid disputes in future, deputations of workmen will be received by their employers, by appointment, for mutual discussion of questions, in the settlement of which both parties are directly concerned. In case of disagreement the local Associations of Employers will negotiate with the local officials of the Trade Unions.

In the event of any Trade Union desiring to raise any question with an Employers' Association, a meeting can be arranged by application to the Secretary of the Employers' Local Association to discuss the question.

Failing settlement by the Local Association and the Trade Union of any question brought before them, the matter shall be forthwith referred to the Executive Board of the Federation and the central authority of the Trade Union; and pending the question being dealt with, there shall be no stoppage of work, either of a partial or a general character, but work shall proceed meantime under the current conditions.

NOTE – A grievance may be brought forward for discussion either by the workman individually concerned, or by him and his fellow workmen, or by the representatives of the Union.

In no instance do the Federated Employers propose conditions which are not at present being worked under by large numbers of the Allied Trade Unions.

The Federated Employers do not want to introduce any new or untried conditions of work, and they have no intention of reducing the rates of wages of skilled men.

These conditions, with relative notes, are to be read and construed together.

It is agreed that there shall be a resumption of work simultaneously in all the workshops of Federated Employers on Monday morning, 31 January 1898.

Parties mutually agree that the foregoing shall be the terms of the settlement.

Source: A.I. Marsh, *Industrial Relations in Engineering* (Oxford, 1965).

Notes

1. Orientations to the analysis of class in Britain

1 For a good example of selection of sources see J. Westergaard and H. Resler, *Class in a Capitalist Society* (1975) especially Part I.
2 Marx's teleological analysis will be examined critically in chapter 4.
3 For example, L. Althusser, *For Marx* (1969, pp. 97–8) and N. Poulantzas, *Classes in Contemporary Capitalism* (1975, p. 42) and *The Crisis of the Dictatorships* (1976, p. 12). For an extended critique of French structuralist Marxism in this context see R.D. Penn, Ph.D. dissertation, 'Skilled Manual Workers in the British Class Structure 1856–1964' (1981, chapter 1).
4 K. Marx, *The Poverty of Philosophy* (1936): 'This mass [the proletariat] is already a class in opposition to capital, but not yet a class for itself' (p. 195).
5 K. Marx and F. Engels, *The German Ideology* (1963): 'The separate individuals form a class in so far as they carry on a common battle against another class; otherwise they are on hostile terms with each other' (p. 48).
6 Marx's famous discussion of the French peasantry.
7 The notion of 'false consciousness' was introduced into Marxism by Engels. Since its inception, it has become a dominant mode of explanation in Marxist accounts.
8 The tendency in Marx's work of the rate of profit to fall is subject to critical scrutiny in chapter 4.
9 Hence the present ultra-leftist attack on the media as the fount of all evils.
10 See R.D. Penn, 'Revolution in Industrial Societies', *Sociology*, 12, 2, 1978.
11 The term 'Marxisant' is taken from J.H. Goldthorpe, 'Class, Status and Party in Modern Britain: some recent interpretations, Marxist and Marxisant', *European Journal of Sociology*, 1972; and refers to social analyses strongly influenced by Marxist assumptions.
12 For example, C. Kerr, J.T. Dunlop, F.H. Harbison and C.A. Myers, *Industrialism and Industrial Man* (1973).
13 Most of these are reproduced in D.J. Treiman, *Occupational Prestige in Comparative Perspective* (1977).
14 Examples of this tradition are Doeringer and Piore (1971), Barron and Norris (1976) and Blackburn and Mann (1979).

15 Apart from Braverman (1974), also of major importance are Friedman (1977a and 1977b), The Brighton Labour Process Group (1977), Cressey and MacInnes (1980) and S. Wood (ed.) (1982).

16 For a critique of Edwards see R.D. Penn, '"The Contested Terrain": a critique of R.C. Edwards' theory of working class fractions and politics' in G. Day (ed.), *Diversity and Decomposition in the Labour Market* (1982). An evaluation of Gordon *et al.* (1982) can be found in P. Nolan and P.K. Edwards, 'Homogenise, Divide and Rule: An Essay on Segmented Work, Divided Workers' (mimeo, 1982, S.S.R.C. Industrial Relations Unit, Warwick University).

17 For reasons given in chapter 9.

2. The traditional working class

1 Many of these are catalogued in J. Klein, *Samples from English Cultures* (Volume 1, 1965).

2 e.g. N. Abercrombie and J. Urry, *Capital, Labour and the Middle Classes* (1983).

3. The labour aristocracy

1 The significance test reported in Foster (1974, Appendix 2, pp. 264–6) is littered with typographical errors. I should like to thank Dr R. Blackburn of the Cambridge University Department of Applied Economics and Mr D.C. Dawkins of the Department of Mathematics, City University for their assistance in sorting out these errors.

2 It is not intended to imply that significance levels of 0.2 are inherently stupid or that levels of 0.05 are automatically correct. Many social scientists have canonized the 0.05 level, but in reality it is only a convention and one strongly influenced by the opinion of R.A. Fisher, the great statistician, 'that the writer prefers to set a low standard of significance at the 5% point and ignore entirely all results which fail to reach that level. A scientific fact should be regarded as experimentally established only if a properly designed experiment rarely fails to give this level of significance' (R.A. Fisher, 'The Arrangement of Field Experiments', *Journal of the Ministry of Agriculture of Great Britain*, 33, 1926, p. 504). The objection is not to the breaking of conventions in social science but to the sleight of hand involved in Foster's unconventionality and to his misunderstanding of the real meaning of significance tests.

3 I am indebted to Mr Geoffrey Hawthorn, Professor John Barnes, Dr R. Blackburn, all of Cambridge University, for assistance with understanding this difficult area and, in particular, to the time spent with me by Mr David Dawkins of City University verifying my critical comments in this section.

4 cf. Y. Bishop, S. Fienberg and P.W. Polland, *Discrete Multivariate Analysis* (1975), pp. 97–101.

5 As can be seen, Foster's dichotomy is reminiscent of the kinds of arguments discussed in the preceding chapter on the 'Traditional Working Class'.

6 A. Gorz, *Socialism and Revolution* (1975), chapter 6, 'Colonialism at Home and Abroad', defines the entire Western working class as a labour aristocracy

confronting the exploited peripheral third world. M. Gronan, 'Die Angestellte technische Intelligenz – eine Lohnarbeiterschichte', *Marxismus Digest*, 1, 1971, argues that the administrative and clerical employees plus the lower strata of the intelligentsia constitute a 'new labour aristocracy', (p. 128). This latter conception has been rejected by T. Toivonen in 'Aristocracy of Labour: Some Old and New Problems', *Acta Sociologica*, 21, 3, 1978.

4. Theoretical orientations to skill

1 Another conference on these themes held in Manchester in March 1983, with the title 'Organization and Control of the Labour Process', attracted nearly 200 participants.
2 cf. H. Scullion, 'The Skilled Revolt against General Unionism: The Case of the B.L. Toolroom Committee', *Industrial Relations Journal*, XII, 3, 1981.
3 P. Cressey and J. MacInnes, 'Voting for Ford: Industrial Democracy and the Control of Labour', *Capital and Class*, 11, Summer 1980 provides an interesting Marxist analysis of the dual processes of 'skilling' and 'de-skilling' in the capitalist mode of production.
4 cf. A. Stewart, K. Prandy and R.M. Blackburn, *Social Stratification and Occupations* (1980).
5 e.g. *The Guardian*, 20 September 1979, 'Skilled Labour Gap Blamed on Pay Level' and *BBC 1*, 'The Risk Business: A Job for Life?', 14 March 1979.
6 cf. C. Cockburn, *Brothers: Male Dominance and Technological Change* (1983), J. Child, *Industrial Relations in the British Printing Industry* (1967), and K. Sisson, *Industrial Relations in Fleet Street* (1975). Apprenticeships in printing are now four years: having declined from seven to five to four over the last century. However, today full craft status is only attained after the passing of formal tests. I would like to thank Mr G.D. Lawday, Head of Research for the National Graphical Association, for information on these points.
7 There is no adequate analysis of the modern building industry on a par with R. Postgate's classic *The Builder's History* (1923). Nevertheless, apprenticeships in the building industry were reduced from five years to four on 6 April, 1965, and from four years to three on 2 September 1974, with the exception of those crafts like plumbing, electrical and mechanical engineering which are governed by the Joint Industrial Board (J.I.B.). However, it is also possible to attain full craft status and pay by means of a course at a Government Training Centre. After a 26 week course, the trainee will be eligible for craft work at a rate of pay equivalent to 85% of the full craft rate. This increases by 5% every six months until the full rate is achieved after two years. I would like to thank the National Joint Council for the Building Industry and Mr Alex Hay of Lancaster University for assistance with these points.
8 cf. J. McColdrick, 'The Inter-War Crisis in Clydeside Shipbuilding: Technical Change and the Negotiation of the Labour Process' (mimeo, Department of Sociology, Glasgow University, April 1981).
9 A six month training diploma from a G.T.C. provides the trainee with a basic training in a 'skilled' craft. In the construction industry, an agreement between

the Confederation of British Industry and the building unions permits the trainee to be employed on the same jobs as apprentice-served men and to be classified as 'skilled'. However, the trainee receives less than the full craft rate for the job, which is only attained after 78 weeks. In other words, a G.T.C. trainee only achieves the full craft rate after 2 years (78 + 26 weeks). In the case of engineering trades, the situation is different. Trainees leave the Centres as 'semi-skilled' and depending upon the structure of local labour markets, they may be engaged as semi-skilled 'dilutees' for the performance of 'skilled' jobs at the full craft rate. I would like to thank Mr Royle, Manpower Services, Preston, for help on the question of G.T.C.s and skill. See chapter 8 for a thorough discussion of the points made in this note.

10 Marx held that the product (w) was expressed in value terms as:

$$c + v + s = w$$

where c = constant capital
v = variable capital
s = surplus

From this relationship, Marx derived three ratios:

i) rate of exploitation $(s') = \dfrac{s}{v}$

ii) organic composition of capital $(q) = \dfrac{c \rightarrow}{c + v}$

iii) rate of profit $(p) = \dfrac{s \rightarrow}{c + v}$

Marx based his conception of the falling rate of profit upon two assumptions. Firstly, the rate of exploitation tended to remain constant and, secondly, the organic composition of capital tended to rise as a result of progressive mechanization. Sweezy, in *The Theory of Capitalist Development* (1942, p. 68), has demonstrated the internal links between these three concepts such that:

$$p = (s')(1 - q)$$

It is evident that if (s') remains constant then p is inversely related to q. In other words, as q rises towards unity, (which presupposes that v is increasingly less as a proportion of c) then p falls towards zero. However, if v is increasingly less of a proportion of c, this means that workers are expending proportionately less labour in producing the same commodity (w). In other words, labour productivity is increasing; but this violates the assumption of subsistence wages. In fact, as Sweezy states: 'a rising organic composition of capital goes hand in hand with increasing labour productivity. If the rate of surplus value remains constant, this means that a rise in real wages takes place which is exactly proportional to the increase in labor productivity' (Sweezy, p. 100).

11 cf. G. Hodgson, 'The Theory of the Falling Rate of Profit', *New Left Review*, 84, March–April 1974.

12 This has been pointed out by a series of critics, notably Maarten de Kadt in *Review of Radical Political Economics*, 7, 1, 1975, and by Paul Goldman in *Insurgent Sociologist*, VI, 1, Fall 1975. For a detailed examination of the impact of Braverman's work see the collected papers from the 1978 Windsor

Conference on 'De-Skilling' edited by Stephen Wood in *The Degradation of Work* (1982).

13 This is very much the result of Braverman's self-imposed project which was to examine technological developments in the labour process based upon his conviction that P. Baran and P. Sweezy had already completed the political economy of advanced capitalism in their *Monopoly Capital* (1966). Braverman makes this explicit on p. 53, second footnote, of *Labor and Monopoly Capital* (1974).

14 Neo-Ricardian economics refers to economics strongly influenced by P. Sraffa. Sraffa's early critique of Marshallian micro-economic assumptions in 'The Laws of Return under Competitive Conditions', *Economic Journal*, XXXVI, December 1926, was followed by his major theoretical contribution, *Production of Commodities by Means of Commodities* (1960). Neo-Ricardian theories have been presented to a wider social scientific audience through the medium of the *Bulletin of the Conference of Socialist Economists* and by the works of I. Steedman and A. Glyn and R. Sutcliffe. Steedman's main work is *Marx after Sraffa* (1977) and Glyn and Sutcliffe's is *British Capitalism, Workers and the Profits Squeeze* (1972). Post-Keynesian economics refers to a corpus of works connected with Joan Robinson, Nicholas Kaldor, Michal Kalecki and Roy Harrod. Valuable introductions to this school are Alfred S. Eichner, *A Guide to Post-Keynesian Economics* (1979) and J.A. Kregel, *The Reconstruction of Political Economy: An Introduction to Post-Keynesian Economics* (1973).

15 Max Weber, *Economy and Society* (1968). Of particular interest is Weber's contention that class structuration may or may not produce class action depending upon empirical circumstances.

16 The model outlined assumes a competitive labour market. Chapter 5 will discuss the validity of such an assumption in Rochdale during the period under review and chapter 8 will assess the evidence in relation to the model.

17 Formal organization is a function of an array of complex political and legal factors. Informal organization can never be eradicated but it can be hindered by the overall politico-judicial climate.

18 Clearly, forms of labour organization are crucial to an understanding of different kinds of capital/labour relationships. Chapter 8 will discuss these issues in greater detail.

19 cf. H.A. Turner, G. Clack and G. Roberts, *Labour Relations in the Motor Industry* (1967).

5. Aspects of the social structure of Rochdale, 1856–1964

1 See Table 5.1.

2 I have relied on a large number of works for this brief history of the Rochdale industrial structure and they are listed in full in the bibliography, under the sub-section 'Local Sources'. However, the most important works incorporated in this part of the research are: *Rochdale Official Handbook* (1954); David M. Smith, *The North West* (1969); R. Robson, *The Cotton Industry in Britain*

(1957); T.W. Freeman, H.B. Rodgers and R.H. Kinvig, *Lancashire, Cheshire and the Isle of Man* (1966).

3 The Census definitions change over time: the categories used for the generation of Table 5.1 are listed here:

a) *1861 Census*: (Rochdale district), for Men and Women aged 20 and above:

Research categories	*Census categories*
Engineering	= Iron manufacture, whitesmith, blacksmith and nail manufacture
Cotton	= Cotton manufacture
Wool	= Wool manufacture

Clearly, the engineering section is under-represented given the absence of machine making; and the numbers in textiles are under-represented by the exclusion of non-adults.

b) *1871 Census*: no data given for Rochdale (it was not included among the 'Principal Towns' of Lancashire).

c) *1881 Census*: (Rochdale Urban Sanitary District), for Males and Females. Ages not given.

Engineering	= Machine makers and tool makers (Class V, Section 10)
Cotton	= Cotton (Class V)
Wool	= Wool (Section 17)

d) *1891 Census*: (Rochdale Urban Sanitary District) for Males and Females 10 years and above.

Engineering	= Machine makers and tool makers (Class 5, sub-sections (i) and (ii))
Cotton	= Cotton
Wool	= Wool

e) *1901 Census*: (Rochdale C.B.) for Males and Females 10 years and above.

Engineering	= Engineering and machine making
Cotton	= Cotton manufacture

f) *1911 Census*: (Rochdale C.B.) for Males and Females aged 10 years and upwards.

Engineering	= Metals, machines, implements and conveyances (Category X)
Cotton	= Textile fabrics (Category XVIII)

g) *1921 and 1931 Censuses*: (Rochdale C.B.) for Males and Females aged 12 years and over in 1921 and 14 years and over in 1931.

Engineering	= Metal workers (Category VII)
Cotton	= Textile workers (Category XII)

h) *1951 Census*: (Rochdale C.B.) for Males and Females aged 15 years and over.

Engineering	= Workers in Metal manufacture and engineering (Category VI)
Cotton	= Textile workers (Category VII)

i) *1961 Census*: (Rochdale C.B.) for Males and Females aged 15 years and over. 10% sample results.

Engineering   = Furnace, forge, foundry and rolling mill workers (040–045)
                                   Engineering and allied trades (060–078)

Cotton   = Textile workers (100–108)

From all these variations in definitions and categories, no great reliance should be placed on the changes in absolute numbers given in the table. However, despite the definitional changes, the overall trends are unmistakable and corroborate the argument of the text.

4 R. Robson, 1957, p. 4, provides the following figures on the Japanese and British industries:

World trade in cotton textiles

	1910–3 Million yds	1926–8 Million sq. yds	1936–8 000 quintals
U.K.	6,650	3,940	1,720
Japan	200	1,390	2,510

5 Robson, 1957, p. 10, provides the following figures for India and the U.K.
Trade in cotton piece goods

Average	1909–13 Million linear yds	1929 Million linear yds	1938 Million linear yds
Indian production	1,141	2,358	4,250
U.K. Exports to India	2,669	1,276	258

6 Robson, 1957, p. 338, gives the following dividends as a percentage of equity: 1914 = 6%, 1917 = 7.5%, 1920 = 40.21%, 1923 = 2.27%, 1933 = 1.5%.

Also see A. Hutt, *The Condition of the Working Class in Britain* (1933), and G.W. Daniels and J. Jewkes, 'The Post-War Depression in the Lancashire Cotton Industry', *Journal of the Royal Statistical Society*, Vol. XCL, 1928.

7 The newspapers consulted were: *Rochdale Observer*; *Rochdale Standard*; *Rochdale Pilot*; *Rochdale Labour News*; *Cotton Factory Times*.

8 Of particular use were the Official Handbooks produced by the Town Hall in Rochdale which contained short histories of major firms and also advertisements.

9 The strong Anglican tradition in Rochdale is documented by H. Fishwick, *A History of the Parish of Rochdale* (1889) and also discussed in passing by Rev.

C.E. Warrington, *The History of a Parish* (1968) and Rev. D.A. Tipper, *De Balderston: 1573–1973* (1973).

10 A wedding must be registered to be lawful. It can be registered by the civil registrar or by a clergyman at an officially registered church. In certain circumstances, a marriage can be solemnized in a church not officially registered for marriages and upon these occasions the civil registrar will perform the 'official' part of the marriage. In all marriages there will be at least two copies of the marriage certificate: one for the local, and one for the national, civil registrar. However, in a registered church a third copy will be made and kept on the premises. It was this last set of records, held by the churches in Rochdale, which provided marriage records from which the sample was drawn.

11 Information derived from *Facts and Figures about the Church of England: Prepared by the Statistical Unit of the Central Board of Finance*, ed. R.F. Neuss (1962).

12 Rochdale was relatively well endowed with sittings in churches as a percentage of the population in 1851. Rochdale had 46.4% sittings whereas Oldham had 32.1%, Bolton 35.6% and Manchester 31.6%. These figures are taken from the 1851 Religious Census. The precise reference is as follows: *Accounts and Papers, Vol. LXXXIX Population (Great Britain): Religious Worship (England and Wales)* (1852–3), and the table quoted is 'Table 4: Religious Accommodation in Large Towns', p. CXXIX.

13 Data taken from Neuss (ed.), *op. cit.*

14 Initially the period 1920–1934 was sampled but this was reduced subsequently to 1920–1929.

15 See Appendix B.

16 See Appendix C.

17 See Appendix C.

18 cf. Appendix B: row B: The Annual Reports of the Registrar General provided the data on the total number of marriages in Rochdale. Unfortunately, the series is incomplete. No total is given for the following years: 1857, 1860, 1861, 1931, 1932, 1933 and 1934. No reasons are given for these gaps.

19 cf. Appendix B: row C.

6. The trade union structure in the Rochdale cotton and engineering industries

1 These secondary materials will be catalogued in the footnotes to the appropriate sections of this chapter.

2 Trade unions directly consulted were:
General Union of Associations of Loom Overlookers
Amalgamated Weavers Association
Amalgamated Union of Engineering Workers
Amalgamated Association of Operative Cotton Spinners

3 *Date of the foundation of the cotton amalgamations*

	Foundation
a) *Spinning section*	
Amalgamated Association of Operative Spinners and Twiners	1870
National Association of Card, Blowing and Ring Room Operatives	1886

b) *Weaving section*

Amalgamated Association of Beamers, Twisters and Drawers	1890
Amalgamated Weavers Association	1884
General Union of Associations of Loom Overlookers	1885
Lancashire Amalgamated Tape Sizers' Association	1880

4 Evidence given by R. Smith, 'History of the Lancashire Cotton Industry, Between the Years 1873 and 1896', Ph.D. thesis, 1954, p. 322, states that the 'Spinners Amalgamation demanded the highest per capita contribution'. He gives the following figures on page 347: 1869 average basic contribution = 26s. per annum, 1896 average = £4 per annum.

5 The Oldham List (1876) was a document that governed the payment of piece rates to minders and also specified piecers' wages. It incorporated a basic notional weekly wage and a series of additional payments per piece of cloth: cf. S.J. Chapman, 'The Regulation of Wages by Lists in the Spinning Industry', *Economic Journal*, IX, 1899.

6 The 'Brooklands' Agreement was an agreement between the Spinners and the mill owners made in 1893 at the Brooklands Hotel. It settled a massive lock-out in the spinning section over a proposed wage reduction and agreed that general wage rates could only be varied at yearly intervals and that any change could not be more than 5% in either direction. It also provided new conciliation procedures. For an assessment of the Agreement, see J.H. Porter, 'Industrial Peace in the Cotton Trade, 1875–1913', *Yorkshire Bulletin of Economic and Social Research*, 19, 1, 1967; and J. White, *The Limits of Trade Union Militancy: The Lancashire Textile Workers, 1910–1914* (1978).

7 For example by C. Bücher, *Industrial Evolution*, ed. S.M. Wickett (1901).

8 I am obliged to Mr Joseph Richardson, General Secretary of The Amalgamated Association of Operative Cotton Spinners and Twiners for assistance on these points.

9 I have relied extensively, as can be seen, on H.A. Turner, *Trade Union Growth, Structure and Policy* (1962), for much of my information on the cardroom. It has proved difficult to enlarge upon his account and there is considerable need for more monographs on subjects like the Cardroom Association.

10 cf. Turner (1962, p. 145).

11 Turner (1962, p. 165) describes this apprenticeship as follows: 'The method varies a little between districts, but its essence is that a would-be recruit must be accepted into the union and work for some time before a specified age (in Bolton, twelve months before seventeen) as a "can-tenter" – a boy assistant. If he completes that period, he will be put on a district rota for vacancies as "junior" or "apprentice grinder", and can meanwhile work at any other job. When a vacancy turns up (which may, even now, take quite a few years) he does two years "learning" at a little below the full rate.'

12 Again, we must rely on Turner's (1962, p. 164) tantalizingly brief description: 'But following the successful initiation of the Cardroom Amalgamation, the

strippers-and-grinders set about a determined attempt to elevate themselves. One of the Amalgamation's first acts was to press for (and secure) a preferential wage-increase on their behalf; its Second Annual Report noted that ".... their status and position as skilled artisans has during the year made gigantic strides towards the ideal that increasing numbers think it should be". And to that aim both the unions and the operatives concerned worked persistently. The two then separate occupations of stripper and grinder were gradually merged from the 1880's on. Their members exploited every minor technical change in carding to increase their responsibility: while according to the Amalgamation's present General Secretary, strippers-and-grinders in his own original district had taken in the 1920's, to setting their own machines despite managerial prohibition.'

13 Unknown author, *A History of the Rochdale Weavers* (no date).
14 Evidence on these practices taken from Hopwood (1969).
15 Evidence for the Overlookers comes mainly from Mr Harold Brown, General Secretary of the United Association of Powerloom Overlookers, in Rochdale.
16 Evidence for the Tapesizers taken from Turner (1962, p. 257 and p. 274).
17 For example, A.I. Marsh, E.O. Evans and P. Garcia, *Workplace Industrial Relations in Engineering* (1971) estimate that the A.E.U. contained 41% of manual worker trade unionists in 432 establishments investigated by them. The T.G.W.U. (Transport and General Workers Union) had 13.6%, the G.M.W.U. (General and Municipal Workers Union) 8.8%, the E.T.U. (Electrical Trade Union) 4.3%, the National Society of Metal Mechanics 2.1%, the Boilermakers, Shipwrights and Blacksmiths 1.5% and the N.U.V.B. (National Union of Vehicle Builders) 1.2%. There were also twenty unions with membership between 0.99% and 0.01%, and ten unions with less than 0.01% (Table 15, pp. 93–4).
18 The major primary source for the 1852 Lock-out is T. Hughes, 'An Account of the Lock-out of Engineers in 1851–2' in *Trades' Societies and Strikes* (1860). I have also relied upon a series of secondary sources on the dispute; of major use were: J. Jefferys (1945) and E. Wigham, *The Power to Manage: A History of the Engineering Employers' Federation* (1973). Also of relevance are H. Pelling, *A History of British Trade Unionism* (1963); K. Burgess, 'Technological Change and the 1852 Lock-out in the British Engineering Industry', *International Review of Social History*, XIV, 1969; P.J. Murphy, 'The Origins of the 1852 Lock-out in the British Engineering Industry Re-considered', *International Review of Social History*, XXIII, 1978 and K. Burgess, *The Origins of British Industrial Relations* (1975).
19 The 1871 strike has been described by J. Burnett, *A History of the Engineers' Strike in Newcastle and Gateshead* (1872). It has also been re-analysed by E. Allan, J.F. Clarke, N. McCord and D.J. Rowe, *The North-East Engineers' Strikes of 1871: The Nine Hours' League* (1971).
20 Information taken from E. Wigham (1973, p. 12).
21 An account of the Sunderland dispute is provided by J. Jefferys (1945, pp. 102–3) and E. Wigham (1973, p. 18).

22 The membership of the A.S.E. in 1891 was 71,221 (Jefferys, 1945, p. 93) and the Census of the same year gave the number employed in engineering and shipbuilding as just over a million (Jefferys, p. 118).

23 Machinery exports rose from £15.2 million in 1892 to £37.0 million in 1913; source, Jefferys (1945, p. 118).

24 Employment in engineering, shipbuilding and kindred trades rose from 1,094,000 in 1891 to 1,447,000 in 1901, to 1,773,000 in 1911; source, Jefferys (1945, p. 118).

25 The first industrial revolution involved the application of steam-power to machinery: its central industries were textiles, iron and railways. The 'second' industrial revolution involved the application of electricity to machinery: its central industries were steel, electrical engineering, and chemicals. For a more extended analysis see either E. Mandel, *Late Capitalism* (1975), chapter 6, or Derek H. Aldcroft and H.W. Richardson, *The British Economy 1870–1939* (1969).

26 The importance of German and American competition has been analysed by S.B. Saul, 'The Engineering Industry' in Derek H. Aldcroft (ed.), *The Development of British Industry and Foreign Competition 1875–1914* (1968).

27 These remained the basic engineering tools until the emergence of computerized tools in the late 1960's.

28 Taylorism has been dealt with extensively by H. Braverman in *Labor and Monopoly Capital* (1974) and by C. Littler, *The Development of the Labour Process in Capitalist Societies* (1982).

29 See H. Pelling, *The Origins of the Labour Party, 1880–1900* (1965). Also of interest is Alan J. Ainsworth, 'The Evolution of Socialism in Later Nineteenth Century Britain: A Study of Social Structure and Working Class Belief', Ph.D. Thesis, 1978; 'Aspects of Socialism at Branch Level 1890–1900', *North West Labour History Bulletin*, 5, 1976, and 'Religion in the Working Class Community and the Evolution of Socialism in Late Nineteenth Century Lancashire: A Case of Working Class Consciousness', *Histoire Sociale: Social History*, XI, November 1977.

30 This information derives from talks given at the North West Labour History Group meeting on 'Trades Councils, 1880–1900' held in October 1975. Socialist engineering workers appear to have been particularly prominent in the organization of other trades in Eccles during the 1890's.

31 cf. Barnes' autobiography, *From Workshop to War Cabinet* (1923).

32 See the *Rochdale Labour News*, 10 February 1922.

33 For example, see the biography of Stanley Burgess in *Rochdale Labour News*, 28 October 1922.

34 The North-East employers were in the forefront of late nineteenth century struggles with the A.S.E. Armstrong's, the armaments manufacturers, provided the first two Presidents of the Employers' Federation after their initiatives in organizing the Federation and, in the person of Colonel Dyer, masterminding the Lock-out.

35 Evidence from Jefferys (1945, p. 145).

36 Source, Jefferys (1945, p. 145).

37 The Free Labour Association has been described by William Collison, *The Apostle of Free Labour* (1913) and recently by G. Alderman, in 'The National Free Labour Association', *International Review of Social History*, XXI, 1976. It has been discussed also by John Saville, 'Trade Unions and Free Labour' in *Essay in Labour History, Volume 1* (1960). Colonel Dyer helped to found the Free Labour Protection Association which was also a strike-breaking organization. Wigham (1973, p. 52) cites F. Millar, the secretary, who told the Royal Commission on Trades Disputes 'that the association had a large force of police at their disposal who could be sent anywhere at a few hours' notice and sworn in as special constables where necessary'. Clearly, the spiritual precursor of Colonel Stirling and General Walker!

38 Quoted in Clarke (1957, p. 134).

39 Evidence from The Amalgamated Society of Engineers, *The Engineering Trade Lock-Out, 1897–8* (1898).

40 These difficulties between the skilled engineers and the non-skilled labourers have been dealt with in the context of Barrow by N. Todd, 'Trade Unions and the Engineering Industry Dispute at Barrow-in-Furness, 1897–98', *International Review of Social History*, XX, 1975. Todd states that: 'The unions' trade and organizational sectionalism, their internal political and tactical disagreements and the sharp hostility between skilled workers and labourers were all clearly revealed in the testing experience of the dispute' (p. 34).

41 The A.S.E. remained outside the T.U.C. until 1918, apart from a period between 1905 and 1907.

42 cf. R. Croucher, 'The Amalgamated Society of Engineers and Local Autonomy, 1898–1914', M.A. Thesis, 1971: B.C.M. Weekes, 'The Amalgamated Society of Engineers, 1880–1914: A Study of Trade Union Government, Politics and Industrial Policy', Ph.D. Thesis, 1970 and J. Zeitlin, 'Craft control and the division of labour: engineers and compositors in Britain, 1890–1930', *Cambridge Journal of Economics*, 3, 1979.

43 For the history of the Workers' Union see R. Hyman, *The Workers Union* (1971).

44 For histories of the N.A.U.L. and G.M.W.U. see H.A. Clegg, *General Union, a Study of the Union of General and Municipal Workers* (1954) and H.A. Clegg, *General Union in a Changing Society* (1964).

45 See H.A. Clegg, Alan Fox and A.F. Thompson, *A History of British Trade Unions since 1889: Volume 1, 1889–1910* (1964, pp. 428–39).

46 The triple disturbances associated with Irish Nationalists, Suffragettes and militant trade unionism. For a valuable account despite its age see George Dangerfield, *The Strange Death of Liberal England* (1935), especially 'Part Three: The Crisis'. For the importance of Syndicalism, see R. Holton, *British Syndicalism 1900–14: Myths and Realities* (1976).

47 This account is based upon J. Hinton's *The First Shop Stewards' Movement* (1973), pp. 60–2.

48 The behaviour of the state during the 1914–1918 war justified Beveridge's

assertion that it, and particularly the Ministry of Munitions, was 'from first to last a businessman's organization'. It was directly a capitalist state in the strongest sense, recruiting leading capitalists to man the state apparatuses (cf. Hinton, 1973, p. 30). Certainly, there was no great emphasis on the need to be seen as impartial, which suggests that Claus Offe's functionalist imperative of the capitalist state to 'appear' as a neutral agency is not a functional invariant but the result of complex historical social factors, not the least important of which is the power of organized labour. The contrast between the intervention of the state in the First World War and that in 1939–1945 demonstrates the validity of the above point. Offe's arguments are presented in 'Advanced Capitalism and the Welfare State', *Politics and Society*, 2, 1972, and 'Political Authority and Class Structures – An Analysis of Late Capitalist Societies', *International Journal of Sociology*, 2, 1, 1972. However, despite the glaring reality of one-sidedness of state intervention, the employers often failed to recognize its benefits since they equated state intervention in capitalist economies with socialism: a point of view shared by Fabians and the Conservative Party leadership in the early 1980's. For an interesting analysis of how state involvement in capitalist production can be welcomed by capitalists, see the account of Japanese 'state capitalism' in Henry Stokes, *The Japanese Competitor* (1976), especially pp. 79–80, where he deals with what is termed 'the concerted economy'.

49 This can be seen as the first concrete example of a tripartite 'corporatist' structure. The contention by J. Winkler in his article, 'Corporatism', in *European Journal of Sociology*, 17, 1976, that Corporatism is fascism with a human face, is not borne out by this wartime configuration which, far from destroying the organizations of labour and replacing them by state-run syndicates as happened under fascism, attempted to integrate all three elements into a unified structure. The growth of rank-and-file opposition to the incorporation of the union leadership into such structures is the normal expression of hostility by union membership and is not the form which dissatisfaction with fascist syndicates can take.

50 The rise and fall of the Clyde struggles during the War has been analysed in Hinton (1973, chapters 3 and 4), and also by the same author in his article, 'The Clyde Workers' Committee and the Dilution Struggle', which can be found in *Essays in Labour History*, ed. A. Briggs and J. Saville (1971).

51 An extended account of these events can be found in Hinton (1973, chapter 5).

52 Also see R.D. Penn, '"The Contested Terrain": A critique of R.C. Edwards' theory of working class fractions and politics' in D. Dunkerley and G. Salaman (eds.), *The International Yearbook of Organization Studies: 1981* (1982): reprinted in G. Day (ed.), *Diversity and Decomposition in the Labour Market* (1982).

53 This account of the 1922 Engineering Lock-out relies heavily upon E. Wigham's (1973) history of the Engineering Employers' Federation and J. Jefferys' (1945) history of the Engineering Union.

54 Jefferys (1945, p. 222).

55 Jefferys (1945, p. 225).
56 Membership figures from Jefferys (1945, p. 260).
57 Information from Jefferys (1945, p. 205).
58 Clearly there is a need to check local E.E.F. figures with local employment records. None were available. It is also worth pointing out that much of our knowledge of employment conditions and the 'battle for skill' derives from reports by men like Fairbairn, Nasmyth, and Thomas Wood, who give information, generally, about the largest factories. There is a considerable gap in knowledge of those medium and small engineering establishments which have dominated employment in the industry until the present.
59 *The Report of the Royal Commission on Trade Unions and Employers' Associations 1965–1968* (Cmnd. 3623, 1971), p. 91.
60 *A.U.E.W. Annual Report*, 1973, p. 12.
61 See Appendix D.
62 See preceding chapter.
63 cf. G.W. Daniels and J. Jewkes, 'The Post-War Depression in the Lancashire Cotton Industry', *Journal of the Royal Statistical Society*, XCL, 1928, especially 'Section 5 – Finance of the Industry, 1919–27'.
64 See preceding chapter.
65 e.g. the 1936 'Spindles Act' and the 1939 'Cotton Reorganization Act'. For a discussion of post-war state intervention, see C. Miles, 'Protection of the British Textile Industry' in W.M. Corden and G. Fels (eds.), *Public Assistance to Industry: Protection and Subsidies in Britain and Germany* (1976).
66 B. Vitkovitch, 'The U.K. Cotton Industry, 1937–54', *Journal of Industrial Economics*, 3, 3, 1955 and C. Miles, *Lancashire Textiles: A Case Study of Industrial Change* (1968), are of some use.
67 cf. R. Robson, *The Man-Made Fibre Industry* (1958).
68 Indeed, the recent Amalgamation of the Boilermakers' Union with the General and Municipal Workers Union is partly a residue of this historic antagonism.

7. The course of wage differentials in Rochdale during the period 1856–1964

1 *Labour Statistics – Returns of Wages 1930–1886* (1887).
2 It is only 11 miles from Manchester.
3 For an elaboration of the conceptual problems involved in the analysis of wage rates and earnings, see the works of A. Bowley, especially *Wages and Income in the U.K. since 1860* (1937) and *Wages in the U.K. in the Nineteenth Century* (1900). This research operationalizes wage differentials in terms of gross weekly earnings.
4 *Labour Statistics* (1887).
5 *Miscellaneous Statistics*, Part II, 1859, p. 299, column three and *Miscellaneous Statistics*, Part X, 1879, p. 394.
6 The spinners' average in 1859 in Bowley's text appears to include as a component spinners on time counts who are, in fact, hand-mule spinners. They vary from 23s 0d to 45s 0d per week. Piecers in 1859 earned between 6s 0d and

10s 0d per week which fails to explain Bowley's estimate of 6s 0d for small piecers. Indeed, the distinction between 'big' and 'little' piecer was not made in the returns. Nor was it made in 1879, which does not give any data on hand-mule piecers. The earnings of hand-mule spinners ranged from 40s 0d to 55s 0d per week, and again seem to have featured in Bowley's estimates of spinners' overall average earnings.

7 *Wage Census,* 1886 (1889), 'Cotton Manufacture' and 'Engineering and Machinery Works'.

8 Accounts and Papers, 'Report of an Enquiry by the Board of Trade into Earnings and Hours of Labour of Workpeople of the United Kingdom', Vol. LXXX, 1909, *Textiles*; Vol. LXXXVIII, 1911, *Engineering and Boilermaking.*

9 *The Cotton Spinning Industry: Report of a Commission set up to review the Wages Arrangements and Methods of Organization of Work, and to make Recommendations* (1945).

10 There has been a considerable literature on this subject in the U.S.A. Central statements, of varying kinds, can be found in: E.E. Muntz, 'The Decline of Wage Differentials Based on Skill in the United States', *International Labour Review*, 71, 1955; R. Ozanne, 'A Century of Occupational Differentials in Manufacturing', *The Review of Economics and Statistics*, Vol. XLIV, 1962; R. Perlman, *Labor Theory* (1969), especially chapter IV, 'The Skill Differential' and Peter R. Skergold, 'Wage Differentials Based on Skill in the United States, 1899–1914: A Case Study', *Labor History*, 18, 1977. Two articles in the first issue of the *International Journal of Social Economics* in 1974 attempt to produce economic arguments to cover the structure of economic differentials within industrial societies: 'Interpretations of Pay Structure', by G.G.C. Routh and 'The Human Capital Approach to Occupational Differentials' by Malcolm R. Fisher. The conclusions derived in this chapter about the mechanisms that determine intra-class differentials in Rochdale around the axis of skill offer little support to such 'macro' formulations.

11 For this period see A. Tatlow, 'The Underlying Issues of the 1949–50 Engineering Wage Claim', *Manchester School*, XXI, 1953. Also, E. Wigham, *The Power to Manage* (1973), chapter 8.

12 See M. Pithers, 'The Pounding of the Toolmaker's Pocket', *The Guardian*, 9 May 1977.

13 See *The Guardian* newspaper for much of April 1977.

14 K.G.J.C. Knowles and D.J. Robertson, 'Differences between the Wages of Skilled and Unskilled Workers, 1880–1950', *Oxford Bulletin of Statistics*, 13, April 1951.

15 Knowles and Robertson, 'Earnings in Engineering, 1926–1948', *Oxford Bulletin of Statistics*, 13, June 1951.

16 cf. E. Wigham, *Strikes and the Government* (1976), chapter 6.

17 The a-typicality of the 1948 figures is also revealed in Hart and MacKay (1975) where they produce the following figures for fitters' earnings as a percentage of labourers' earnings:

	Skill differential	(Average weekly earnings in British engineering including overtime both time-workers and piece-workers included)
1914	165.4	
1923	138.3	
1925	138.0	
1930	144.2	
1935	141.8	
1940	148.9	
1948	125.4	
1951	127.1	
1955	129.8	
1960	135.1	
1965	138.2	
1968	140.2	

Source: R.A. Hart and D.I. MacKay, 'Engineering Earnings in Britain, 1914–68', *Journal of the Royal Statistical Society*, Series A, 138, Part 1, 1975, pp. 44–6.

These figures also feature in William Brown's 'Incomes Policy and Pay Differentials', *Oxford Bulletin of Economics and Statistics*, Vol. 58, 1, February 1976; and the table above is taken from his article, p. 41. Such data also confirm the typicality of the patterns uncovered in the Rochdale evidence on engineering earnings.

18 Knowles and Robertson, 'Some Notes on Engineering Earnings', *Oxford Bulletin of Statistics*, 13, July 1951.
19 Knowles and T.P. Hill, 'The Structure of Engineering Earnings', *Oxford Bulletin of Statistics*, 9 and 10, September and October 1954.
20 H.A. Turner, 'Trade Unions, Differentials and the Levelling of Wages', *Manchester School*, XX, 3, September 1952.
21 H.A. Turner, 'Inflation and Wage Differentials in Great Britain' in *The Theory of Wage Determination*, ed. J. Dunlop (1964).
22 See Wilkinson (1977), Howard (1973) and Docherty (1983).
23 Money wages rose by a factor of ten between 1914 and 1964 whilst inflation rose by a factor of four. This means that real wages rose by around 250%. Source: *British Labour Statistics: Historical Abstract 1886–1968* (1971).
24 Especially R. Spicer, *British Engineering Wages* (1928) and M. Yates, *Wages and Labour Conditions in British Engineering* (1937).
25 Published under the auspices of the Carnegie Endowment for International Peace. Of special interest are A.L. Bowley, *Prices and Wages in the U.K., 1914–20* (1921), H. Wolfe, *Labour Supply and Regulation* (1923), G.D.H. Cole, *Workshop Organization* (1923) and G.D.H. Cole, *Trade Unionism and Munitions* (1923).

26 Indeed, as the census data in table 5.1 showed, the very definition of an engineering industry has proved very difficult. For a thorough account of the problems see G.D.H. Cole, *Trade Unionism and Munitions* (1923, chapter 2). For the purposes of this book, engineering is defined as the production of metal goods by means of machinery and maintenance work on all machinery.

27 See Cole (1923a), chapters 9 and 10.

28 For an analysis of this structural 'divide', see A.I. Marsh, *Industrial Relations in Engineering* (1965).

29 The remote sense is that increased piecework was made *possible* by technological developments but not *necessary*.

30 Their 'silence' reflects the persistent inability of the employers and unions in engineering to formalize wage payments tc semi-skilled workers at a national level. A. Tatlow in 'The Underlying Issues of the 1949–50 Engineering Wage Claim', *Manchester School*, XXI, 1953, p. 265, makes the following perceptive remarks: 'There are still no district, let alone national rates for the semi-skilled. Individual rates still vary from shop to shop according to relative bargaining strength between foremen and workers. The rates reflect historical differences and individual pressure, instead of being related to present productivity and negotiated by agreed channels.'

31 See Clegg (1979), Clegg *et al.* (1964), Burgess (1975), Martin (1981) and Willman (1982).

32 Here the major absence lies in the area of spinning. The only figures on earnings in spinning are the Ministry of Labour six-monthly inquiries but these give only differences according to sex and age, and no occupational breakdown. Hence, they are no use for an investigation of inter-occupational differentials. For an attempt to use those figures that do exist, in a different context, see G. Evans, 'Wage Rates and Earnings in the Cotton Industry from 1946 to 1951', *Manchester School*, XXI, 1953.

33 The Oldham piece-list gave the lion's share of any increased earnings to the minder. As S.J. Chapman wrote in 'The Regulation of Wages by Lists in the Spinning Industry', *Economic Journal*, IX, 1899: 'Piecers' wages, however, are still definite weekly amounts; even at Oldham, in practice, although the masters in 1876 forced the spinners to pay the piecers a definite proportion of their weekly takings, for the Oldham spinners were strong enough after the dispute of 1876 to retain all extras for themselves, and so to leave the piecers in much the same position as before' (pp. 597–8).

34 It might appear as if the overall trend between 1859 and 1964 supports the hypothesis of a long-term secular decline in earnings differentials between skilled and non-skilled engineering workers. However, this is not the most plausible model with which to fit the data. The most plausible is a 'changed-point' model which argues that there is a situation of constancy prior to World War I and another state of constancy after 1920. The intervening period represents the change of state. I should like to thank Mr David Dawkins of the Department of Mathematics, City University for his help on this point.

35 The cotton textile industry has long been concentrated in Lancashire and north Cheshire. A.J. Taylor has described the early concentration of the industry in

this north-western area in his article, 'Concentration and Specialization in the Lancashire Cotton Industry, 1825–1850', *Economic History Review*, 2nd series, Vol. 1 (2–3), 1949. See also S.J. Chapman, in *The Lancashire Cotton Industry: A Study in Economic Development* (1904).
36 cf. Howard (1973), and Wilkinson (1983).

8. Skilled manual workers in the labour process

1 A.E. Musson, *British Trade Unions, 1800–1875* (1972); A.E. Musson, *Trade Union and Social History* (1974); and A.E. Musson, 'Class Struggle and the Labour Aristocracy, 1830–60', *Social History*, 3, 1, 1976.
2 cf. H. Phelps-Brown, *The Inequality of Pay* (1977), especially chapter 3, section 1, 'Changes in the Differential for Manual Skill'.
3 cf. E.P. Thompson, 'Time, Work Discipline and the Industrial Revolution', *Past and Present*, 38, 1967, and also S. Pollard, 'Factory Discipline in the Industrial Revolution', *Economic History Review*, 16, 1963–64.
4 This 'orthodox' view is a construct and comprises an amalgam of Marxist and traditional economic history. It is implicit in much research but can be seen most clearly in C. Bücher, *Industrial Evolution* (1901) and the Webbs' *History of Trade Unionism* (1920). Also see W.H. Chaloner, *The Skilled Artisan During the Industrial Revolution, 1750–1850* (1969) and J.L. and B. Hammond, *The Skilled Labourer: 1760–1832* (1919).
5 I prefer 'oligopolistic' capitalism to the Marxist term 'monopoly' capitalism, since the latter is an incorrect characterization of the industrial structure of twentieth century capitalism.
6 I am distinguishing between mechanized and automatic factory production. This is a difference of degree. The hand-mules in spinning and early lathes like Maudslay's in engineering were not automatic and required considerable intervention by operatives.
7 Lazonick (1979, p. 232).
8 cf. G.H. Wood, *The History of Wages in the Cotton Trade During the Past Hundred Years* (1910), pp. 24–6.
9 Turner (1962, p. 116), 'The difference between the hand-mule and the self-actor when the latter came was small; they were both powered machines, but the former was only semi-automatic . . . and the operators of both machines were to be found together in the same factory and even in the same workroom.'
10 cf. Cuca (1977).
11 For a discussion of these issues at an abstract level, see F. Parkin, *Marxism and Class Theory: A Bourgeois Critique* (1979, chapter 6, 'Dual Closure').
12 I would like to thank officials of the Operative Cotton Spinners Association for information on this point.
13 Neil Smelser in *Social Change in the Industrial Revolution* (1959) was the first sociologist to comment on the effects of structural differentiation on the British cotton industry. However, his main focus was on the separation of family and production functions rather than the emergence of a separate managerial function.

14 For France, see P. Fridenson, 'France–États-Unis: Genèse de l'usine nouvelle', *Recherches*, September 1978, and also P. Fridenson, 'The Coming of the Assembly Line to Europe' in E.T. Layton (ed.), *The Dynamics of Science and Technology*, (1978), pp. 159–75, and B. Coriat, *L'Atelier et Le Chronomètre: Essai sur le Taylorisme, le Fordisme et la Production de Masse* (1979).

15 For Germany, see Dick Geary, 'Radicalism and the Worker: Metalworkers and Revolution 1914–23', in R. Evans (ed.), *Society and Politics in Germany* (1978); R.A. Comfort, *Revolutionary Hamburg: Labor Politics in the Weimar Republic* (1966) and Charles, Louise and Richard Tilly, *The Rebellious Century, 1830–1930* (1975).

16 Evidence on Italy can be found in S. Spriano, *The Occupation of the Factories* (1975) and Gwyn A. Williams, 'Proletarian Forms', *New Edinburgh Review*, Vol. 1, 1975.

17 *Earnings differentials within textiles 1950–1963*:

	1950	1958	1962/3
Weavers (average)	100	100	100
Winders (pion: cotton and rayon)	84	88	84
Overlookers (Lancashire looms)	168	170	161
Tape-sizers	142	151	143
Weftmen and tape labourers	96	98	92
Adult battery fillers	78	82	78

18 I am indebted to officials of the A.U.E.W. both in Rochdale and elsewhere in Lancashire for information on the points in this paragraph. Also, I would like to thank Mr Royle of Preston Manpower Services Commission for assistance on contemporary evidence.

19 Notably, Robert J. Bezucha, 'The "Pre-industrial" Worker Movement: The Canuts of Lyons' in *Modern European Social History*, ed. R.J. Bezucha (1972) and Bernard H. Moss, *Origins of the French Labor Movement 1830–1914: The Socialism of Skilled Workers* (1976).

20 This information has been gained from the *Rochdale Labour News*. The main focus of the empirical research did not deal systematically with the relationships of the skilled with political parties in Rochdale, partly because of problems of gaining evidence but also as a consequence of the need to delimit the area of research.

21 I have gained much of this information from *General Engineering Workshop Practice: A Guide to the Principles and Practice of Workshop Procedure* (n.d.). I would like to thank my father for making this book available to me.

22 Such a viewpoint has been supported by evidence from the U.S.A. by David F. Noble, 'Social Choice in Machine Design: The Case of Automatically Controlled Machine Tools, and a Challenge for Labor', *Politics and Society*, 8, 3–4, 1978.

23 A functional type of argument cannot constitute an explanation of the genesis

of any phenomena; nevertheless, it can suggest possible generative hypotheses.

24 There has been a massive debate amongst (predominantly) social historians about the factors that determine variations in workers' militancy. Joan W. Scott, William Sewell Jnr and Charles and Louise Tilly all emphasize the significance of work situations as the single most salient variable. However, writers like Bernard Moss and Margot B. Stein argue that such writers have tended to ignore the autonomous importance of political and ideological changes in the structuration of workers' responses to changes enforced by capitalist management at the point of production. My argument attempts to connect the influence of socialism on skilled craftsmen in Britain with the rhythms of managerial assaults on their exclusive supports to 'skill', and in particular their discretionary power over the actual forms of producing, cf. Joan W. Scott, *The Glassworkers of Carmaux* (1974); William J. Sewell Jnr, 'La classe ouvrière de Marseille sous la Seconde République', *Le Mouvement Social*, 76, July–September 1971; Bernard Moss, 'Workers' Ideology and French Social History', *International Labor and Working Class History*, 11, May 1977 and Margot B. Stein, 'The Meaning of Skill: The Case of the French Engine-Drivers, 1837–1917', *Politics and Society*, 8, nos. 3–4, 1978. Clearly, more evidence is needed about the links between socialist politics, technological change and skilled workers. The lack of any connection in the mid-nineteenth century indicates the significance of the 'political factor' as an independent variable.

25 I am not using the term 'ideology' with any pejorative connotation, but simply to refer to a system of ideas.

26 'Negative' from the perspective of socialist ideology.

27 This general approach of conceptualizing the dynamics of class structure in terms of 'managerial strategies' and 'workers' resistance' can be seen in A.L. Friedman, *Industry and Labour* (1977a). Also see the journal *Capital and Class*, number 1, 1977, for articles by Friedman on 'Responsible Autonomy versus Direct Control over the Labour Process' and by the Brighton Labour Process Group on 'The Capitalist Labour Process'. A recent attempt to utilize these concepts in an American context can be seen in P. Goldman and D.R. Van Houten, 'Managerial strategies and the worker', *Sociological Quarterly*, 18, Winter 1977.

28 cf. data provided by Peter Kellner in the *New Statesman*, 18 May 1979, based upon Market and Opinion Research International Polls. Also see Ken Coates, *What Went Wrong?* (1979). For evidence on relativities see W. Brown, 'Incomes Policy and Pay Differentials', *Oxford Bulletin of Economics and Statistics*, 58, 1, 1976.

29 For an analysis of the left-right split within the A.U.E.W. see R. Undy, 'The Electoral Influence of the Opposition Party in the A.U.E.W. Engineering Section 1960–75', *British Journal of Industrial Relations*, XVII, 1, 1979.

30 This point has been emphasized by Ken Green in his paper presented to the Windsor S.S.R.C. Conference on 'De-skilling' in December 1978, entitled 'Group Technology in Small Batch Engineering' (mimeo).

31 *Classification of Occupations, 1970* (1970).

32 See I. Reid, *Social Class Differences in Britain* (1977), J.H. Goldthorpe and K. Hope, *The Social Grading of Occupations: A New Approach and Scale* (1974) and G. Routh, *Occupation and Pay in Great Britain, 1906–60* (1965).

33 For a discussion of the development of the Census occupational categorization see T.H.C. Stevenson, 'The Vital Statistics of Wealth and Poverty', *Journal of the Royal Statistical Society*, Vol. XC1, 1928.

34 *Registrar General's Annual Report, 1911* (1911), p. xli.

35 The tendency of the Registrar General to lump non-skilled assistants with skilled workers is evident also in the case of the blacksmith and his striker. However, in general, the Registrar General's classification is a better guide to basic occupational divisions in the engineering and metal trades than in the cotton textile industry.

36 The newspapers consulted were: *Rochdale Observer, Rochdale Standard, Rochdale Pilot, Rochdale Labour News, Cotton Factory Times.*

37 For example, Turner and Wood for cotton and Yates and Spicer for engineering (see chapters 6 and 7).

38 Unions consulted were: General Union of Associations of Loom Overlookers, Amalgamated Weavers' Association, Amalgamated Union of Engineering Workers, Amalgamated Association of Operative Cotton Spinners.

39 I would like to thank Mr Brown, Secretary of the Rochdale Overlookers for information on these and following points.

40 In Liverpool, the docking workforce, though casualized until the 1960's, was riven by a Protestant/Catholic divide which meant that men only sought work in their respective religious 'territory'.

41 cf. D. Lee, 'Very Small Firms and the Training of Engineering Craftsmen – Some Recent Findings', *British Journal of Industrial Relations*, X, 1972.

42 Based upon the data presented in chapter 7.

43 This would appear to be a misconception of either a phenomenological or culturalist argument. The former asserts that actors are *actively* engaged in the reproduction of social structure and that their intentions are central to any form of meaningful interpretation but not that action occurs at will or in a structureless vacuum. The latter, culturalist argument, holds that definitions are structured by culture and that action is determined in some degree by this matrix of meanings. Both sets of arguments encounter difficulties but not those suggested by Lee since neither theory would argue that actors simply create their world *ab initio* in a structureless void. At the very least language itself makes such a viewpoint meaningless.

44 i.e. the top, left-hand corner.

45 cf. A. Giddens, *Central Problems in Sociological Theory* (1979).

46 cf. The disputes between the National Graphical Association and Times Newspapers. Atlantic Richfield (owners of the *Observer*) and the owners of the *Nottingham Evening Post*. P. Sadler's 'Sociological Aspects of Skill', *British Journal of Industrial Relations*, VIII, 1970, remains the best introduction to the battle for skill in contemporary printing.

47 The laggers' dispute at the Isle of Grain power station centred around the battle for 'skill'. An interesting account of the rise to 'skill' of the laggers and the power

relationships involved is found in J. Fryer and P. Rodgers, 'Why They All Want To Smash The Laggers'. *Sunday Times*, 1 June 1980.

48 See the article by B. Jones, 'Destruction or Re-Distribution of Engineering Skills? The Case of Numerical Control', in S. Wood (ed.) (1982). Also of interest is K. Hall and I. Miller, 'Industrial Attitudes to Skills Dilution'. *British Journal of Industrial Relations*, IX, 1971, and the reply to this article by J.J. Hughes, 'Industrial Attitudes to Skills Dilution: A Comment', *British Journal of Industrial Relations*, X, 1972.

49 For a discussion of how to *measure* skills (not a notable feature of most of the discussion of de-skilling) see A. Jones and P. Whittaker, *Testing Industrial Skills* (1975).

9. Classes, strata and occupations

1 For a discussion of these multiple meanings see A. Marwick, *Class: Image and Reality: In Britain, France and the U.S.A. Since 1930* (1980) and also, in a much more lighthearted vein, J. Cooper, *Class: A View from Middle England* (1979).

2 This is connected with Weber's commitment to neo-classical, marginalist economics rather than classical political economy.

3 Max Weber, *Economy and Society* (1968), pp. 302–7 and 926–39.

4 Examples of this rejection include P. Anderson, *Considerations of Western Marxism* (1976) where he argues that 'another uneasy aspect of the whole theory of value is the distinction between productive and unproductive labour itself, which although essential to it, has never yet been codified theoretically or established empirically by Marx or his successors' (p. 115).

5 A clear indication of its weakness is a general failure to produce empirical research structured by the notions of productive and unproductive labour.

6 Examples include: labour aristocracy = the entire western working class: F. Fanon, *The Wretched of the Earth* (1961); labour aristocracy = schoolteachers and blackcoated workers: A. Gramsci, *Prison Notebooks* (1971); and labour aristocracy = the intelligentsia plus lower level clerical and administrative workers: M. Gronan, 'Die Angestellte technische Intelligenz – eine Lohnarbeiterschichte', *Marxismus Digest*, 1, 1971.

7 Office of Population Censuses and Surveys, *Classification of Occupations 1970* (1970).

8 Department of Employment, *Classification of Occupations and Directory of Occupational Titles* (C.O.D.O.T.) (1972).

9 cf. A. Stewart, K. Prandy and R.M. Blackburn, *Social Stratification and Occupations* (1980).

10 Department of Employment, *Skilled Engineering Shortages in A High Demand Area: An Inquiry in the Leicester Area; May/June 1970* (1971); National Economic Development Office, *Engineering Craftsmen: Shortages and Related Problems* (1977); and National Economic Development Office, *Focus on Engineering Craftsmen* (1980). The N.E.D.O. Reports in particular demonstrate the employment insecurity of skilled engineering craftsmen. Runciman and Lockwood have both cast doubt on the relative employment

security of lower level non-manual workers, but their evidence is far from persuasive. See W.G. Runciman, 'Occupational class and the assessment of economic inequality in Britain' in D. Wedderburn (ed.), *Poverty, Inequality and Class Structure* (1974), p. 99 and p. 105, fn. 26; and D. Lockwood, *The Blackcoated Worker: A Study in Class Consciousness* (1958), pp. 55–57. Clearly, far more empirical research is needed on this subject.

11 F. Bechhofer, B. Elliott and D. McCrone, 'Structure, consciousness and action: a sociological profile of the British middle class', *British Journal of Sociology*, 4, 1978 and F. Bechhofer, B. Elliott, M. Rushforth and M. Bland, 'The Petits Bourgeois in the Class Structure: the Case of the Small Shopkeepers', in F. Parkin (ed.) (1974).

12 K. Renner, 'The Service Class' in T. Bottomore and P. Goode (eds.), *Austro-Marxism* (1978), pp. 249–52.

13 The term 'co-ordinator' has also been used by M. Albert and R. Hahnel, 'A Ticket to Ride: More Locations on the Class Map' in P. Walker (ed.), *Between Labour and Capital* (1979).

14 R.M. Blackburn, 'Occupations, Definitions and Coding for Social Research', unpublished manuscript. I would like to thank Dr Blackburn for allowing me to consult this document.

15 The entire list of occupations collected in the Rochdale research and their exact location in the seventeen categories can be found in Appendix J of my Ph.D. dissertation 'Skilled Manual Workers in the British Class Structure 1856–1964'. (1981).

16 For a critique of the Nuffield class model along these lines see R.D. Penn 'The Nuffield Class Categorization: some critical remarks', *Sociology*, 1981 and also J.H. Goldthorpe's reply immediately following it.

10. Class analysis and marital endogamy

1 For example, August B. Hollingshead, 'Cultural Factors in the Selection of Marriage Mates', *American Sociological Review*, 15, 1950, pp. 619–27.

2 For example, William J. Goode, 'The Theoretical Importance of Love', *American Sociological Review*, 24, 1959, pp. 38–47.

3 cf. Thomas P. Monahan, 'The Occupational Class of Couples Entering into Interracial Marriages', *Journal of Comparative Family Studies*, VII, 2, 1976.

4 The classic statement about residential propinquity and endogamy is James H.S. Bossard's 'Residential Propinquity as a Factor in Mate Selection', *American Journal of Sociology*, 38, 1932; and the same author's 'The Age Factor in Marriage: A Philadelphia Study 1931', *American Journal of Sociology*, 38, 1933. More recent studies are Alvin M. Katz and Reuben Hill, 'Residential Propinquity and Marital Selection: A Review of Theory, Method and Fact', *Journal of Marriage and the Family*, 20, 1958, pp. 27–35, and Alan C. Kerckhoff, 'Patterns of Homogamy and the Field of Eligibles', *Social Forces*, 32, 1964.

5 For example, R. Centers, 'Marital selection and occupational strata', *American Journal of Sociology*, 54, 1949, pp. 530–5, and Zick Rubin, 'Do American Women Marry Up?', *American Sociological Review*, 1968, 5, 33, pp. 750–60.

6 The most detailed exposition of this theory is Robert F. Winch, *Mate Selection* (1958).

7 For example, P. Laslett, *Household and Family in Past Time* (1972), and P. Laslett, *Family Life and Illicit Love in Earlier Generations* (1977).

8 For example, F.M.L. Thompson, *English Landed Society in the Nineteenth Century* (1963).

9 The terminology used in this research is as follows: Endogamy—marriage within a social category; Exogamy—marriage outside a social category; Hypergamy—marriage into a social category ranked higher than the individual's own position; Hypogamy—marriage into a social category ranked lower, Homogamy—(assortative mating): the tendency for persons to select mates with similar social characteristics; Heterogamy—the tendency to select mates with dissimilar social characteristics.

10 cf. Lévi-Strauss (1973, p. 293), 'of a much more direct bearing on current anthropological research is the recent work of two French demographers who by using Dahlberg's demonstration that the size of an isolate (that is a group of intermarrying people) can be computed from the frequency of marriage between cross-cousins, have succeeded in computing the average size of isolates in all French "departments", thus throwing open to anthropological investigation the marriage system of a complex modern society'.

11 The concentration of mobility or exogamy in adjacent status categories has been a general finding of mobility researchers. See, amongst others, S.M. Miller, 'Comparative Social Mobility: A trend report and bibliography', *Current Sociology*, IX, 1, 1960; Peter M. Blau and O.D. Duncan, *The American Occupational Structure* (1967); C.J. Richardson. *Contemporary Social Mobility* (1977) and A. Daumard and F. Furet, *Structures et Relations Sociales à Paris: au milieu du XVIIIe siècle* (1961).

11. Intermarriage in Rochdale: Class endogamy of brides and grooms

1 A marriage certificate possesses space for four pieces of occupational data—the occupation of bride, groom, father of the bride and father of the groom.

2 e.g. F. Parkin. *Class Inequality and Political Order* (1971).

3 'Essentialism' in class analyses involves making inferences about the structuration of one sphere of the class structure from evidence derived from another, distinct sphere.

4 In my Ph.D. dissertation 'Skilled Manual Workers in the British Class Structure 1856–1964' (1981), the class aspect of intermarriage was looked at from three different angles. Marital endogamy was examined in terms of the relationship between bride and groom, father of bride and father of groom, and father of bride and groom. The final operationalization is not reported in this research since the results for the relationship of grooms and fathers of brides did not differ significantly from those reported in this chapter on the data pertaining to brides and grooms.

5 Absolute endogamy refers to the total number of endogamous marriages: relative endogamy to the degree to which intermarriage deviates from some statistical expectation.

6 These summaries of the matrices are not meant to be exhaustive but merely general guides to their broad parameters. For an extended discussion of the matrices see R.D. Penn (1981, chapters 11, 12 and 13).
7 My dissertation 'Skilled Manual Workers in the British Class Structure 1856–1964' (1981) made use both of Glass and Boudon indices of association. However a clearer picture is forthcoming with the use of Yule's Q. I should like to thank Dr K. Prandy and Dr R.M. Blackburn of the Department of Applied Economics, Cambridge University, for advice on the use of this measure.
8

	x	y
x	A	B
y	C	D

N

The cross-products are A.D. and B.C. The formula for Q is A.D − B.C

$$\frac{A.D - B.C}{A.D + B.C}$$

9 This was because the number of skilled endogamous marriages in the sub-samples for 1856–1865 was zero and for 1875–1884 was only 3. Consequently, the paucity of the data led to their exclusion from the analysis.

12. Intermarriage in Rochdale: class endogamy of fathers of brides and fathers of grooms

1 This conclusion is mirrored in the log-linear analysis conducted on the data reported in this chapter by R.D. Penn and D.C. Dawkins, 'Structural Transformations in the British Class Structure 1856–1964', *Sociology*, November 1983. This analysis also discovered a positive class association over the period under review but no evidence to support a theory of a changing pattern of class association over time.
2 Indeed, this is the conclusion in Penn and Dawkins (forthcoming). Part of the difference in results derives from the fact that Penn and Dawkins make use of the seven-fold categorization of occupations whereas this chapter limits itself to the investigation of dichotomous class aggregations.

13. Skilled manual workers in the British class structure

1 See R.D. Penn, 'Technological Change, Skilled Manual Work and the Division of Labour', *Sociological Review* (forthcoming).
2 This is the conclusion of S. Lash, *The Militant Worker* (1984).
3 An interesting recent article on this issue is J. Gennard and S. Dunn, 'The Impact of New Technology on the Structure and Organisation of Craft Unions in the Printing Industry', *British Journal of Industrial Relations*, XXI, 1, March 1983. Also of relevance is B. Wilkinson, *The Shopfloor Politics of New Technology* (1983) and R.D. Penn, 'Automation and Skilled workers in Contemporary Britain', *Automation*, August 1984.

Bibliography

This bibliography comprises five sections. The first lists local sources consulted, apart from newspapers. The second covers the local press. The third lists the local trade unions consulted. The fourth gives all dissertations consulted, and the final section provides a catalogue of all the secondary sources referred to in the footnotes.

1. Local sources

Brown, W.H., *The Rochdale Pioneers: A Century of Co-operation in Rochdale, 1844–1944* (Manchester, 1944).

Collins, H.C., *Rochdale Roundabout* (Rochdale, 1960).

Fishwick, H., *A History of the Parish of Rochdale* (Rochdale, 1889).

Hopwood, E., *A History of the Lancashire Cotton Industry and the Amalgamated Weavers' Association* (Manchester, 1969).

Kershaw, H., *Over my Shoulder* (Rochdale, 1974).

Milne, J., *Rochdale, As It Was* (Nelson, 1973).

Rochdale Civic Society, *Rochdale to Remember* (Rochdale, 1972).

Rochdale Corporation, *Rochdale Jubilee: A Record of Fifty Years' Municipal Work, 1856–1906* (Manchester, 1906).

Rochdale Official Handbook, various years. In Rochdale Town Library Reference Section.

Taylor, R.P., *Rochdale Retrospect* (Rochdale, 1956).

Tipper, Rev. D.A., *De Balderston: 1573–1973* (Rochdale, 1973).

Unknown author, *A History of the Rochdale Weavers* (no date, in the possession of R. Penn).

Warrington, Rev. C.E., *The History of a Parish* (Rochdale, 1968).

2. Local newspapers

Rochdale Observer
Rochdale Standard
Rochdale Pilot
Rochdale Labour News
Cotton Factory Times

3. Local trade unions consulted

General Union of Associations of Loom Overlookers
Amalgamated Weavers Association
Amalgamated Union of Engineering Workers
Amalgamated Association of Operative Cotton Spinners

4. Dissertations consulted

Textiles

Farnie, D., 'The English Cotton Industry 1850–1896', University of Manchester, M.A. Thesis, 1953.

Smith, R., 'History of the Lancashire Cotton Industry Between the Years 1873 and 1896', University of Birmingham, Ph.D. Thesis, 1954.

Engineering

Croucher, R., 'The Amalgamated Society of Engineers and Local Autonomy, 1898–1914', University of Warwick, M.A. Thesis, 1971.

Croucher, R., 'Communist Politics and Shop Stewards in Engineering, 1935–46', University of Warwick, Ph.D. Thesis, 1977.

Weekes, B.C.M., 'The Amalgamated Society of Engineers, 1880–1914. A Study of Trade Union Government, Politics and Industrial Policy', University of Warwick, Ph.D. Thesis, 1970.

General

Ainsworth, A., 'The Evolution of Socialism in Later Nineteenth Century Britain: A Study of Social Structure and Working Class Belief', University of Warwick, Ph.D. Thesis, 1978.

Bloor, T., 'Trade Union Control Through Apprenticeship Training: The Case of The Printing Industry', University of Manchester, M.A. Thesis, 1965.

5. Secondary sources

(Entries with the same first author are in date order.)

Abercrombie, N. and Urry, J., *Capital, Labour and the Middle Classes* (London, 1983).

Accounts and Papers, 'Population (Great Britain): Religious Worship (England and Wales)', Vol. LXXXIX (London, H.M.S.O., 1852–3).

Accounts and Papers, 'Report of an Enquiry by the Board of Trade into Earnings and Hours of Labour of Workpeople of the United Kingdom', Vol. LXXXVIII, 1911, *Engineering and Boilermaking*.

Accounts and Papers, 'Report of an Enquiry by the Board of Trade into Earnings and Hours of Labour of Workpeople of the United Kingdom', Vol. LXXX, 1909, *Textiles*.

Ainsworth, A.J., 'Aspects of Socialism at Branch Level 1890–1900', *North West Labour History Bulletin*, 5, 1976.

Ainsworth, A.J., 'Religion in the Working Class Community and the Evolution of Socialism in Late Nineteenth Century Lancashire: A Case of Working Class Consciousness', *Histoire Sociale: Social History*, XI (Nov.), 1977.

Albert, M. and Hahnel, R., 'A Ticket To Ride: More Locations on the Class Map' in P. Walker (ed.), *Between Labour and Capital* (Hassocks, Sussex, 1979).

Aldcroft, D.H. (ed.), *The Development of British Industry and Foreign Competition 1875–1914* (London, 1968).

Aldcroft, D.H. and Richardson, H.W., *The British Economy, 1870–1939* (London, 1969).

Alderman, G., 'The National Free Labour Association', *International Review of Social History*, XXI, 1976.

Allan, E., Clarke, J.F., McCord, N. and Rowe, D.J., *The North-East Engineers' Strikes of 1871: The Nine Hours' League* (Newcastle, 1971).

Althusser, L., *For Marx* (Harmondsworth, 1969).

Althusser, L. and Balibar, E., *Reading Capital* (London, 1972).

Amalgamated Society of Engineers, *The Engineering Trade Lock-Out, 1897–8* (London, 1898).

Amalgamated Union of Engineering Workers, *Annual Report, 1973.*

Anderson, P. and Blackburn, R. (eds.), *Towards Socialism* (London, 1965).

Anderson, P., 'Origins of the Present Crisis' in P. Anderson and R. Blackburn (eds.), *Towards Socialism* (London, 1965).

Anderson, P., 'Socialism and Pseudo-Empiricism', *New Left Review*, 35, 1966.

Anderson, P., *Considerations of Western Marxism* (London, 1976).

Ashton, T.S., 'The Growth of Textile Businesses in the Oldham District', *Journal of the Royal Statistical Society*, LXXXIX, 1926.

Baran, P. and Sweezy, P., *Monopoly Capital* (New York 1966).

Barber, B., *Social Stratification* (New York, 1957).

Barnes, G., *From Workshop to War Cabinet* (London, 1923).

Barron, R.D. and Norris, G.M., 'Sexual Divisions and the Dual Labour Market' in D.L. Barker and S. Allen (eds.), *Dependence and Exploitation in Work and Marriage* (London, 1976).

Bechhofer, F., Elliott, B., Rushforth, M. and Bland, M., 'The Petits Bourgeois in the Class Structure: The Case of the Small Shopkeepers' in F. Parkin (ed.), *The Social Analysis of Class Structure* (London, 1974).

Bechhofer, F., Elliott, B., and McCrone, D., 'Structure, consciousness and action: a sociological profile of the British middle class', *British Journal of Sociology*, 4, 1978.

Becker, G., *Human Capital* (New York, 1964).

Beechey, V., 'Labor and Monopoly Capital: Notes Towards a Marxist Feminist Critique' (mimeo, 1978).

Bell, D., 'Notes on the Post-Industrial Society', *The Public Interest*, 6, 1967.

Bell, D., *The Coming of Post-Industrial Society* (London, 1974).

Bell, D., 'The Return of the Sacred?', *British Journal of Sociology*, XXVIII, 4, 1977.

Bendix, R. and Lipset, S.M., *Class, Status and Power* (first edition, Glencoe, Ill., 1953; second edition, London, 1967).

Bendix, R., *Work and Authority in Industry* (Berkeley, 1974).

Berent, J., 'Social Mobility and Marriage: A Study of Trends in England and Wales' in D. Glass (ed.), *Social Mobility in Britain* (London, 1954).

Bezucha, R.J., 'The "Pre-industrial" Worker Movement: The Canuts of Lyons' in R.J. Bezucha (ed.), *Modern European Social History* (Lexington, Mass., 1972).

Binns, D., *Beyond the Sociology of Conflict* (London, 1977).

Bishop, Y., Fienberg, S. and Polland, P.W., *Discrete Multivariate Analysis* (Boston, 1975).

Blackburn, R.M. and Mann, M., *The Working Class in the Labour Market* (London, 1979).

Blackburn, R.M., 'Occupations: Definitions and Coding for Social Research' (mimeo).

Blalock, H.M., *Social Statistics* (second edition, New York, 1972).

Blau, P.M. and Duncan, O.D., *The American Occupational Structure* (New York, 1967).

Blauner, R., *Alienation and Freedom: The Factory Worker and His Industry* (Chicago, 1964).

Bloomfield, J. (ed.), *Class, Hegemony and Party* (London, 1977).

Booth, C., *Life and Labour in London* (London, 1902).

Bossard, J.H.S., 'Residential Propinquity as a Factor in Mate Selection', *American Journal of Sociology*, 38, 1932.

Bossard, J.H.S., 'The Age Factor in Marriage: A Philadelphia Study 1931', *American Journal of Sociology*, 38, 1933.

Bott, E., *Family and Social Network* (London, 1957).

Bottomore, T. and Goode, P. (eds.), *Austro-Marxism* (Oxford, 1978).

Boudon, R., *Mathematical Structures of Social Mobility* (Amsterdam, 1973).

Bowley, A.L., *Wages in the U.K. in the Nineteenth Century* (Cambridge, 1900).

Bowley, A.L. and Burnett-Hurst, A.R., *Livelihood and Poverty* (London, 1915).

Bowley, A.L., *Prices and Wages in the U.K. 1914–20* (Oxford, 1921).

Bowley, A.L., *Wages and Income in the U.K. since 1860* (Cambridge, 1937).

Braverman, H., *Labor and Monopoly Capital: The Degradation of Work in the Twentieth Century* (New York, 1974).

Briggs, A., 'The Language of "Class" in Early Nineteenth Century England' in A. Briggs and J. Saville (eds.), *Essays in Labour History* (London, 1960).

Briggs, A. and Saville, J. (eds.), *Essays in Labour History, 1886–1923* (London, 1971).

Briggs, A. and Saville, J. (eds.), *Essays in Labour History, 1918–1939* (London, 1977).

Brighton Labour Process Group, 'The Capitalist Labour Process', *Capital and Class*, 1, 1977.

British Labour Statistics: Historical Abstract 1886–1968 (London, 1971).

Brown, R. and Brannen, P., 'Social Relations and Social Perspectives amongst Shipbuilding Workers – a Preliminary Statement', *Sociology*, 4, 1970.

Brown, R.K., Brannen, P., Cousins, K. and Samphier, M.L., 'The Contours of Solidarity: Social Stratification and Industrial Relations in Shipbuilding',

British Journal of Industrial Relations, X, 1, 1972.

Brown, W., 'Incomes Policy and Pay Differentials', *Oxford Bulletin of Economics and Statistics*, 58, 1, 1976.

Bücher, C., *Industrial Evolution*, ed. S.M. Wickett (London, 1901).

Bulmer, M. (ed.), *Working Class Images of Society* (London, 1975).

Burgess, K., 'Technological Change and the 1852 Lock-out in the British Engineering Industry', *International Review of Social History*, XIV, 1969.

Burgess, K., 'Trade Union Policy and the 1852 Lock-out in the British Engineering Industry', *International Review of Social History*, XVII, 1972.

Burgess, K., *The Origins of British Industrial Relations* (London, 1975).

Burnett, J., *A History of the Engineers' Strike in Newcastle and Gateshead* (Newcastle, 1872).

Butler, D. and Pinto-Duschinsky, M., *The British General Election of 1970* (London. 1971).

Carchedi, G., 'On the Economic Identification of the New Middle Class', *Economy and Society*, 4, 1, 1975.

Carr Committee Report, *Training for Skill* (London, 1958).

Catling, H., *The Spinning Mule* (Newton Abbot, 1969).

Centers, R., 'Marital selection and occupational strata', *American Journal of Sociology*, 54, 1949.

Centers, R., *The Psychology of Social Classes* (Princeton, 1959).

Chaloner, W.H., *The Skilled Artisan During the Industrial Revolution 1750–1850* (History Association, 1969).

Chapman, S.J., 'The Regulation of Wages by Lists in the Spinning Industry', *Economic Journal*, IX, 1899.

Chapman, S.J., 'Some Policies of the Cotton Spinners' Trade Unions', *Economic Journal*, X, 1900.

Chapman, S.J., *The Lancashire Cotton Industry: A Study in Economic Development* (Manchester, 1904).

Child, J., *Industrial Relations in the British Printing Industry* (London, 1967).

Clarke, R.O., 'The dispute in the British engineering industry, 1897–8: an evaluation', *Economica*, XXIV, 1957.

Clegg, H.A., *General Union, a study of the Union of General and Municipal Workers* (Oxford, 1954).

Clegg, H.A., *General Union in a Changing Society* (Oxford, 1964).

Clegg, H.A., *The Changing System of Industrial Relations in Great Britain* (Oxford, 1979).

Clegg, H.A., Fox, A. and Thompson, A.F., *A History of British Trade Unions since 1889: Volume 1, 1889–1910* (Oxford, 1964).

Coates, K., *What Went Wrong?* (Nottingham, 1979).

Cockburn, C., *Brothers: Male Dominance and Technological Change* (London, 1983).

Cole, G.D.H., *Trade Unionism and Munitions* (Oxford, 1923a).

Cole, G.D.H., *Workshop Organization* (Oxford, 1923b).

Collison, W., *The Apostle of Free Labour* (London, 1913).

Comfort, R., *Revolutionary Hamburg: Labor Politics in the Weimar Republic* (Stanford, 1966).

Cooper, J., *Class: A View from Middle England* (London, 1979).

Corden, W.M. and Fels, G. (eds.), *Public Assistance to Industry: Protection and Subsidies in Britain and Germany* (London, 1976).

Coriat, B., *L'Atelier et le Chronomètre: Essai sur le Taylorisme, le Fordisme et la Production de Masse* (Paris, 1979).

Corrigan, P., *Schooling the Smash-Street Kids* (London, 1979).

Cotton Spinning Industry, 'Report of a Commission set up to Review the Wage Arrangements and Methods of Organization of Work, and to Make Recommendations', (London, H.M.S.O. 1945).

Coxon, A. and Jones, C.L., *The Images of Occupational Prestige: A Study in Social Cognition* (London, 1978).

Cressey, P. and MacInnes, J., 'Voting for Ford: Industrial Democracy and the Control of Labour', *Capital and Class*, 11, 1980.

Crompton, R., 'The deskilling of clerical work' (mimeo, 1978).

Crompton, R. and Gubbay, J., *Economy and Class Structure* (London, 1977).

Crosland, A., *Can Labour Win?*, Fabian Tract 324 (London, 1960).

Cuca, J.R., 'Industrial Change and the Progress of Labor in the English Cotton Industry', *International Review of Social History*, XXII, 1977.

Cutler, A., Hindess, B., Hirst, P. and Hussain, A., *Marx's Capital and Capitalism Today, Volume 1* (London, 1977).

Dahrendorf, R., *Class and Class Conflict in Industrial Society* (Stanford, 1959).

Dahrendorf, R., 'Recent Changes in the Class Structure of European Societies', *Daedalus*, Winter 1964.

Dahrendorf, R., 'The Collapse of Class Spawns a New Politics', *The Guardian*, 15 September 1980a.

Dahrendorf, R., 'Twenty-Five Years of Socio-Political Analysis: Notes and Reflections', *Government and Opposition*, 15, 3/4, 1980b.

Dangerfield, G., *The Strange Death of Liberal England* (London, 1935).

Daniels, G.W. and Jewkes, J., 'The Post-War Depression in the Lancashire Cotton Industry', *Journal of the Royal Statistical Society*, XCL, 1928.

Daumard, A. and Furet, F., *Structures et Relations Sociales à Paris: au milieu du XVIIIe siècle* (Paris, 1961).

Davis, J.A., *Elementary Survey Analysis* (Englewood Cliffs, N.J., 1971).

Davis, K. and Moore, W., 'Some Principles of Stratification' in R. Bendix and S.M. Lipset (eds.), *Class, Status and Power* (second edition, London, 1967).

Davis, R.L. and Cousins, J., 'The "New Working Class" and the Old' in M. Bulmer (ed.), *Working Class Images of Society* (London, 1975).

Department of Employment, *Skilled Engineering Shortages in a High Demand Area: An Inquiry into the Leicester Area; May/June 1970* (Manpower Papers, No. 3, London, H.M.S.O., 1971).

Department of Employment, *Classification of Occupations and Directory of Occupational Titles* (London, H.M.S.O., 1972).

Docherty, C., *Steel and Steelworkers: The Sons of Vulcan* (London, 1983).

Doeringer, P., and Piore, M., *Internal Labour Markets and Manpower Analysis* (Lexington, Mass., 1971).

Downing, H., 'Word Processors and the Oppression of Women' in T. Forester (ed.), *The Microelectronics Revolution* (Oxford, 1980).

Edwards, R.C., *Contested Terrain: The Transformation of the Workplace in the Twentieth Century* (New York, 1979).

Eichner, A.S., *A Guide to Post-Keynesian Economics* (London, 1979).

Elbaum, B., Lazonick, W., Wilkinson, F., and Zeitlin, J., 'The Labour Process, Market Structure and Marxist Theory: A Symposium', *Cambridge Journal of Economics*, 3, 1979.

Engels, F., 'England in 1845 and 1885' in K. Marx and F. Engels, *On Britain* (London, 1953).

Evans, G., 'Wage Rates and Earnings in the Cotton Industry from 1946 to 1951', *Manchester School*, XXI, 1953.

Fanon, F., *The Wretched of the Earth* (Paris, 1961).

Farrell, M., *Northern Ireland: The Orange State* (London, 1976).

Fisher, M.R., 'The Human Capital Approach to Occupational Differentials', *International Journal of Social Economics*, 1, 1974.

Fisher, R.A., 'The Arrangement of Field Experiments', *Journal of the Ministry of Agriculture of Great Britain*, 33, 1926.

Flanders, A., *Management and Unions* (London, 1970).

Fong, H., *Triumph of Factory System in England* (Tientsin, 1930).

Foster, J., *Class Struggle and the Industrial Revolution: Early Industrial Capitalism in Three English Towns* (London, 1974).

Foster, J., 'British Imperialism and the Labour Aristocracy', in R. Skelley (ed.), *The General Strike* (London, 1976).

Fox, A., *Beyond Contract: Work, Power and Trust Relations* (London, 1974).

Frankenberg, R., *Communities in Britain* (London, 1966).

Freeman, T.W., Rodgers, H.B. and Kinvig, R.H., *Lancashire, Cheshire and the Isle of Man* (London, 1966).

Fridenson, P., 'France–États-Unis: Genèse de l'usine nouvelle', *Recherches* September 1978.

Fridenson, P., 'The Coming of the Assembly Line to Europe', in E.T. Layton (ed.), *The Dynamics of Science and Technology* (Amsterdam, 1978).

Friedman, A., *Industry and Labour* (London, 1977a).

Friedman, A., 'Responsible Autonomy versus Direct Control over the Labour Process', *Capital and Class*, 1, 1977b.

Fryer, J. and Rodgers, P., 'Why they all want to Smash the Laggers', *Sunday Times*, 1 June 1980.

Fuchs, V.R., *The Service Economy* (New York, 1968).

Galbraith, J.K., *The New Industrial State* (London, 1967).

Gallie, D., *In Search of the New Working Class* (Cambridge, 1978).

Garnsey, E., 'Women's Work and Theories of Class Stratification', *Sociology*, 12, 2, May 1978.

Geary, R., 'Radicalism and the Worker: Metalworkers and Revolution 1914–23' in R. Evans (ed.), *Society and Politics in Germany* (London, 1978).

General Engineering Workshop Practice (London, n.d).

Gennard, J. and Dunn, S., 'The Impact of New Technology on the Structure and Organisation of Craft Unions in the Printing Industry', *British Journal of Industrial Relations*, XXI, 1, March 1983.

Giddens, A., *The Class Structure of the Advanced Societies* (London, 1973).

Giddens, A., *Studies in Social and Political Theory* (London, 1977).

Giddens, A., *Central Problems in Sociological Theory* (London, 1979).

Class, D. (ed.), *Social Mobility in Britain* (London, 1954).

Glyn, A. and Sutcliffe, R., *British Capitalism, Workers and the Profits Squeeze* (Harmondsworth, 1972).

Goldman, P. and van Houten, D.R., 'Managerial strategies and the worker', *Sociological Quarterly*, 18, Winter 1977.

Goldthorpe, J.H., 'Social Stratification in Industrial Society' in R. Bendix and S.M. Lipset (eds.), *Class, Status and Power* (second edition, London, 1967).

Goldthorpe, J.H., Lockwood, D., Bechhofer, F. and Platt, J., *The Affluent Worker: Industrial Attitudes and Behaviour* (Cambridge, 1968).

Goldthorpe, J.H., Lockwood, D., Bechhofer, F. and Platt, J., *The Affluent Worker: Political Attitudes and Behaviour* (Cambridge, 1968).

Goldthorpe, J.H., Lockwood, D., Bechhofer, F. and Platt, J., *The Affluent Worker in the Class Structure* (Cambridge, 1969).

Goldthorpe, J.H., 'Theories of Industrial Society', *Archives Européenne de Sociologie*, 12, 2, 1971.

Goldthorpe, J.H., 'Class, Status and Party in Modern Britain: some recent interpretations, Marxist and Marxisant', *European Journal of Sociology* 1972.

Goldthorpe, J.H. and Hope, K., 'Occupational Grading and Occupational Prestige' in K. Hope (ed.), *The Analysis of Social Mobility: Methods and Approaches* (Oxford, 1972).

Goldthorpe, J.H. and Hope, K. (eds.), *The Social Grading of Occupations: A New Approach and Scale* (Oxford, 1974).

Goldthorpe, J.H. and Bevan, P., 'The Study of Social Stratification in Britain: 1945–1975', Nuffield College, 1975 (mimeo).

Goldthorpe, J.H. and Llewellyn, C., 'Class Mobility in Modern Britain: Three Theses Examined', *Sociology*, 11, 2, 1977.

Goldthorpe, J.H. and Llewellyn, C., 'Class Mobility and Worklife Patterns', *British Journal of Sociology*, XXVIII, 3, 1977.

Goldthorpe, J.H., Payne, C. and Llewellyn, C., 'Trends in Class Mobility', *Sociology*, 12, 3, 1978.

Goldthorpe, J.H., Llewellyn, C., and Payne, C., *Social Mobility and Class Structure in Modern Britain* (Oxford, 1980).

Goode, W.J., 'The Theoretical Importance of Love', *American Sociological Review*, 24, February 1959.

Goode, W., *World Revolution and Family Patterns* (New York, 1963).

Goodman, L. and Kurskal, W., 'Measures of Associations for Cross Classifications', *Journal of the American Statistical Association*, 49, 1954.

Goody, J., Thirsk, J. and Thompson, E.P. (eds.), *Family and Inheritance: Rural Society in Western Europe 1200–1800* (Cambridge, 1976).

Gordon, D.M., Edwards, R. and Reich, M., *Segmented Work, Divided Workers* (Cambridge, 1982).

Gorz, A., *Socialism and Revolution* (London, 1975).

Gouldner, A., *The Coming Crisis of Western Sociology* (London, 1971).

Gramsci, A., *Selections from the Prison Notebooks* (London, 1971).

Gray, E.M., *The Weaver's Wage* (Manchester, 1937).

Gray, R.Q., 'The Labour Aristocracy in the Victorian Class Structure' in F. Parkin (ed.), *The Social Analysis of Class Structure* (London, 1974).

Gray, R.Q., *The Labour Aristocracy in Victorian Edinburgh* (Oxford, 1976).

Green, K., 'Group Technology in Small Batch Engineering', paper presented to the S.S.R.C. Conference on 'De-skilling', December 1978, Windsor (mimeo).

Greenwood, W., *Love on the Dole* (London, 1933).

Gronan, M., 'Die Angestellte technische Intelligenz – eine Lohnarbeiterschichte', *Marxismus Digest*, 1, 1971.

Gurr, T., *Why Men Rebel* (Princeton, 1971).

Gustafsson, B. (ed.), *Post-Industrial Society* (London, 1979).

Habermas, J., *Legitimation Crisis* (London, 1976).

Hall, K. and Miller, I., 'Industrial Attitudes to Skills Dilution', *British Journal of Industrial Relations*, IX, 1971.

Halsey, A.H., 'Towards Meritocracy? The Case of Britain' in A.H. Halsey and J. Karabel (eds.), *Power and Ideology in Education* (Oxford, 1977).

Halsey, A.H., Heath, A.F. and Ridge, J.M., *Origins and Destinations: Family, Class and Education in Modern Britain* (Oxford, 1980).

Hammond, J.L. and Hammond, B., *The Skilled Labourer, 1760–1832* (London, 1919).

Hart, R.A. and MacKay, D.I., 'Engineering Earnings in Britain, 1914–68', *Journal, of the Royal Statistical Society*, A, 138, Part 1, 1975.

Hindess, B., 'The Concept of Class in Marxist Theory and Marxist Politics' in J. Bloomfield (ed.), *Class, Hegemony and Party* (London, 1977).

Hinton, J., 'The Clyde Workers' Committee and the Dilution Struggle' in A. Briggs and J. Saville (eds.), *Essays in Labour History, 1886–1923* (London, 1971).

Hinton, J., *The First Shop Stewards' Movement* (London, 1973).

Hirst, P., 'Economic Classes and Politics' in A. Hunt (ed.), *Class and Class Structure* (London, 1977).

Hobsbawm, E., *Labouring Men* (London, 1964).

Hodgson, G., 'The Theory of the Falling Rate of Profit', *New Left Review*, 84, 1974.

Hoggart, R., *The Uses of Literacy* (Harmondsworth, 1959).

Hoggart, R. and Williams, R., 'Working Class Attitudes', *New Left Review*, 1, 1960.

Holbrook-Jones, M., *Supremacy and Subordination of Labour* (London, 1982).

Hollingshead, A.B., 'Cultural Factors in the Selection of Marriage Mates', *American Sociological Review*, 15, 1950.

Hollingsworth, T.H., 'The demography of the British peerage', *Population Studies*, 1964.

Holton, R., *British Syndicalism 1900-14: Myths and Realities* (London, 1976).

Hope, K. (ed.), *The Analysis of Social Mobility: Methods and Approaches* (Oxford, 1972).

Howard, M.C. and King, J.E., *The Political Economy of Marx* (London, 1975).

Howard, N.P., 'The Strikes and Lockouts in the Iron Industry and the Formation of the Ironworkers' Unions, 1862–1869', *International Review of Social History*, 1973.

Hughes, J.J., 'Industrial Attitudes to Skills Dilution: A Comment', *British Journal of Industrial Relations*, X, 1972.

Hughes, T., 'An Account of the Lock-out of Engineers in 1851–2' in *Trades' Societies and Strikes* (London, 1860).

Hunt, A. (ed.), *Class and Class Structure* (London, 1977).

Hutt, A., *The Condition of the Working Class in Britain* (London, 1933).

Hyman, R., *The Workers Union* (London, 1971).

Inkeles, A. and Rossi, P., 'National Comparisons of Occupational Prestige', *American Journal of Sociology*, 61, 1956.

Jaques, E., *Measurement of Responsibility* (London, 1956).

Jefferys, J.B., *The Story of the Engineers* (London, 1945).

Jenkins, M., 'Early Days in the Y.C.L.', *Marxism Today*, February 1972.

Jewkes, J. and Gray, E.M., *Wage and Labour in the Cotton Spinning Industry* (Manchester, 1935).

Jones, A. and Whittaker, P., *Testing Industrial Skills* (Epping, 1975).

Jones, B., 'Destruction or Re-distribution of Engineering Skills? The Case of Numerical Control' in S. Wood (ed.), *The Degradation of Work* (London, 1982).

Kalecki, M., 'Political Aspects of Full Employment', *Political Quarterly*, 1943.

Katz, A.M. and Hill, R., 'Residential Propinquity and Marital Selection: A Review of Theory, Method and Fact', *Journal of Marriage, and the Family*, 20, 1958.

Kerckhoff, A.C., 'Patterns of Homogamy and the Field of Eligibles', *Social Forces*, 32, 1964.

Kerr, C., Dunlop, J.T., Harbison, F.H. and Myers, C.A., *Industrialism and Industrial Man* (Harmondsworth, 1973).

Klare, K. and Howard, D. (eds.), *The Unknown Dimension* (New York, 1972).

Klein, J., *Samples from English Cultures* (Volume 1, London, 1965).

Klingender, F.D., *The Condition of Clerical Labour in Britain* (London, 1935).

Knowles, K.G.J.C. and Robertson, D.J., 'Differences between the Wages of Skilled and Unskilled Workers, 1880–1950', *Oxford Bulletin of Statistics*, 13, April 1951.

Knowles, K.G.J.C. and Robertson, D.J., 'Earnings in Engineering, 1926–1948', *Oxford Bulletin of Statistics*, 13, June 1951.

Knowles, K.G.J.C. and Robertson, D.J., 'Some Notes on Engineering Earnings', *Oxford Bulletin of Statistics*, 13, July 1951.

Knowles, K.G.J.C. and Hill, T.P., 'The Structure of Engineering Earnings', *Oxford Bulletin of Statistics*, 9 and 10, September and October 1954.

Kregel, J.A., *The Reconstruction of Political Economy: An Introduction to Post-Keynesian Economics* (London, 1973).

Kumar, K., 'Revolution and Industrial Society: An Historical Perspective', *Sociology*, 10, 2, 1976.

Kumar, K., *Prophecy and Progress: The Sociology of Industrial and Post-Industrial Society* (Harmondsworth, 1978).
Labour Statistics – Returns of Wages 1830–1886, C-5172 (London, H.M.S.O., 1887).
Labrousse, H., *Esquisse du mouvement des prix et des revenus en France en XVIIIe siècle* (Paris, 1933).
Lash, S. M., *The Militant Worker* (London, 1984).
Laslett, P., *Household and Family in Past Time* (Cambridge, 1972).
Laslett, P., *Family Life and Illicit Love in Earlier Generations* (Cambridge, 1977).
Lazonick, W., 'Industrial Relations and Technical Change: The Case of the Self-Acting Mule', *Cambridge Journal of Economics*, 3, 1979.
Lee, D., 'Very Small Firms and the Training of Engineering Craftsmen – Some Recent Findings', *British Journal of Industrial Relations*, X, 1972.
Lee, D., 'Craft Unions and the Force of Tradition', *British Journal of Industrial Relations*, XVII, 1, March 1979.
Lee, D., 'Skill, Conflict and Class: A Theoretical Critique and a Deviant Case', *Sociology*, 1981.
Lenin, V.I., 'Imperialism: The Highest Stage of Capitalism' in *Selected Works*, (Moscow, 1971).
Lenin, V.I., *Selected Works* (Moscow, 1971).
Lévi-Strauss, C., *Structural Anthropology* (New York, 1973).
Lichtheim, G., *From Marx to Hegel* (London, 1967).
Liepman, K., *Apprenticeship: An Enquiry into its Adequacy under Modern Conditions* (London, 1958).
Lindberg, L.N., Alford, R., Crouch, C. and Offe, C., *Stress and Contradiction in Modern Capitalism: Public Policy and the Theory of the State* (Lexington, Mass., 1975).
Lindberg, L.N., *Politics and the Future of Industrial Society* (New York, 1978).
Littler, C., *The Development of the Labour Process in Capitalist Societies* (London, 1982).
Lockwood, D., *The Blackcoated Worker: A Study in Class Consciousness* (London, 1958).
Lockwood, D., 'The "New Working Class"', *European Journal of Sociology*, 1, 2, 1960.
Lockwood, D., 'Sources of Variation in Working Class Images of Society', *Sociological Review*, 14, 3, 1966.
Low-Beer, J.R., *Protest and Participation* (Cambridge, 1978).
Lucas, E., *Arbeiterradikalismus: Zwei Formen von Radikalismus in der deutschen Arbeiterbewegung* (Frankfurt-am-Main, 1976).
Lukács, G., *History and Class Consciousness* (London, 1971).
Mackenzie, G., *The Aristocracy of Labor: The Position of Skilled Craftsmen in the American Class Structure* (Cambridge, 1973).
Mackenzie, G., 'The Affluent Worker Study: An Evaluation and Critique' in F. Parkin (ed.), *The Social Analysis of Class Structure* (London, 1974).
Maitland, I., 'Disorder in the British Workplace: The Limits of Consensus', *British Journal of Industrial Relations*, XVIII, 1980.

Maitland, I., *The Causes of Industrial Disorder: A Comparison of a British and a German Factory* (London, 1983).

Mallet, S., *La Nouvelle Classe Ouvrière* (Paris, 1963).

Mandel, E., *Late Capitalism* (London, 1975).

Mann, M., 'The Social Cohesion of Liberal Democracy', *American Sociological Review*, 35, 3 June 1970.

Mann, M., 'The Ideology of Intellectuals and Other People in the Development of Capitalism', in Leon N. Lindberg, R. Alford, C. Crouch and C. Offe (eds.), *Stress and Contradiction in Modern Capitalism: Public Policy and the Theory of the State* (Lexington, Mass., 1975).

Marcuse, H., *One Dimensional Man* (London, 1964).

Marsh, A.I., *Industrial Relations in Engineering* (Oxford, 1965).

Marsh, A.I., Evans, E.O. and Garcia, P., *Workplace Industrial Relations in Engineering* (London, 1971).

Marshall, T.H., *Sociology at the Crossroads and other Essays* (London, 1963).

Martin, R., *New Technology and Industrial Relations in Fleet Street* (Oxford, 1981).

Marwick, A., *Class: Image and Reality* (London, 1980).

Marx, K., *The Eighteenth Brumaire of Louis Bonaparte* (London, 1926).

Marx, K., *The Poverty of Philosophy* (London, 1936).

Marx, K., *Capital: Volume 1* (Moscow, 1970).

Marx, K., *Capital: Volume 3* (London–Moscow, 1970).

Marx, K. and Engels, F., *On Britain* (London, 1953).

Marx, K. and Engels, F., *The German Ideology* (Moscow, 1963).

Mayhew, H., *London Labour and the London Poor*, Vol. III (London, 1861).

McColdrick, J., 'The Interwar Crisis in Clydeside Shipbuilding: Technical Change and the Negotiation of the Labour Process' (mimeo., Department of Sociology, Glasgow University, April 1981).

Michels, R., 'Psychologie der antikapitalistischen Massenbewegungen', *Grundriss der Sozialökonomik*, IX, 1926.

Miles, C., *Lancashire Textiles: A Case Study of Industrial Change* (Cambridge, 1968).

Miles, C., 'Protection of the British Textile Industry' in W.M. Corden and G. Fels (eds.), *Public Assistance to Industry: Protection and Subsidies in Britain and Germany* (London, 1976).

Miller, S.M., 'Comparative Social Mobility: A trend report and bibliography', *Current Sociology*, IX, 1, 1960.

Millett, K., *Sexual Politics* (New York, 1969).

Monahan, T.P., 'The Occupational Class of Couples Entering into Interracial Marriages', *Journal of Comparative Family Studies*, VII, 2, 1976.

Montgomery, D., 'Workers' Control of Machine Production in the Nineteenth Century', *Labor History*, Fall 1976.

Moorhouse, H.F., 'The Marxist Theory of the Labour Aristocracy', *Social History*, 3, 1, 1978.

More, C., *Skill and the English Working Class, 1870–1914* (London, 1980).

Moss, B., *The Origins of the French Labor Movement 1830–1914: The Socialism of Skilled Workers* (Berkeley, 1976).

Moss, B., 'Workers' Ideology and French Social History', *International Labor and Working Class History*, 11, May 1977.

Muntz, E.E., 'The Decline of Wage Differentials Based on Skill in the United States', *International Labor Review*, 71, 1955.

Murphy, P.J., 'The Origins of the 1852 Lock-Out in the British Engineering Industry Reconsidered', *International Review of Social History*, XXIII, 1978.

Musson, A.E., *British Trade Unions, 1800–1875* (London, 1972).

Musson, A.E., *Trade Union and Social History* (London, 1974).

Musson, A.E., 'Class Struggle and the Labour Aristocracy 1830–60', *Social History*, 3, 1, 1976.

Nairn, T., 'The Nature of the Labour Party', *New Left Review*, 27 and 28, 1964.

Nairn, T., 'Labour Imperialism', *New Left Review*, 32, 1965.

National Economic Development Office, *Engineering Craftsmen: Shortages and Related Problems* (London, 1977).

National Economic Development Office, *Focus on Engineering Craftsmen* (London, 1980).

National Opinion Research Center, 'Jobs and Occupations: A Popular Evaluation' in R. Bendix and S.M. Lipset (eds.), *Class, Status and Power* (first edition, Glencoe, Ill., 1953).

Neale, R.S., *Class and Ideology in the Nineteenth Century* (London, 1972).

Nelson, D., *Managers and Workers: The Origins of the New Factory System in The United States* (Madison, 1975).

Neuss, R.F. (ed.), *Facts and Figures about the Church of England: Prepared by The Statistical Unit of the Central Board of Finance* (Oxford, 1962).

Noble, D.F., 'Social Choice in Machine Design: The Case of Automatically Controlled Machine Tools, and a Challenge for Labor', *Politics and Society*, 8, 3–4, 1978.

Nolan, P. and Edwards P.K., 'Homogenise, Divide and Rule: An Essay on Segmented Work, Divided Workers' (Mimeo, 1982, Warwick University).

Offe, C., 'Advanced Capitalism and the Welfare State', *Politics and Society*, 2, 1972.

Offe, C., 'Political Authority and Class Structures – An Analysis of Late Capitalist Societies', *International Journal of Sociology*, 2, 1, 1972.

Office of Population, Censuses and Surveys, *Classification of Occupations, 1970*, (London, H.M.S.O., 1970).

Ossowski, S., *Class Structure in the Social Consciousness* (New York, 1965).

Ozanne, R., 'A Century of Occupational Differentials in Manufacturing', *The Review of Economics and Statistics*, XLIV, 1962.

Pareto, V., *The Rise and Fall of Elites* (Totowa, N.J., 1968).

Parkin, F., *Class Inequality and Political Order* (London, 1971).

Parkin, F., 'Strategies of Social Closure in Class Formation' in F. Parkin (ed.) *The Social Analysis of Class Structure* (London, 1974).

Parkin, F. (ed.), *The Social Analysis of Class Structure* (London, 1974).

Parkin, F., *Marxism and Class Theory: A Bourgeois Critique* (London, 1979).

Parsons, T., 'An Analytical Approach to the Theory of Social Stratification', in T. Parsons (ed.), *Essays in Sociological Theory* (Glencoe, Ill., 1949).

Parsons, T. (ed.), *Essays in Sociological Theory* (Glencoe, Ill., 1949).

Parsons, T., 'A Revised Analytical Approach to the Theory of Social Stratification' in R. Bendix and S.M. Lipset (eds.), *Class, Status and Power* (first edition, Glencoe, Ill., 1953).

Pelling, H., *A History of British Trade Unionism* (Harmondsworth, 1963).

Pelling, H., *The Origins of the Labour Party, 1880–1900* (Oxford, 1965).

Pelling, H., *Popular Politics and Society in Late Victorian Britain* (London, 1968).

Penn, R.D., 'Occupational Prestige: A Great Empirical Invariant?', *Social Forces*, 1975.

Penn, R.D., 'Revolution in Industrial Societies', *Sociology*, 12, 2, 1978.

Penn, R.D., 'The Nuffield Class Categorization: Some Critical Remarks', *Sociology*, 15, 2, 1981.

Penn, R.D., 'Skilled Manual Workers in the Labour Process, 1856–1964' in S. Wood (ed.), *The Degradation of Work* (London, 1982).

Penn, R.D., '"The Contested Terrain": a critique of R.C. Edwards' theory of working class fractions and politics' in G. Day (ed.), *Diversity and Decomposition in the Labour Market* (London, 1982).

Penn, R.D., 'Trade Union Organization and Skill in the Cotton and Engineering Industries in Britain, 1850–1960', *Social History*, 8, 1, 1983.

Penn, R.D., 'Theories of Skill and Class Structure', *Sociological Review*, 31, 1, 1983.

Penn, R.D., 'The Course of Wage Differentials between Skilled and Non-skilled Manual Workers in Britain between 1856 and 1964', *British Journal of Industrial Relations*, XXI, 1, 1983.

Penn, R.D. and Dawkins, D., 'Structural Transformations in the British Class Structure, 1856–1964', *Sociology*, November 1983.

Penn, R.D., 'Automation and Skilled Manual Workers in Contemporary Britain', *Automation*, August 1984.

Penn, R.D., 'Technological Change, Skilled Manual Work and the Division of Labour', *Sociological Review* (forthcoming).

Perlman, R., *Labor Theory* (New York, 1969).

Phelps-Brown, H., *The Inequality of Pay* (Oxford, 1977).

Pithers, M., 'The Pounding of the Toolmaker's Pocket', *The Guardian*, 9 May 1977.

Piva, M.J., 'The Aristocracy of the English Working Class; Help for an Historical Debate in Difficulties', *Histoire Sociale: Social History*, 1975.

Pollard, S., 'Factory Discipline in the Industrial Revolution', *Economic History Review*, 16, 1963–64.

Popitz, H., Bahrdt, H.P., Jueres, E.A. and Kesting, A., *Das Gesellschaftsbild des Arbeiters* (Tubingen, 1957).

Porter, J.H., 'Industrial Peace in the Cotton Trade, 1875–1913', *Yorkshire Bulletin of Economic and Social Research*, 19, 1, 1967.

Postgate, R., *The Builder's History* (London, 1923).

Poulantzas, N., 'Marxist Political Theory in Great Britain', *New Left Review*, 43, 1967.

Poulantzas, N., *Political Power and Social Classes* (London, 1973).

Poulantzas, N., *Fascism and Dictatorship* (London, 1974).

Poulantzas, N., *Classes in Contemporary Capitalism* (London, 1975).

Poulantzas, N., *The Crisis of the Dictatorships* (London, 1976).

Reid, A., 'Politics and Economics in the Formation of the British Working Class: A Response to H.F. Moorhouse', *Social History*, 3, 3, 1978.

Reid, I., *Social Class Differences in Britain* (London, 1977).

Renner, K., 'The Service Class' in T. Bottomore and P. Goode (eds.), *Austro-Marxism* (Oxford, 1978).

Report of the Royal Commission on Trade Unions and Employers' Associations 1965–1968 (Chairman, Lord Donovan) (London, 1971, Cmnd. 3623).

Ricardo, D., *Principles of Political Economy and Taxation* (London, 1973).

Richardson, C.J., *Contemporary Social Mobility* (London, 1977).

Ridge, J.M. (ed.), *Mobility in Britain Reconsidered* (Oxford, 1974).

Roberts, K., Cook, F.G., Clark, S.C. and Semeonoff, E., *The Fragmentary Class Structure* (London, 1977).

Roberts, R., *The Classic Slum* (Manchester, 1971).

Robinson, J., *An Essay in Marxian Economics* (London, 1942).

Robson, R., *The Cotton Industry in Britain* (London, 1957).

Robson, R., *The Man-Made Fibre Industry* (London, 1958).

Rogoff, N., *Recent Trends in Occupational Mobility* (New York, 1953).

Routh, G., *Occupation and Pay in Great Britain, 1906–60* (Cambridge, 1965).

Routh, G.G.C., 'Interpretations of Pay Structure', *International Journal of Social Economics*, 1, 1974.

Rowntree, B.S., *Poverty* (London, 1902).

Rubin, Z., 'Do American Women Marry Up?', *American Sociological Review*, 33, 1968.

Runciman, W.G., 'Class, Status and Power?' in J. Jackson (ed.), *Social Stratification* (Cambridge, 1968).

Runciman, W.G., 'Occupational Class and the Assessment of Economic Inequality in Britain' in D. Wedderburn (ed.), *Poverty, Inequality and Class Structure* (Cambridge, 1974).

Ryndina, L. and Chernikov, G. (eds.), *The Political Economy of Capitalism* (Moscow, 1974).

Sadler, P., 'Sociological Aspects of Skill', *British Journal of Industrial Relations*, VIII, 1970.

Saul, S.B., 'The Engineering Industry' in Derek H. Aldcroft (ed.), *The Development of British Industry and Foreign Competition 1875–1914* (London, 1968).

Saul, S.B., *The Myth of the Great Depression* (London, 1969).

Saville, J., 'Trade Unions and Free Labour' in A. Briggs and J. Saville (eds.), *Essays in Labour History: Volume 1* (London, 1960).

Schultz, T.W., 'Investment in Human Capital', *American Economic Review*, 51, March 1961.

Schulze-Gaevernitz, G. von, *The Cotton Trade in England and on the Continent* (London, 1895).

Scott, J.W., *The Glassworkers of Carmaux* (Cambridge, 1974).

Scullion, H., 'The Skilled Revolt against General Unionism: The Case of the B.L. Toolroom Committee', *Industrial Relations Journal*, XII, 1981.

Sewell, W.J. Jnr, 'La classe ouvrière de Marseille sous la Seconde République', *Le Mouvement Social*, 76, 1971.

Shorter, E. and Tilly, C., *Strikes in France* (Cambridge, 1974).

Sisson, K., *Industrial Relations in Fleet Street* (Oxford, 1975).

Skelley, R. (ed.), *The General Strike* (London, 1976).

Skergold, P.R., 'Wage Differentials Based on Skill in the United States, 1899–1914: A Case Study', *Labor History*, 18, 1977.

Smelser, N., *Social Change in the Industrial Revolution* (Chicago, 1959).

Smith, D.M., *The North West* (Newton Abbot, 1969).

Sorokin, P., *Social Mobility* (New York, 1927).

Sorokin, P., *Social and Cultural Mobility* (New York, 1959).

Spicer, R., *British Engineering Wages* (London, 1928).

Spriano, S., *The Occupation of the Factories* (London, 1975).

Sraffa, P., 'The Laws of Return under Competitive Conditions', *Economic Journal* XXXVI, 1926.

Sraffa, P., *The Production of Commodities by Means of Commodities* (Cambridge, 1960).

Steedman, I., *Marx after Sraffa* (London, 1977).

Stein, M.B., 'The Meaning of Skill: The Case of the French Engine-Drivers, 1837–1917', *Politics and Society*, 8, 3–4, 1978.

Stevenson, T.H.C., 'The Vital Statistics of Wealth and Poverty', *Journal of The Royal Statistical Society*, Vol. XCI, 1928.

Stewart, A., Prandy, K. and Blackburn, R.M., 'Measuring the Class Structure', *Nature*, vol. 245. 1973.

Stewart, A., Prandy, K. and Blackburn, R.M., *Social Stratification and Occupations* (London, 1980).

Stokes, H., *The Japanese Competitor* (London, 1976).

Stone, K., 'The Origin of Job Structures in the Steel Industry', *Radical America*, 7, 6, 1973.

Stone, L., *Family, Sex and Marriage in England 1500–1800* (London, 1977).

Sutter, J. and Tabah, L., 'Les notions de l'isolat et de population minimum', *Population*, 1951.

Sweezy, P., *The Theory of Capitalist Development* (New York, 1942).

Tatlow, A., 'The Underlying Issues of the 1949–50 Engineering Wage Claim', *Manchester School*, XXI, 1953.

Taylor, A.J., 'Concentration and Specialization in the Lancashire Cotton Industry 1825–1850', *Economic History Review, 2nd Series*, 1, 2–3, 1949.

Therbörn, G., 'What does the Ruling Class do when it Rules?', *Insurgent Sociologist*, VI, 3, 1976.

Thomas, D., 'The Social Origins of Marriage Partners of the British Peerage in the Eighteenth and Nineteenth Centuries', *Population Studies*, 1972.

Thompson, E.P., *The Making of the English Working Class* (London, 1963).

Thompson, E.P., 'The Peculiarities of the English', *Socialist Register* (London, 1965).

Thompson, E.P., 'Time, Work Discipline and the Industrial Revolution', *Past and Present*, 38, 1967.

Thompson, F.M.L., *English Landed Society in the Nineteenth Century* (London, 1963).

Tilly, C., Tilly, L. and Tilly, R. *The Rebellious Century, 1830–1930* (Harvard, 1975).

Todd, N., 'Trade Unions and the Engineering Industry Dispute at Barrow-in-Furness, 1897–98', *International Review of Social History*, XX, 1975.

Toivonen, T., 'Aristocracy of Labour: Some Old and New Problems', *Acta Sociologica*, 21, 3, 1978.

Touraine, A., *La Conscience Ouvrière* (Paris, 1966).

Touraine, A., *La Société Post-Industrielle* (Paris, 1969).

Treiman, D.J., *Occupational Prestige in Comparative Perspective* (New York, 1977).

Trotsky, L., *History of the Russian Revolution* (London, 1934).

Tumin, M., 'Some Principles of Stratification: A Critical Analysis', *American Sociological Review*, 18, 1953.

Turner, H.A., 'Trade Unions, Differentials and the Levelling of Wages', *Manchester School*, XX, 3, September 1952.

Turner, H.A., *Trade Union Growth, Structure and Policy* (London, 1962).

Turner, H.A., 'Inflation and Wage Differentials in Great Britain' in J. Dunlop (ed.), *The Theory of Wage Determination* (London, 1964).

Turner, H.A., Clack, G. and Roberts, G., *Labour Relations in the Motor Industry* (London, 1967).

Tyson, R.E., 'The Cotton Industry' in D.H. Aldcroft (ed.), *The Development of British Industry and Foreign Competition 1875–1914* (London, 1968).

Undy, R., 'The Electoral Influence of the Opposition Party in the A.U.E.W. Engineering Section, 1960–75', *British Journal of Industrial Relations*, XVII, 1, 1979.

Vitkovitch, B., 'The U.K. Cotton Industry, 1937–54', *Journal of Industrial Economics*, 3, 3, 1955.

Wage Census, 1886, C-5807 (London, H.M.S.O., 1889).

Webb, S. and Webb, B., *The History of Trade Unionism* (London, 1920).

Weber, M., *General Economic History*, trans, F.H. Knight (New York, 1961).

Weber, M., *Economy and Society* (3 volumes, edited by G. Roth and C. Wittich, New York, 1968).

Wedderburn, D. and Craig, C., 'Relative Deprivation in Work' in D. Wedderburn (ed.), *Poverty, Inequality and Class Structure* (Cambridge, 1974).

Westergaard, J. and Resler, H., *Class in a Capitalist Society* (London, 1975).

White, J., *The Limits of Trade Union Militancy: The Lancashire Textile Workers, 1910–1914* (London, 1978).

Wigham, E., *The Power to Manage: A History of the Engineering Employers' Federation* (London, 1973).

Wigham, E., *Strikes and the Government* (London, 1976).

Wilkinson, B., *The Shopfloor Politics of New Technology* (London, 1983).

Wilkinson, F., 'Collective Bargaining in the Steel Industry in the 1920's' in A. Briggs and J. Saville (eds.), *Essays in Labour History, 1918–1939* (London, 1977).

Willener, A., *Images de la Société et Classes Sociales* (Berne, 1957).

Williams, G., *Recruitment to Skilled Trades* (London, 1958).

Williams, G., 'Proletarian Forms', *New Edinburgh Review*, 1, 1975.

Williams, G., 'Gramsci': a series of three articles in *New Edinburgh Review*, 1975–1976.

Williams, R., *Culture and Society* (London, 1958).

Willis, P.E., *Learning to Labour* (Farnborough, 1977).

Willman, P., *Fairness, Collective Bargaining and Incomes Policy* (Oxford, 1982).

Willmott, P. and Young, M., 'Social Grading by Manual Workers', *British Journal of Sociology*, 7, 1956.

Winch, R.F., *Mate Selection* (New York, 1958).

Winkler, J., 'Corporatism', *European Journal of Sociology*, 17, 1976.

Wolfe, H., *Labour Supply and Regulation* (Oxford, 1923).

Wood, G.H., *The History of Wages in the Cotton Trade During the Past Hundred Years* (London, 1910).

Wood, S. (ed.), *The Degradation of Work* (London, 1982).

Wootton, B., *The Social Foundations of Wage Policy* (London, 1954).

Wright, E.O., 'Class Boundaries in Advanced Capitalist Societies', *New Left Review*, 98, 1976.

Wright, T., ('The Journeyman Engineer') 'Our New Masters', *The Reformer*, 29 March 1873.

Wrong, D., 'The Functional Theory of Stratification: Two Decades of Controversy', *Inquiry*, 9, 1966.

Yasuda, S., 'A Methodological Inquiry into Social Mobility', *American Sociological Review*, 29, 1964.

Yates, M., *Wages and Labour Conditions in British Engineering* (London, 1937).

Young, N., 'Prometheans or Troglodytes? The English Working Class and the Dialectics of Incorporation', *Berkeley Journal of Sociology*, XII, 1967.

Yule, G.U., 'On the methods of measuring association between two attributes.' *Journal of the Royal Statistical Society*, 75, 1912.

Zeitlin, J, 'Craft control and the division of labour: engineers and compositors in Britain, 1890–1930', *Cambridge Journal of Economics*, 3, 1979.

Zweig, F., *The Worker in an Affluent Society* (London, 1961).

Index